BLACK

ENOUGH

MAN

ENOUGH

———

Embracing My Mixed Race
and Fluid Sexuality

GEE SMALLS

Marketing and Branding Consultant: Daniel P. Calderon

Cover design: Lindsay Starr, lindsaystarr.com

Cover and author photos: Nadia Nima, vanitystudios.co

Interior design: Jera Publishing, www.self-pub.net

ISBN: 978-1-7330828-0-8

Published by Juan & Gee Enterprises, LLC

This book is dedicated to *you*.

I hope my story inspires you to live in love and authenticity.

~ Gee

FOREWORD

There are many things about Gee, my partner in life and business, that I'm attracted to — besides his good looks and glowing smile, that is (wink). He is extremely charismatic, witty, and driven; the type of person that never meets a stranger, can always make me laugh and exudes confidence. He's a gifted visionary whose purpose-filled life is an inspiration to people across the globe, partly due to the aforementioned characteristics, but mostly because of his commitment to being self-aware, his generous spirit, and his unabashed transparency. This sentiment is made evident through his work as Co-Founder of The Gentlemen's Foundation, as Chef/Owner of Virgil's Gullah Kitchen & Bar, and is echoed throughout the pages of Black Enough, Man Enough.

In this socially relevant recounting of his life, Gee offers himself in the most vulnerable of ways, immediately captivating the reader with the vivid imagery of him "playing teacher" as a kid, then taking them on a whirlwind journey through the ups and downs of a biracial man in the south yearning for what most of us desire, to be ENOUGH. With each page, he engages the reader in a heart-to-heart conversation on race, class, sexual identity, self-discovery, parenthood and many other universal truths, inviting you deeper and deeper into the sacred depths of his soul with every transformative word.

It was such a privilege to witness the years-long process of his writing this book. The long nights, numerous edits, psychological stress and emotional turmoil might have deterred others, but not Gee. He knew that this important work would educate, inspire, and incite a vibrational shift just as his other endeavors have. So, he endured. With every edit he was forced to relive each life-changing event, regurgitate every emotion, recount every heartache and relish every triumph.

He put in the work.
And he delivered.
And I'm so proud.

Each time I've read a draft of this memoir — and I've read a few of them — I experienced a gamut of emotions. I laughed. I cried. I became angry and overjoyed and turned-on and by the end, after the tears had dried and my laughter subsided, my heart overflowed with empathy, compassion and love. Reading this book reminded me why I fell in love with Gee: his pure heart. So, get ready for a deeply honest, beautifully raw and poignant voyage into the life of my dear husband. I know you will enjoy the ride as much as I did.

Juan Smalls
Co-Owner, Virgil's Gullah Kitchen & Bar
Co-Founder, The Gentlemen's Foundation

CONTENTS

1

DIFFERENT

I WAS A VERY animated kid, always dancing, always singing, always acting out a random character from TV. Often, after locking myself up in my bedroom, I would imitate one of my school teachers, who were all women, leading a class. I loved playing the teacher, probably because I liked being bossy and in control.

And I loved the boy group, The Boys. I remember seeing them on Soul Train one Saturday morning and wishing I could be on that stage with them. I was always jealous of them, not only because they were famous for singing and dancing, but also because they were all brothers. I loved my sister to death, but I always wanted a brother.

I also remember when Aunt Pam visited us, and I performed a dance routine for her to Whitney Houston's "I Wanna Dance With Somebody." I always loved Whitney Houston, and I loved that song. I can still see my skinny arms and legs flying up and down as I ran my fingers through my Debarge-Esque hair, as Whitney did in her videos.

"Boy, Greg, you sure can dance! You should be a professional dancer," my Aunt Pam said." Look at him go, Rita, and he doesn't stop!" she said to my mom, her sister.

I'm not quite sure if I was ever really any good or not. I mean, coming from a middle-aged White woman, her compliment didn't mean much. What would Aunt Pam have known about dancing, right? Anyway, I think her comment may have been more about mocking my "girly" dance moves and not so much about my dance skills. She never did have a problem pointing out that I wasn't exactly a normal boy, even once telling my mom that I ran like a girl. After overhearing her comment, I wondered how boys were supposed to run and why I wasn't running like one.

As a child, I wanted to grow up to be an actor, at least until the age of seven or eight, when I attended my first and last casting for a child's role. The Post and Courier was looking for young Black boys between the ages seven to ten to act in an upcoming Hollywood film. I can't quite remember if it was my mom that found the ad about it or me. Why were they casting it in my hometown of Charleston, South Carolina? No clue, but I didn't care because it was my chance to be in a big Hollywood movie!

When we arrived at the casting—in some business office down the road from where we lived—there was only one other young boy seated waiting to be called. The boy happened to be a distant cousin of mine. A distant cousin was one of those cousins that you weren't quite sure how you were related to them, but somebody's momma or daddy said you were, so you just accepted it. In Charleston, it seemed most everyone was my cousin.

"Hi, Carlton," I said as I waved to him and his mom.

"Hi," he said softly. The waiting area was small and quiet, smelled like dusty old furniture, and it resembled the waiting area of a small dentist's office.

I could tell Carlton was nervous. I felt more anxious than anything. My mom spoke to Carlton's mother while we sat and waited.

"You nervous, honey?" my mom asked, looking at me with eager eyes.

"No, not really. Just ready to get it over with," I replied while Carlton and his mom disappeared down the long hallway after his name was called. I didn't see anyone else come out.

I swung my legs back and forth in the chair with my hands folded for about ten minutes before Carlton came back. I could not tell from his face how things went. I'm not sure Carlton knew either.

"They asked for me to tell you to go back there, Greg," Carlton's mom said to me. She looked happy. "Last room on the right. You are the last one to audition. Good luck!"

"Ready, Gregory?" My mom asked. She rarely called me Gregory. It always made me blush when she did.

"Yep! Let's go!" I replied as I popped out of my chair.

As I walked into the small conference room, there was a young White woman with blonde hair seated at the table alongside an older White man with gray hair who briefly glanced up before looking down again at his paperwork.

"Hi, Greg! I'm Amber!" the excited young woman said. "And you must be Mom! Why don't the two of you have a seat?"

Her excitement started to make me nervous.

"Hi, thank you!" my mom said as we both took a seat. "Say hi, Greg." "Hello."

"This is my colleague Dan, and we are going to be working with you today. We won't take up too much time. It will be really quick. We just need you to read these few lines here."

Amber handed me a sheet of paper with the scene on it. Dan didn't look up or utter a word.

"I am going to start, and you will read the lines that say, Darnell. Do you see that there? Can you do that for me?"

My mom looked over to see what Amber was referring to and pointed at Darnell's first line.

"I see em, Mommy," I whispered to her, then I said to Amber, "Yea, I can do em."

"Okay, perfect! Here we go!"

Amber read the first line, I replied with the next, and so on. I think I did a pretty decent job, but I wasn't quite sure. Before I knew it, it was over.

"You did a great job, Greg! Why don't you step outside while we talk to Mom? It'll just be a minute or two."

"Okay." I walked out of the room nervously, thinking that they must want me if they wanted to talk to Mommy. I started getting excited at the thoughts of taking my first plane trip to Hollywood.

In less than a minute, my mom exited the conference room. I could tell it was not good news. Disappointed, she put her hand on the top of my back and led me out of the office building.

"Wah dey say, Mommy?" I asked after buckling my seatbelt.

"They said they thought you did a good job, but..."

I could tell my mom didn't quite know how to deliver the bad news to me.

"...they are looking for someone who looks a little more Black—someone who has hair and skin like the other Black boys. You are different than the rest of them. I'm sorry. Maybe next time."

My light, bright skin, and soft wavy hair would not make the cut as a 'Darnell.'

Since that day in 1984, I never had another chance to audition for a Hollywood movie in Charleston. It wasn't because opportunities to act never came, but because of what happened that day—I never again found the courage. What role would I play?

I couldn't play a White boy even though my mom is White. I couldn't play a Black boy, even though my father is Black. Who am I? What am I? As far as I've seen, no one looks like me on TV or anywhere else for that matter. On that day, I gained the realization of being 'different.' This was the first time I felt that way.

As a youngster, not only did I learn that I would never be Black enough, I also learned that I would also never be "boy" enough. Aunt Pam surely wasn't the only one that pointed out that I "acted" like a girl, walked like a girl, and even looked like a girl. Not much longer after auditioning for the role of 'Darnell,' an older White woman, maybe in her 60s, walked up to my mom and me while we were in the mall shopping for school clothes.

"Excuse me, Ma'am," the older White woman said to my mom. "May I ask you a question?"

"Hi. Okay, sure," my mom said with a confused look on her face.

"My friend and I have a bet going. She seems to think this little girl is a boy, and I keep trying to tell her she is a girl! Can you help settle this for us?"

My mom laughed and said, "Oh, no, your friend is actually right. He is a boy!"

"Oh, my gosh, he is! He is so pretty, and oh, my gosh, look at all that hair!"

I turned my head down and looked at the brown tiles that were cemented to the floor beneath my feet, at The Citadel Mall. I didn't get the same amusement that she and my mom seemed to have got out of the bet.

When the lady walked away, my mom said to me while laughing, "Man, I should have asked what was in it for me since they were betting on my son!"

I didn't want to act as if my feelings were hurt, so I laughed along with her as if the exchange didn't just crush me. I learned early on that "laughing things off" would be one of my go-to defense mechanisms. I now wonder if it was something I learned from my mom. Maybe her feelings were also hurt, and her laughter was a way of protecting herself too.

I'm not sure if I got teased more for being a "half-breed" or a "faggot," but what I do know is that both made a significant impression on the fabric of my being. At that time, me never being Black enough or Man enough quickly became the foundation for my lack of self-identity, self-love, and self-confidence, through growing up and into adulthood.

2

THE SMALLS FAMILY

WHAT Y'ALL THINK about Rita Faye having a baby for that nigger?!" my drunk Uncle Tommy yelled out as he burst into my grandmother's home on the night before Thanksgiving in 1974.

Rita, my mom, had just left after bringing my sister over to her mom's house so everyone could see her new baby. My half White/half Black sister was only a few weeks old, and like most Black babies, her real skin color had not come in. This meant that she could "pass" as White; at least that's what my mom had hoped on that Thanksgiving Eve. After her mother, Ruby, teased her about her new baby looking a little "Chinese" and asked why her cuticles looked so dark, Rita snatched the baby out of her mother's arms and left. The reason was revealed later when her brother Tommy busted through the door.

My grandmother Ruby was mortified. "A nigger? A nigger! She had a nigger in my house?! You tell Rita Faye to never come back or bring that nigger baby into my house again! She is not my daughter!"

Rita never had a great relationship with her mother. Her mother hated her guts. Ruby would never let Rita leave the house, and if she did not have to clean up the house, Ruby would make her stay in her room. Her three brothers and two sisters got to do what they wished and what they wanted while Rita got treated like shit. One time, her mother bought her shoes that were two sizes too small, and when Rita told her about it, Ruby made her wear them anyway. It was the only pair of shoes she had, and she had to wear them as she walked three miles to school every day. I remember my dad, Virgil, always teasing my mom about how her pinky toe would curl over the neighboring toe while my sister and I pointed and laughed at it. My mom laughed along, but I'm sure that deep down, it triggered the anger she must have held against her mom for being so cruel.

Ruby whipped and cussed at Rita like she was a servant. She embarrassed her in front of her friends when they came over and never let her see boys. When Rita was about five months old, Ruby put Rita and her siblings up for adoption after she divorced their father. Of the more than ten kids my grandmother had, I only met three because every time Ruby would meet a man, she would have a kid or two, break up with him, and go back home to Nanny, my mom's grandmother. Nanny was a strict Catholic, and although she would allow Ruby to come back home, the kids could not because they were born out of wedlock. They were bastards, so Ruby would quickly give up her kids to go back home until she met another man and had more kids.

My mom's father happened to marry Ruby. That meant Rita, her sister Pam, and brother Tommy were not bastards. My great grandmother, 'Nanny,' welcomed them in her home and subsequently got them out of foster care. Not only was my mom welcomed, but Nanny also treated her the best. I believe she saw how Ruby treated my mom and tried to over-compensate for it, which only made Ruby treat her worse after my mom and her siblings returned home with her once she found another man. My mom and Nanny were close until the day she died in 1988. Nanny was the only one that showed my mom real love growing up.

After that Thanksgiving Eve, when she brought my sister over, it would be more than a decade before my mom saw her mother again. I'm not sure how they reconnected, but when Ruby finally came around and visited for the first time, I remember my mom being anxious the entire visit. I had to be about eight or nine, and I had never seen my mom so uncomfortable. She scrubbed the house like never before and even redecorated.

It was like she wanted to do all she could to ensure her mom liked her and everything about her life. I even remember when one of Mom's best friends was on her way over to visit, and my mom said to Ruby, "I want you to meet my good friend, Yvonne. She is a very well-mannered Black girl that lives around the corner and teaches at Tawny and Greg's school."

At the time, I couldn't understand why I felt so uncomfortable with those words that came out of her mouth. I see now that she was warning her mom that Yvonne was Black, but she did all she could to let her know Yvonne was not one of the "Blacks" who her mom would think of when hearing that. She was a "good Black." I also know now that my mom was still trying to please her mother. She always wanted acceptance from her.

Although my mom's family was racist, real rednecks from the back-woods of St. Mary's County, Maryland, my mom never got that gene. My mom gravitated more towards Black people in school since the Black kids made her feel the most accepted, and it was a relief from all the rejection she received at home. It had gotten so bad at home that my mom dropped out of high school in her junior year and moved in with her older sister Pam, who had moved to Washington, D.C. A few years later, at age 19, she met my father, Virgil Fred Smalls, through one of her Black girlfriends who worked with her at the dry cleaners. I was surprised when I learned this because I always assumed it was my dad who hung around a lot of White people that led him to meet my mom.

Unlike my grandmother Ruby, who I just called Ruby until the day she died, my paternal Grandma Mable fully accepted my White mom and her biracial granddaughter. She was only worried about my sister coming out with too many toes and fingers because that's what she had heard about the babies of White and Black parents. She had never seen one for herself around James Island, South Carolina, the only place she had ever lived and where she raised my father. It is also where my parents raised me.

James Island is a small island connected by a bridge across the Ashley River and off the coast of Charleston, South Carolina. James Island was home to about 9% of Charleston's population of roughly 65,000 during this time. Charleston was the nation's capital for the slave trade, where many enslaved Africans first landed in the New World. The old slave plantations and even the auction block, where many slaves were sold just hours after being escorted off slave ships, are historically preserved and open to visitors. By 1860, 400,000 slaves lived in South Carolina, which was 10% of the four million slaves living as property in the United States. Because my ancestors did not have access to the mainland until the late 1890s to early 1900s, they were able to preserve much of our African heritage, including crafts and folktales. Gullah Geechee people, as we are called, can easily be identified by the way we speak and for our cuisine, especially our love of white rice, which was Charleston's largest cash crop. We are often mistaken for being from the Bahamas, Jamaica, or New Orleans because of our creole culture, although Gullah Geechee culture is the first Black culture in America.

I have always been very proud to be Gullah Geechee, but with such rich culture and history in the city, it came along with its fair share of challenges, especially being biracial. I had no idea as a child, but towards the end of slavery, slaves could earn their freedom in a few ways: by purchasing their freedom, by providing service to the state or local community, or by being freed by their masters, who could free them at any time. Many were freed by last will and testament after their master's death. Slave owners would often free their mistresses and illegitimate children, and by 1860, 75% of freed Blacks were mulattoes or people like me with one White and one Black parent. I can only imagine the tension and separation this caused amongst Black people in Charleston, which undoubtedly still plays a part in many experiences of our people today, just as it does in my experience of what I carry from growing up as a child of mixed race.

On James Island, my father was one of nine siblings from a single mother who cleaned White people's homes after finishing her day job in the school cafeteria. Grandma Mable was my grandfather's mistress, who lived down the street from him and his family. She had three boys during her relationship with him. Grandma Mable used to make my dad and his two brothers go up to his dad's house as kids and ask for money, only to get the door slammed in his face by their father or father's wife.

That must have had to break him over and over again. I cannot imagine how that would affect a kid—my father. To be disowned and have the door slammed in his face over and over by his own father. And for my grandmother to make my dad do that must have meant she was in a very hurt place. My father's father died when my dad was in his early teens.

With Dad rejected by his father and Mom rejected by her mother, my parents met in 1973, just six short years after mixed-race marriage became legal, and only four years after my dad graduated high school and moved to Washington, D.C., where he was stationed in the Navy. After a year, my sister was born in Prince George's General Hospital, and just two and a half years later, on March 24, 1977, I was born at the very same hospital. Everyone thought I was going to be a girl, but they were all wrong. When my dad found out, he went screaming through the hospital with joy. He had always wanted a son who would carry the Smalls name. That was important to him, and my sister Tawny, who I've called "Kony" ever since learning to talk, could never do it. My mom decided to name me "Gregory" because of a big strong, good looking man, her best friend had met at a bar a few years ago. "Guys named Gregory are always so strong and good looking," and so I became Gregory with the middle name Virgil after my father.

My mom wasn't as happy as my father was when I was born. She cried after the doctor placed me in her arms for the very first time because she thought I looked like an ugly little Asian baby. "Tawny was such a cute baby when she was born. I was so shocked when I saw you! But you turned out to be handsome, Gregory," is what she would often say to me whenever the memory came up. Maybe I did look ugly, but her breakdown had little to with my looks and more to do with the start of her postpartum depression.

The summer after I was born, my parents moved to James Island because Grandma Mable was sick with cancer, and my dad wanted to be near her. He grew up very close to his mother. She was his world. The entire family called her "Mother" because of the way she took care of everyone. She did not make it long after they moved, only surviving until the end of the year. I always imagined her being the super affectionate, bake-you-some-biscuits, loving type of grandmother. Despite not remembering her, I still missed her and would often even talk to her through prayer as a kid. I think I longed for her even more because my living grandmother rejected me. Also, after Ruby came around, I still felt rejected and never bonded with her. She was just Ruby to me. I know Grandma Mable would have been different; Mother would have loved me.

Moving to the south as an interracial couple in the '70s was not easy for my parents, especially for my mom since James Island was not her home. She had to make an entirely new life in a new place where Whites often hated her because she was married to my Black father, and also hated by Blacks, especially Black women, for the same reason. My father was pretty well known around James Island and was considered one of the successful Black men in the community who "made it out" and had a good job after leaving the military. A White woman snatching him up from the abundance of eligible single Black women did not go over too well with many, not to mention there were still a lot of people, Black and White, who did not believe that Blacks and Whites should marry. Although unbeknownst to most, my parents had yet to marry, but that did not stop them from telling everyone they were when they moved to town together.

I've always been told that my parents didn't care to get married, which is why it took them so long. But I found out in my adult years that when my mom got pregnant with my sister, my dad wanted to marry her right away; however, my mom was not ready. Shortly after I was born, she told my dad that she was ready, but he declined as a way to get back at her. *Her words, not mine.* Fast forward six years to the weekend my father decided to sleep out, with another woman, without so much as a phone call to my mom. She was so pissed when he returned that she pushed him into his mother Mable's old china closet that sat in the dining room and screamed at him,

"I'll be damned if I moved all the way down here away from my family to be with you, and you are out with some other woman! If you don't marry me, I'm leaving!"

The very next day, my parents went to the courthouse and got married. That would satisfy my mom for a short while, but it would not be long before she was out getting my father back for what he had done to her. This tit-for-tat cheating game went on for as long as I can remember, but the only difference is my dad was a lot more discreet about it than my mom. Around age 7, I recall seeing my mom slow dancing and kissing her boyfriend, Wayne, in the living room of her friend's house while my sister and I peeked at them from the back bedroom. She would also take us over to her boyfriend's house sometimes. It was also nothing for her to sneak him in the house late at night when my dad was away on one of his Navy Reserve assignments. She never knew I was up, but I always heard him. When she left my dad for a year, Wayne was spending nights with us at our new apartment. I always hated Wayne. I once woke in the middle of the night to my sister, pounding him on his back and screaming, "Let go of my Momma!" as he held her in a headlock. After peaking around the corner to see what was going on, I quickly ran back to bed and hid under the covers, too afraid to do anything. I remember feeling like such a punk for not being able to save my mom.

Around age 12, when Mom and Dad separated for the second time, my mom put me in the middle of their fight. This time it was him that moved out of our family home and rented an apartment across town. One night, my mom had shared with us that she had just left Dad's apartment to go and "beat his girlfriend's ass," who was also my classmate's mom.

I wasn't surprised that my mom was "beatin' ass." I had seen my mom fight countless times. She once pulled into the median in the middle of the highway, got out of the car, and told some woman in another car, "Come and beat my ass if you bad!" She was something else, but as the only White girl on James Island dating a Black man, she had to be *tough*. She used to try and make me *tough*, but it never worked. Like the time I allowed a boy in the neighborhood to take the tube out of my bike tire. When my mom found out, she made me jump in the car with her to go to his house to get the tube back. She said if I did not get it, she was going to beat my ass. I was terrified of both, but I decided to get my tube. Luckily, he gave it back when he saw my mom in the driveway.

I guess after catching my dad with his girlfriend and beating her up, my mom was sure to let him know, in real "a woman scorned" fashion, she was going to 'blast him' to us. It wasn't uncommon for my mom to share with us all the bad news she had on my father. I'm not sure if it was her way of justifying her bad behavior and getting us on her side, or maybe she was just vulnerable. Either way, it came from a place of hurt. She also knew how my father felt about his kids, so she used it against him.

That night after Mom beat his girlfriend's ass, Dad called me. "Hello?" I heard him take a puff from one of his Kool cigarettes. "Bubba, you okay?"

He released the smoke. His voice was low, and I could sense there was discomfort, even a bit of fear in his voice. As I reflect, I can only imagine how hard it was to make that call.

"Yes, I'm okay. I want you to come home," I begged.

"I know you do, Bub, I know. And if it wasn't for you kids, me and your mom would have been divorced a long time ago. I love you, okay? No matter what your mother tells you, you know that I love you, right?"

I cried. And with all the strength I could muster, I replied, "Yes." It was the first time my dad had ever told me he loved me. Nothing else mattered to me at the moment. The truth is it didn't bother me that much that he moved out. I liked going over to visit him. There was much more peace over at his place. When he left, my Mom had started going back to church again to "get her life right," and seemed to be in a better mood. It also didn't bother me that he had a girlfriend. The way I had seen my mom cheat on my dad throughout my childhood years, I thought he had the right. I never knew he started cheating first.

The morning after that call with my dad, my mom convinced me to stay home from school. She said I was too upset about what happened the day before with her and my dad. It didn't take much convincing; I loved staying home from school. My sister decided not to say home. She always loved school. As I expected, my mom took me over to my dad's apartment.

"Look at your son! He couldn't even go to school today. He was so upset! Is that what you want for him? You busy around here with your

new apartment and your little girlfriend, wh
again, just living the life!"

My father knew she had orchestrated th
not amused.

She started to rustle through the cabinets, panᴛ
"Oh, you got wine and fancy wine glasses! You don't b\

I couldn't take it anymore. Whenever I got back from
with my dad, my mom always questioned me about what woᴍᴀ.
have been over there or any "woman's hair" that may have been in the
shower drain. This time she was going too far.

"Stop it!" I yelled. "This ain't yo 'partment, 'n' you can be doin' that!
Leave Daddy's stuff 'lone! And Daddy, I yo son 'n' dis yo wife, and you
can't be doin' wah you doin'!" My mom had gotten to me, and she won. I
could genuinely not give a shit that my dad was fucking another woman.
"Get yours" is what I felt, but I did feel sorry for my mom.

"I'm sorry, Greg. I won't do that again. I don't want to upset you," my
mom apologized as she had never apologized in her life. I never saw such
fake compassion. She had gotten exactly what she wanted—my emotional
reaction and my father feeling like shit. She expected my father to apologize, but he didn't. My mom and her 'gangsta ways' DID eventually get
her man (my dad) back home—in about three months.

Besides my sister, I was probably the only kid at school that had a White
mother and a Black father. If you weren't White or "all the way" Black,
you stood out. I tried my best to fit in as if I lived in a "regular" Black
household, but that never stopped kids from asking me what it felt like to
have a White mother. "What does it feel like having a Black mother?" was
my usual response. Neither Kony nor I ever really could answer, although
I would always make sure that they knew my mom was the only White
person around, and she acted like a Black mom in knowing how to cook,
scream at us, and whip my ass when she needed to. I also couldn't go without
letting them know that all of her friends were Black. All along while trying

chem, I was trying to convince myself. I just wanted to fit in
never really felt like I was similar to anyone else other than Kony.
c as what's been passed down to most of us, I have always heard,
drop of Black makes you Black," and that you go by the father's race.
owever, I wasn't made to feel like a Black boy by many, except for White
people. If my sister and I were with my mom in public, people would often
point and stare at us. Their staring sometimes made my mom respond,
"Yes, these are my kids!" Although sometimes shocked I had a White
mom, I'm not sure that any of the White kids at school made mention of
my colorful family. Conversely, the Black kids didn't hold back with the
teasing and tormenting.

"Look at the Zebra! The half-breed! The mutt!"

I've heard all of those things and more. Along with the occasional
"honkey," they would say: "house nigga, White boy," and the list goes
on. I used to get so embarrassed when my mom would have to come up
to the school. I was always reminded, to their standard, that I was not
Black enough, and that "fact" would never really allow any space for me
to fit in anywhere. Starting around age eight or nine, I would lie out in
the sun in the backyard religiously, or at times with my mom on Folly
Beach, which was down the road from our house, trying to get as dark as
possible. I wanted my skin to be the color of the other kids. I grew up in
a Black neighborhood around my extended Black family, and I identified
only with Black culture but still never wholly felt comfortable or accepted
as a part of the Black community. I was often questioned about my race,
by adults, and sometimes even by my family members.

Upstairs in her house, I was arguing with my first cousin Tawanna, both of
us about eight years old. She said I acted like a girl, and that pissed me off.

"Shetup wit yo black self! You luuk like a burn-up bisket," I shot back
at her loudly in my Geechee boy's voice.

A Black person calling another Black person "black" where I'm from
was used to insult someone for having dark skin. Nobody seemed to

have wanted dark skin except me. Adults would even check the ears of newborn babies to see how dark they would be as if it were a measurement for beauty. It seems that everyone was obsessed with skin color, and the blacker was never the better, so it was the perfect insult for my dark chocolate cousin. I had always heard kids and adults say this, so it came naturally.

My cousin's mom and sisters overheard me saying this and called me downstairs to the living room.

"Greg, wah yuu say to her?" my Aunt Nita asked in a nasty tone. Nita was married to my father's younger brother, Uncle Larry, who was in the kitchen listening.

"I say shetup, cuz she say I act like a girl," I said fearfully.

"No, wen yuu said, 'yo black self!' Wah colah yuu think you is?" she asked with slight curiousness and annoyance in her voice.

I was stumped. *What did I say wrong?* My cousin Tawanna did have dark skin. I had even overheard my Aunt Nita and her sisters call other people "black" before. My aunt also didn't like Tawanna playing in the sun because she didn't want her to get any darker. This sentiment around skin color was common for many parents of the kids in my community. I was also confused about how to answer the question. What color did I think I was? Different people always told me different things. When having to fill out forms at school, I never knew which choice to select. I felt more Black'—whatever that was supposed to feel like—so I always chose it. I even remember circling both 'Black' and 'White' a few times.

After a few seconds, I muttered, "I mix."

See, my mom always reminded me that I was mixed. Not Black, not White, but mixed. Now, I understand why she made sure I knew I was mixed. She was adamant and did not want us to forget we were also a part of her. I get it. My dad? Well, he didn't say much about it. It wasn't until high school when I was deciding what to do after I graduated that I heard him refer to me as Black.

"The Navy ain't no place for a Black man, son," he secretly told me after strong advisement from my mom to join the military. My father always made it very clear that the military did not treat Black men very well. He never would elaborate on any stories on the topic. Neither of my parents talked to us about race, Black culture, or history, nor instilled the fact that we were Black kids in the eyes of America—regardless of our White mother. What they did do was: prepare us for the backlash we would receive for having parents who were of different races. They made it known that not many people would approve of their marriage. I was always prepared not to be liked or accepted.

Carrying this baggage around with me always made me keep my guard up with most of my teachers at school, as well. I would often think the Black teachers didn't like me because my mom was White, or the White teachers didn't like me because my father was Black. To this day, my mom jokes about me using that as a reason for why I wasn't doing well in school. And though she put that fear in me, I know she was trying to prepare me the best she could. Although I always got teased and made fun of, the Black kids in school would always talk about my soft, "pretty" hair and want to touch it, especially girls and adult women—they were always very drawn to me. Boys, when they were friendly, would call me a pretty boy. Deep down inside, I believed all the teasing and name-calling were more of an admiration for my differences and a rejection of their beautiful skin color. We both hated the color of our skin and secretly admired each other for what the other had.

Thinking back the day Aunt Nita asked me about how I racially identify, I realize now she wanted me to know I was a Black kid too. She didn't want me to be fooled into thinking because my mom was White; it made me White as well. But, when I answered and said, "I mix," my Uncle Larry came in the room.

"Nita! What did I tell you about questioning those kids? Leave him alone!"

Aunt Nita didn't say another word. I knew she wanted to say more, and I wanted to hear it. I hated it when adults did that.

Then one year later, during the summer of 1986, while visiting my Aunt Mary, in Beaufort, I was playing with Jeremy—one of the White kids in the neighborhood—in his front yard. His father, apparently a pastor, came out on the porch, dressed in his black and white pastor's clothing.

"Come inside here boy and have a seat," he said to me. I was shocked because his dad had never invited me into the house, and I had no idea why he would want me to come in now. I didn't ask any questions, just said okay, and did as was told. Jeremy followed.

"Jeremy tells me that your parents are a mixed couple. That your mother is White, and your father is Black," he said to me sternly.

"Yeah, I mix," I answered.

"No, you are not. You are not counted as White. You are Black. You are not pure. When Whites mix with niggers, it erases your White race. You are a Black boy, and your parents were never supposed to make you. The Bible says Whites and Blacks are not supposed to mix! Your parents will burn in hell for being together and making you."

Shocked, tears welled up in my eyes, and I ran out of the house. I felt like I was never supposed to be born, and I would be going to hell too. If a pastor said it, it had to be true. I never did tell anyone about that day. I just stopped going over my little White friend Jeremy's house.

———

My parents did the best they could and were the most amazing providers for us. My mom was great at making sure we had nice clothes, fresh from the cleaners where she worked. My mom always cooked dinner, and we never went without. She would also take us out to restaurants for dinner—one of my favorite things to do with her. Whenever I got sick, she would feel my tummy (yes, tummy, not forehead) to see if I had a fever. I always loved it when she did that, partly because she was never the touchy-feely type, and I yearned for that type of attention. Sometimes I would even fake sick to get it, or I even once threatened my dad and said I was going to run away.

"You gon' run away? Wah you runnin away foe?" my dad asked while I rubbed my eyes.

"cause nobody love me."

"Ha! You hear dat Tawny? He say nobody love him. Want me show you how much I love you?!" My dad said, laughing as he began removing his belt as if he was going to whip me.

He never did whip me, so I knew he was only kidding.

"Gon run way! You gon' run right back hea!"

And so, I ran down the street, only to come back five to six hours later before dark after no one came to look for me. I hated that I had to go back home, almost validating my feelings of loving them more than they loved me. That wasn't true, but I didn't know at the time that "laughing things off" was my parents' way of showing love.

Every Easter, my mom ensured we had a new outfit and Easter basket, and on the Fourth of July, Dad always had our annual BBQ and fireworks. We didn't take many vacations, but when we did, my mom usually packed us up for a weekend at Myrtle Beach or somewhere else close enough to drive while my dad stayed behind. Although he would spend time with us here and there, we were mostly with our mom while my dad worked or slept to prepare to go to work.

Thanksgiving was our favorite holiday, especially Dad's. He would love to carve the turkey and take the first bite. "Man, dis turkey jam up!" was always his favorite thing to say, adding, "Ya know ya gotta let 'em soak overnight, so the seasonings go through it. Right, Rita Faye?"

My mom would always gloat at the compliment. Making sure my dad had a good meal was something that she took seriously as a wife. Kony and I would always have to write and recite the Thanksgiving blessing, which everyone would follow with what they were thankful for before we could eat. And Santa Claus never missed our house on Christmas. When I reached ten, they would let us sip sherry wine during the Christmas dinner toast. My dad would always take me fishing and even came to my first baseball and basketball game. I never made the second game of either before quitting. Although not the tender, loving, emotional type, my parents put forth their best, and overall, I believe they did a great job.

Mom and Dad, picture booth, Ocean City, MD, 1975

Dad and Mom in their first apartment, 1975

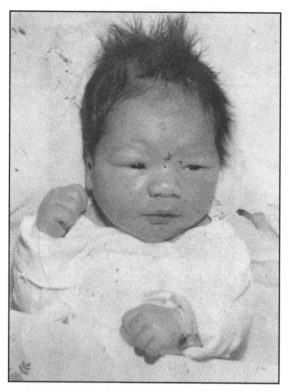

Gee, newborn, Prince George's County Hospital, Cheverly, MD, 1977

Gee and sister 'Kony,' Easter Sunday in front yard, James Island, SC, 1979

Gee, Frampton Elementary School, Head Start, Charleston, SC, 1981

Gee and Kony with Dad after his softball game, 1983

Gee photobombs Mommy before she goes to the club, 1983

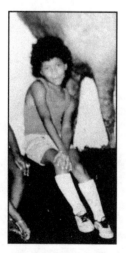

Gee, Charlestown Landing, 1984

Gee in favorite Pepsi shirt, 1985

3

FAGGOT-ASS HALF-BREED

YOU DON'T NEED that College Prep English class. That's for students who are preparing to go to college. I am going to recommend you for the general level English class." Mrs. Brown, my eighth-grade English teacher, a chunky Black woman in her mid-forties with thick glasses and a Jheri curl, uttered those words as I was signing up for my freshman classes. I held my head down with shame as a feeling of defeat overtook my body, and I told myself, "I am not smart enough for college." Those very words defined how I thought of my education during the next few years of high school.

Although my feelings were bruised and my self-esteem was broken, deep down, I couldn't deny how Mrs. Brown's words mirrored the nagging complex I already had about not having been smart enough. Even though neither of my parents went to college, I wanted to go, especially after the show A Different World came out, which was about students at a Historically Black University (HBCU). Maybe I always felt less than smart as a kid because of how my dad would always call me "dummy" as a joke.

"No, dummy! That's not how you do it!" he would say, laughing.

While I would laugh it off, it always made me question whether or not I was dumb, and still to this day, I often call myself that out loud. In my head, sometimes, it was his voice. This negative verbalization contributed to my feelings of not being able to do well in school. It also didn't help that my mom constantly nagged me about not doing as good in school as my sister. Kony, who was nearly three years older than me, was considered the "smart" one. Now that I think of it she was always the "golden child." Rightfully so, because I was a pretty active kid who often got into trouble.

My work ethic and study habits reflected the lack of confidence I had at achieving academic success all through middle school. It didn't help that the school grouped students on how smart we were: Group A being the smartest and Group C being the dumbest, with Group's B1, B2, and B3 falling in between. I was in Group C, which was always the laughing stock of each grade level. I developed a habit, only to do the bare minimum to pass a class. Honestly, I hated school. I always did. I would especially suck at writing and grammar, and my Gullah Geechee dialect did not help. My reading comprehension was so bad; I'd have to read a paragraph five times before being able to understand—often, I still do. I can't say I ever really had great experiences with any of my teachers while I was growing up in Charleston.

The only teacher I enjoyed and worked hard for was my fifth-grade teacher, Mrs. Oliver. She was a younger, hip, Black woman in her early thirties, and she was always very kind to me. I believed she treated me special because she knew I felt different than the rest of the kids. Hell, I was different than the rest of the kids. I can recall one incident in Mrs. Oliver's class, where I sat at my desk and started feeling like I had to defecate. I thought I could hold it, and I did for about two hours. Before I knew it, my Fruit of the Loom tighty whities was full of shit. The entire class was making a fuss about the smell, and she knew it was me. On the way to lunch, she asked if I wanted to call my parents, but I said no. I was too embarrassed to admit it was me. Mrs. Oliver went along with it to save me the embarrassment of the kids finding out.

I can't say many teachers treated me so nicely, or at least I never felt like they did. And Mrs. Brown was no different.

Despite my perception of school, my pride took over, and I became adamant about taking this college-prep English class and signed up for it. I had to prove Mrs. Brown wrong.

On the first day of school in that college prep English class, I met Carla. It was the first period of my freshman year at James Island High School that had just over 1,000 students. I noticed her sitting in the second seat of my row. From in the back, I would catch small glimpses of her face when she turned around to pass some papers back or talk to other classmates. Just a tad bit taller than me, Carla stood about 5'5" with flawless pecan brown skin, straight black shoulder-length hair that she always wore in a ponytail with a long bang over her left eye that reached down to her chin. She had the most beautiful cat eyes that reminded me of Nia Long or Angela Bassett. She weighed about 100 pounds and always seemed bashful. My crush on her was instant and ongoing, yet I could never muster up the courage to do anything about it for that entire fall semester. What would she want with a short, yellow boy with slick, wavy hair and a girly voice? Not to mention, I had eaten my way through middle school stress, which now put me in the "fat boy" category.

There was something unique about Carla. She was unlike any of the girls I ever liked before. She was a talented basketball player, so she was both popular and athletic. Despite her petite frame and dainty demeanor, she exhibited subtle masculinity about the way she carried herself. She didn't cross her legs when she sat, and she never wore dresses or skirts. She neither wore lipstick, nail polish, jewelry, nor would she ever carry a purse. Although popular because of her athletic ability, she was still a bit quiet and did not seem to have many friends that she hung around. I liked this about her.

Why would Carla want me? Fear kept saying to me, "You're no match for her. You don't act like a real man. You're short, fat, and everyone is calling you a faggot." These thoughts paralyzed me, making me afraid to make my feelings known to her. What if people teased me in front of her? I couldn't fathom her bearing witness to the boys on the bus who would yell out the window to me as I walked off, asking to come over later that night.

"Come on, girl, wen you gon' let me ride dat bonkey? Wen you gon' gimme sum? Lemme come ta nite."

"Letting them ride" meant they wanted to have sex with me, and "bonkey" meant butt, both apart of our Gullah Geechee language. The boys did this at least two to three times a week, and it always left me feeling humiliated. I couldn't possibly let Carla see that.

I also knew she had a boyfriend. He was someone she had been dating for two years since the seventh grade. How in the hell was I going to get my chance if she had a boyfriend?

My only saving grace was that he was a year younger and still in middle school. I only saw them together at our school football games, so I knew I'd have plenty of time to make my move. After daily daydreams of our courtship, it wasn't until the winter semester that I finally built enough courage to tell her how I felt. I still don't think she noticed I was in her class. When she would have to speak in front of the class, she would hold her head down and not make eye contact. She carried an air of darkness around with her—a bit of sadness. It was something, I believe, attracted me to her. I, too, was hurting and carried an air of sadness around with me.

How do I approach this girl? I finally thought of the perfect solution: it was always easy for me to write down my feelings, so I decided to send her a secret admirer letter.

December 15, 1991

Dear Carla,

I am writing you this letter because I want to tell you that I like you. I am making it a secret because I know you have a boyfriend, and I do not want to be embarrassed. I see y'all at the football games sitting together and hugging. I still really like you even though you may not like me back or want to cheat on your boyfriend. I am in one of your classes and sit behind you. I always think about you and think you are very pretty with your Chinese eyes and beautiful skin. If you do not mind, maybe we can be secret lovers? I will not tell anybody. I hope that you will write back.

Sincerely,
Your secret admirer

Being Carla's secret lover was acceptable to me. I remember when Atlantic Starr came out with that song "Secret Lovers," and it felt normal. Besides, I had grown up with parents who cheated on each other.

I had a close friend named Christina Latten, who shared class with us. She was also the girlfriend of one of my best childhood friends, JT. Christina knew how much I liked Carla, so I decided I would let her be the one to give it to her. The morning after I wrote the letter, I was so nervous. English was my first-period class, which meant Carla would get it first thing in the morning. I gave Christina strict instructions not to give it to her until the end of class. I could not stand the thought of her reading it while I sat in the same row, six seats behind her. She would know it was me and laugh. I was convinced she would figure out who it was, but she didn't. By lunchtime, Christina had already heard back from Carla and was begging me to give her permission to tell.

"Hey Greg, Carla really wanted to know who the letter's from. Can I please tell her? C'mon, please? She thinks someone is playing a joke on her."

I replied, "Man, I don't know. What if she laughs or embarrasses me? She could tell everyone."

"Well, she acts like she's excited about the letter, and that it doesn't even matter that she already has a boyfriend. I think you have a shot. C'mon, man, let me tell her, please."

"Okay, Christina, go ahead and tell her."

Carla returned the letter with her own words, most of which I don't remember, but it did include her number. She even went on to tell me that she loved my "jet Black, wavy hair." My hair was always a hit with the girls.

Carla was so sweet and innocent, despite her cheating on her boyfriend with me for a couple of weeks.

"We hardly ever talk or see each other. I'll tell him eventually. I don't want to be with him," she would tell me.

Not long after that, she broke up with her boyfriend and started going steady with me on January 10, 1993. I remember the night she broke up with her boyfriend, she called to tell me, and I immediately ask her to be my girlfriend. "Ask me da morrah on da teenth. Dat's my jersey numba."

I thought it was cute that she wanted our anniversary date to match her jersey. Carla had this well thought out.

While I had to attend summer school for failing College Prep English as Mrs. Brown predicted, I understood Carla was my destiny, even at that young age. In my heart, I knew I took that class to meet her. It was the last college prep class I would take.

Her innocence and shyness also attracted me to her. She wasn't like a lot of aggressive and fast girls around the school, which made me feel more comfortable. I wouldn't be pressured into anything or feel like I had to go after sex. I was terrified of sex because I still hadn't started puberty yet and was ashamed.

Carla and I would spend hours talking on the phone and meet each other after every one of her basketball games. She was one of the best players on her team, and I would never miss the opportunity to see her play. While her two sisters were always at her games, her parents never came. Whenever I would call her house, her dad would sound so mean, like he didn't want me calling there. I was terrified to meet him, so I was kind of glad they never came. Carla was from a neighborhood we called "down the island," which was known for being "the hood" and one of the places you would go on James Island to buy drugs. I never liked going "down the island" because that area seemed to have all the toughest boys and meanest adults who picked on me the most. Aside from being afraid they wouldn't accept the way I looked; I think this was also part of the reason I was scared to meet her parents. I do remember, however, seeing them from a distance on "parent appreciation night," but I never officially met them. By the time we had gotten to our sophomore year, Carla had moved in with her great grandmother, Mother Mae, so I always visited her there, and Mother Mae loved me. She always liked my hair too. Although Mother Mae lived in the house directly in front of Carla's parents' house, almost in the front yard, I still would never see them.

We spent so many days and nights on the couch, watching TV and talking. She quickly became my "Pooh," which is the pet name I made up for her. Carla had a gentle, affectionate spirit and way about her that I loved. It was motherly and tender, and she always showed me lots of affection. She gave me nurturing and love I hadn't experienced before. I appreciated her for this.

While all my life, I was called faggot, punk, sissy, and more by kids in the neighborhood, dating Carla didn't make that name-calling go away. It got worse. Instead of me dealing with the vicious taunts of high school boys alone, I introduced a girlfriend to that same pain. I picked up more pressure from having to protect a girl from boys that I knew I could never beat.

Carla and I were often harassed as we walked down the hall. I remember one day, this one boy yelled, "Why do you go with that faggot? You know Greg likes dick up in his bonkey, right?" Bonkey is Geechee for a butt. That remains one of the most embarrassing moments of my life. I was never good at sticking up for myself. My sister always did that for me, and now I had a girlfriend to protect. I was not up for the role.

Carla was never afraid to take up for me, though, almost replacing my sister. "Leave him alone," she shouted. "He is not no faggot! He's more of a man than you will ever be!" While I appreciated her support, I hated she felt compelled to protect me so often. I wished I was not so afraid to stand up to them. I wished I had her courage. Why were they so mean to me? Why were they so set on embarrassing me and making me feel like shit? Couldn't they see I now had a girlfriend, and that proved I was not a faggot? There were a few times I was cornered and asked if we fucked yet, or if I was going with her to say I had a girlfriend. The worst part about what they said was that, deep down, I wondered if it was partially true. I was afraid to have sex with her, so maybe I really was gay.

Did I always keep girlfriends as a protection of my masculinity? Was it the only way I could express anything I deemed to be masculine? I never had a shot at being tough, playing sports, or doing anything remotely related to what it means to be masculine. Still, I sure could date girls and get a girlfriend—I liked girls. Actually, I loved girls! They were always so much fun to be around. I never felt as much pressure to act like something I was not. As a boy who was feminine presenting, being around other boys always filled me with anxiety. I was aware of how I was seen by others, ensuring I did not do or say anything feminine-like. I obviously failed all too often since I did have the reputation of being a sissy.

Even though growing up, I was blessed to have great male friends from my neighborhood who accepted me for me; I still wanted acceptance from all the others who rejected me. It didn't matter that JT, Jerome, Nicky, and Twan never brought up the fact that I was a little "girly" and everyone else was calling me a faggot, I was still conscious of my behavior and mannerisms around them.

Maybe always having a girlfriend was me just doing what I was taught to do. "You got a girlfriend yet?" was a common question asked of little boys. I felt I was supposed to have a girlfriend, but it was never something I ever thought I was doing with intention. And it helped that it was "normal" and what I was supposed to do. I mean, I did genuinely like the girls I dated. I have to admit, I also remember the feeling I experienced once with a boy when I had started middle school.

I remember it was the sixth grade when I was in the boy's bathroom washing my hands. A seventh-grader named Rodrick walked in. He was dark brown with a medium, athletic build, bright white teeth, and a box fade. He had the same bad-boy swag as the rest of his crew. They were all from Sol e Gre, an area of James Island that used to be one of the 17 slave plantations. Most of them would all end up in jail years later for selling drugs. Rodrick was also one of those boys who would call me names and harass me. But it was usually only when he was around his friends, which was not uncommon for most boys. This day, Rodrick was coming into the bathroom as I was walking out, and we ran into each other. Well, it was more like he deliberately got in my way to stop me. He didn't say anything at first; he just kept blocking me as I tried to get around him.

"Weh you goin'?" he asked with a slight smirk.

When he finally did let me pass, he touched me on my butt and smiled at me as I looked back. It was a soft, gentle touch. I was very confused by this gesture, but I remember feeling something I had never felt before. I felt vulnerable but in a good way. I not only felt accepted but desired—by one of the boys who made my life a living hell. It's my first memory of feeling romantic affection from another male. While it was not the first time a boy had touched my butt, it was the first time it felt like an attraction towards me. I remember back when I was growing up between the ages of seven and ten; there were two neighborhood boys I used to play with almost every day. It was not uncommon for us to hump each other in the woods or the bed when we had sleepovers. I had these experiences off and on with three of my neighborhood friends until seventh grade. I never associated this behavior with liking boys, and it never felt like we "liked" each other during these experiences. It just felt explorative, curious, and natural, no different than it felt when I also had these types of experiences with girls. That day in the bathroom of James Island Middle School, though, was different. Rodrick liked me, and I liked him, but that's all it would ever be.

I did have some not-so-comfortable sexual experiences when I was this age, as well. One that comes to mind was with my neighbor Brad. He and his family were the only White family in the neighborhood. I always loved going over their house because his mom was always so nice. Whenever I went over to play, she would let me go into their cabinet and grab a handful of banana chips. To me, they were the best thing ever, as I had never seen banana chips anywhere else. She would also make pimento cheese sandwiches, something else I had never seen in anyone else's house, but could have gone without them. I never did like the taste. To this day, banana chips and pimento cheese sandwiches are something that I associate with White people. What I'm about to say may sound weird since I have a White mother, but I never looked at my family as White or at my mom as a "normal" White person.

Brad also always had the coolest toys and the best bikes. Brad was about two or three years older than me and would always look after me when we played. Brad was also the person that introduced me to "playing doctor." In this game, he would take me to his "examination room," which was a cool fort that his dad built for him in the backyard, and he would ask me to lie down on my stomach so he could examine me. He would then pull down my pants and spread my butt cheeks while sticking a needle from a pine tree between them as if he was poking and prodding to test for irregularities. He never tried to penetrate me; he'd use the pine needles to stick me. While it would make me uncomfortable, Brad never made me feel scared or like he was going to harm me. He was always kind to me and let me play with any of the toys I wanted, so "playing doctor" never bothered me that much. He was nothing like Bernetta.

Bernetta was the daughter of one of the girlfriends that my mom would often hang out with on weekends. Bernetta had an older teenage sister that used to watch us when our moms went out to the clubs. I would often spend the night over at their house, and I always hated it. Although her sister would let us do anything we wanted: from running the streets day or night, jumping on all the beds, running throughout the house, and making and eating all the syrup sandwiches we could eat, I still hated it. I hated going over there mostly because I was terrified of Bernetta. She was about three years older than me, and she was a tomboy. She was very tough and did all the things boys would especially fight. She loved to bully people; boys included, especially me.

One night, while everyone was downstairs, Bernetta told me to come upstairs with her to play Pac-Man on their Atari in the attic, where she and her two older brothers shared a bedroom. She knew how much I loved that game, and I was good at it, too, even at age 7. It was not even two seconds after entering the attic bedroom when she ordered me to pull down my pants as she began pulling down hers while standing near the window by the bed.

"Come here," she demanded, watching the confused look on my face. "I said, come here!"

I began to walk reluctantly towards the window, as the old pissy mattress began to overwhelm my sense of smell. Bernetta was known for peeing the bed.

"Pull your pants down!" she said again, only this time she said it while grinding her teeth as if she was getting angry and trying to keep her voice down so no one could hear her commands.

I trembled with extreme terror, but I began to slowly pull down my "jams," these colorful beach shorts we wore back in the '80s. With my Fruit of the Loom underwear exposed, Bernetta looked at me with dis-appointment as she aggressively pulled my underwear down.

"Press up against me! Come closer!"

Bernetta grabbed me by the waist and pressed my body up against hers. She smelled as bad as the aroma from the mattress. It was almost like a mix of urine, underarm odor, and gym socks.

"Stop!" I cried out as she started to pull on my penis.

"Shet up, you lil faggot, and stop being so loud. You a lil crybaby!"

Bernetta continued to grab, pull, and pinch my penis, pressing it up against her vagina as if she was trying to insert me inside of her.

"Ouch! That hurts! Stop it!" I said as I tried to pull away from her. The pinch from her nails on the head of my penis was excruciating.

"Come hea 'n' jus be quiet! If yo lil ass dick wasn't so soft, I wouldn't have to pull it! I knew you was nothin' but a faggot-ass half-breed!"

Bernetta always pushed me around but never like this. I don't remember how many more times she took me up to that attic.

4

LOVE HER, LOVE HER NOT

CARLA AND I did not share our first kiss until after maybe three months of being together. I was always very slow in making the first move with girls, and it was no different from Carla. I remember I would always talk about kissing her in our love letters but acting as if we never had the opportunity. One night after one of her basketball games freshman year, she called me behind the school and said to me as we walked towards the back, "You gon' kiss me or wah, Greg?" As soon as she said that, I pulled her in and kissed her on the lips. I had kissed my fair share of girls throughout my early adolescent years, but this was the first time I kissed my official girlfriend in a real relationship, in high school. Ever since that night, we never greeted or left each other's presence without a "nab," which was the nickname we made up for a kiss.

"Gimme nab" was one of our most favorite things to say to one another.

Carla and I quickly became codependent. We were in love and spent as much time as we could together. "Make It Last Forever" by Keith Sweat became the first song that became "ours." We had that good ole fashion puppy love with the butterflies to boot. She had also become my security blanket and protection throughout high school. As long as we were together, I had, at least, a small piece of masculinity to claim.

And people weren't teasing me as much, I think, mostly out of respect for Carla. People could and would still assume I was gay, but having a girlfriend added a shadow of a doubt.

One night when I was 16, these two boys who I worked with as a dishwasher at a restaurant called Bushy's forced me to go to this White girl's house instead of taking them straight home. I was driving, but I wouldn't dare tell them no. One of the guys, Jimmy, was my ultimate tormentor in school and at work. I only use to let him ride with me, because I thought that would make him like me. That never happened.

"You gonna prove to us you like pussy and fuck this White girl!" Jimmy said to me, while in the backseat of my 1980 Honda Accord.

"Yea, you always talking about you like girls. Well, you gonna prove it. You bet not be scared either!" the other boy said to me.

"Ain't like I scared, I jus don't be cheatin on my girl like dat." That statement was both true and false. I was scared as shit, but I did not want to cheat on Carla. Luckily the girl never answered the knock at her window, so I did not have to prove that I was not scared or cheat on Carla. I felt so small that night like such a punk.

And although I loved her—loved her more than I had ever loved another girl—I eventually started to feel like something was not complete. I loved having Carla, but by the time we had been together for a year and a half, I started to feel smothered and wanted to explore. I broke up with her for the first time towards the end of our sophomore year of high school.

Soon after, I would try to find another girlfriend. If it went too long without me finding someone else, I would miss Carla and go back to her. Most times, when I went back to her, she was dating another boy, and I took her attention away from him. Carla never rejected me.

However, it wouldn't be long before I would have those same feelings of not wanting to be with her. I would break up with her again because I felt we weren't meant for each other. This cycle continued throughout all our years of high school.

Although Carla and I had been together off and on for years, we made out a lot but still hadn't had sex. Sex terrified me because of my insecurities with my body, but I felt so much pressure to lose my virginity, and I must admit that I was becoming a horny teenage boy.

At 17, I had finally started puberty! I finally had hair "down there," although I still felt like my dick was little. Not being able to see it without lifting my stomach did not help. My voice? Well, that wouldn't change until college, along with facial hair. Many people used to think I was a girl, and because I was overweight, it looked like I had a set of teenage-girl breasts, which would further their confusion when I told them I was a boy. When I worked the drive-thru during my part-time job at Burger King or answered the phone at home, everyone thought I was a girl. I'd hear things like, "Yes, ma'am, that will complete my order," or "Hey Tawny, is your mom home?"

But at least I had pubic hair! I finally built up enough courage and had sex the first time during the summer before starting my senior year of high school, but it wasn't with Carla. It was just some random girl I met at the pool that I used to end my virginity. She was a much larger girl and not so easy on the eyes, so it was easy for me to not worry about rejection with her. Not to mention, she did not know me, and I didn't care what she thought, and it made me feels secure that she was even fatter than me. I felt like she should have been lucky to have me. I feel bad every time I think about her.

Carla and I finally tried to have sex during the middle of my senior year in high school. After returning to school following that summer break, I asked Carla to be my girlfriend again. One rainy Friday night, Mother Mae was in a deep sleep. Carla and I were making out and dry humping on the couch as we did every weekend, until Carla whispered to me, "Let's go to my room. Be really quiet." I got up, and she led me by the hand, tiptoeing across the cherry hardwood floors, down the hall to her bedroom. Carla sat on the edge of the bed and lifted her arms for me to remove her oversized blue and orange James Island Trojans t-shirt. It was the first time I had ever seen her bare breasts. She lay back as I started to caress her small breast and lick her nipples that I had touched so often under her shirt but never in this way. The entire time I was kissing and touching Carla, my dick remained limp. Any other time when we were making out, my dick would stay hard until I left to go home. I couldn't understand what was going on. Now that it was time for action, I could not step up to the plate. Even after us taking off our pants and me grinding on her, I still could not get an erection. I remember trying to force my flaccid penis inside of her, and it reminded me of those days on Bernetta's pissy mattress. And just like in those moments, I began to feel like a failure and less than a man. I had so much anxiety about my body, my penis, and being able to "measure up" that I could not stay in the moment. It was just too much pressure.

"I sorry. I know I tight like a clam." Carla said to me as she rubbed my head while we were lying on the bed. I knew Carla was just trying to make me feel better by taking the blame for what was supposed to be a magical night. I couldn't say a word; I was just too embarrassed. I remember on the way home "I'll Make Love to You" by BoyzIIMen was playing on the radio. I felt like God was laughing at me. To this day, that song reminds me of that moment.

After another unsuccessful attempt at having sex at Mother Mae's house, we finally went through with it at the Evergreen Motel on Savannah Highway in a part of Charleston called West of the Ashley. The Evergreen was known for being the cheap spot you go to have sex. I believe it was about $30 a night. It was awkward at first but quickly felt natural. I didn't have any issues getting an erection like before. I think I was finally able to get more comfortable with the thought of being naked with Carla, and I did not worry so much.

After that first time, we began having sex often. Many times were at The Evergreen, more times were in my Blue 1989 VW Jetta in the school parking lot or at Sol E Gre Boat Landing while listening to Carla's favorite song, "Body and Soul" by Anita Baker, and a few times were in my parents' house.

I believe the fact that we were having sex was the only thing that kept us together most of our senior year. I liked having sex with Carla, and although I loved her, I often felt smothered and wanted out, but having sex was a huge plus to stay in the relationship. I could try to have sex with someone else, but it was way too intimidating to try and get this comfortable again. Having sex also gave me a little confidence. It made me feel like a man, but more importantly, it made me feel a little bit more like all the other boys.

By the time the fall semester of senior year was ending, I had decided I wanted to go to college. I knew I was not going to go to the military, as my mom wanted. Sometimes, I think she thought enlisting would make me into a man or toughen me up. I would never go as it was way too intimidating, and I would never fit in there. Around my neighborhood, the military seemed to be the place most of the Black boys went after high school. It appeared to be a viable option for everyone. I knew that was never going to happen for me, even though a part of me wanted to go. I always imagined the military as another place for me to get bullied. The thought of being around only men in such a hyper-masculine environment terrified the shit out of me.

So, what was I to do now? How could I get into college, only having taken one college prep class and suffered from a 2.0 GPA? My rank was 201 out of 246 students in my class, and I had an SAT score of 720 out of 1600. I did not apply myself enough to get into any traditional colleges or universities. I refused to go to Trident Technical College, the place everyone who didn't leave James Island went but never seemed ever to finish. I wasn't passionate about anything except cooking, but I did not want to go to culinary school. My limited view of being a chef was cooking in a hot kitchen every day, and I didn't want to do that. I knew there was another life out there for me, and I wanted to grab it. My saving grace arrived when DeVry Institute, now DeVry University, recruited at our school during my senior year. I was first in line. All I had to do was take an entrance exam to get in, and even if I failed, I could still attend, by taking extra classes; This was my sure way out of James Island.

Although Carla and I didn't break up as much as we did in our sophomore and junior year, our relationship was still stressed. The truth is, part of me wanted to be with her, and part of me didn't. Carla's neediness did not allow me any freedom that I desperately desired while with her. She was not very social and did not have many friends, only her two sisters—which meant she wanted to spend all of her time with me. I started to feel suffocated and resentful. I enjoyed that we were having sex and I had a girlfriend to spend time with, but I always had the desire to get out. I believed that Carla and I did not have the chemistry I felt when we first met.

After graduating high school, Carla stayed behind in Charleston to work as a manager at McDonald's. At the same time, I went off to a new life in Atlanta. It was July 5, 1995, and I drove my packed 1989 Jetta while my mom and dad followed, heading down to Decatur, Georgia, to start my life as a student majoring in Computer Information Systems. It was the "information age," and if I wanted a "guarantee" to make good money, computers were the way to go. I had taken a few programming classes in high school, and I was good at it. So, I didn't mind pursuing a degree in it, despite having no real passion for it. I hadn't identified anything I was passionate about except making money since I tried out for that role as Darnell years ago.

5

CURIOUS

I N ATLANTA, I had never seen so many Black people in my life! Successful Black people! No longer did driving a Lexus or Mercedes Benz mean the Black person behind the wheel sold drugs like it did in Charleston. I was excited about my possibilities. I also was very rarely asked what I was "mixed with" anymore. With all types of Black people that all looked different, I didn't stand out as much. I loved it. Nobody was interested in touching my hair, but they sure were curious about my accent. I never knew I had an accent until I moved, and people asked if I were from the Bahamas or Jamaica. Aside from receiving the occasional apology after someone in the room talked about White people, which I always hated, it was rare that anyone pointed out that I was not "all the way Black."

When I moved to Atlanta, I came with JT and another friend named Alan. DeVry's student-housing were actual apartments they rented for their students and charged four times the cost. We had a two-bedroom, two-bathroom apartment; Alan and I shared a room, while JT and a guy named Thomas from North Carolina shared a room. It wasn't until after I moved in with these guys that my attraction for men became more apparent.

Alan was very comfortable with his body to the point that he would walk around our room naked, lotion his entire body including dick and balls, and lie around—all in front of me. Even when he would walk around with his boxers on, it was normal to see Alan lying down playing video games with his dick slipping out. This was the first time I had ever experienced anything like this, and it made me so curious. I was nowhere near comfortable with my fat, soft, and overweight body. Still, my attraction and curiosity made me want to do the same. I admired how free he was with his naked body. I remember once after taking a shower, my dick was exposed after I walked out of the bathroom while wearing just a t-shirt. I was not comfortable exposing my man boobs and belly, but I wanted in on the action. I wanted to experience the freedom he seemed to have.

Alan and I never did anything sexual. Alan is straight to my knowledge, but those very innocent experiences were pivotal moments in my life. I discovered I could not deny my sexual attraction any longer. Alan didn't even stay with us very long, dropping out of school after six months. For me, his impact was life changing. Before I had reached the age of 19, less than a year after moving to Atlanta, my same-sex attraction started to get the best of me. Were the kids in Charleston right all along about me? Was I a faggot?

My attraction to the same sex was apparent to the other college kids. I thought, when starting over at a new place, I would be able to escape the gay rumors. The rumors seemed to get increasingly worse, and over the next three years, I fought hard against them. The gossiping and tormenting about me being gay only escalated. The fact that Carla, my girlfriend and security blanket, was so far away only made it worse. She couldn't protect me anymore. No one could see I had a real girlfriend and couldn't possibly be gay. People often accused me of making her up.

Carla and I had planned to maintain a long-distance relationship at first until I broke up with her again and again as we danced the same dance we did in high school. I would go back to her, then break up with her because the relationship was not "right," but then run back to her again when things got uncomfortable just like I did in high school. Only this time, I was also dealing with my growing attraction towards men.

As the arguments ensued, I started to resent Carla again. I felt like she was trying to hold me back. Since moving to Atlanta, Carla became needy and jealous that I was in another city without her. She even wanted to move to Atlanta to be with me, which sounded ridiculous to me since we were only 18. I think she saw me as her escape away from the hell she lived at home, but I was not ready to be that person for her.

I remember she caught the Greyhound bus to Atlanta once to see me about eight months after I moved. The night she arrived, I broke up with her because I was dating my next-door neighbor, Veronica, who also attended DeVry. I didn't tell Carla that was the reason. I didn't even intend to break up with her because Veronica also had a boyfriend back home, and we agreed to this situation. I hated cheating on Carla, and I would have broken up with her, but I believe I held on to her because Veronica didn't break up with her boyfriend. However, after Carla tried having sex with me in her hotel room that night after dinner, I started feeling too guilty and couldn't fake it.

"What's wrong?" she asked while grinding on top of me, in her sexy lingerie—something she had never worn in the past. She could tell I was not into it, which had never happened before.

"I just can't do this anymore. I feel like we've grown apart," I lied, knowing that I was hurting Carla once again.

I left her in the hotel room that night and went to sleep with Veronica. I took Carla back to the bus station early that next day. That was fucked up of me to treat her that way. I remember my mom telling me how unfair it was of me to break up with Carla because Veronica didn't break up with her boyfriend. She never once told me it was wrong to cheat on her, though.

Veronica was a "bad" girl. She was the "hoe" in her high school, and this was only confirmed after I once found her sex diary, where she kept a record of all her sexual experiences, and *damn*, there were a lot of times and partners. Yet, this didn't bother me because not only did I admire her liberation—she was a fine and fast girl, all the guys wanted her, and she wanted me. She also was a freak and gave great sex. Carla used to suck my dick occasionally, but only out of obligation. Veronica did it out of love for the dick, and she was the first person to tell me my dick was big. For a "hoe" to say that to me, I knew it had to be true. Despite my late puberty, I now knew I had a big dick. I fell quickly and madly in love with Veronica. Six months into our courtship, Veronica got pregnant by me and wanted to have an abortion. I wanted Veronica to keep the baby, but she was convinced her dad would kill her.

Even though I did not want her to abort the baby, I had to pay for the procedure—$300. I remember walking into the family planning clinic on Buford Highway, where Veronica made the appointment, the cheapest place she could find at the time—no surprise why. The place was small, with a crowded lobby area with about four or five rooms in the back where they performed all kinds of medical procedures for women. Most of the staff were Asian and spoke very little English. After I paid, we were led to one of the small, cold rooms that smelled like Band-Aids. They made Veronica change into a patient's robe and place each leg on the stirrups that sat on her left and right side.

"Looks like you are about twelve weeks pregnant with a boy. We can go ahead and perform this procedure. Do you still want to go through with this?" The Doctor looked over at Veronica, and Veronica looked over at me. I looked at the ultrasound machine screen and held my head down. All I could think about was what would be my son, in her belly—soon to be taken away from me. I didn't understand my immediate attachment or the sadness I felt. I just knew I wanted him—a son.

"Yes, I do," Veronica firmly replied without hesitation, and moments later, she was squeezing my hand as I listened to him being sucked out of her by what looked like to be a long vacuum cleaner hose. I held her hand, bearing witness as the sponsor of the experience.

Days later, I had phoned my mom, who was in the dark about the whole ordeal. I was afraid to tell her but couldn't hold it in any longer. I was sad.

"Veronica had an abortion a couple of weeks ago."

"She what, Greg? Oh gosh, how do you know it was yours? I knew Veronica was a little loose."

"I knew it was, Momma." I started to choke up, and she could hear it.

46

"You wanted her to keep the baby, Greg?"

"Yes, but Veronica said her Dad would kill her, and she didn't want to keep it."

"Aww. I wish I would have known Greg. I'm sorry. She was probably just scared, but we would have all come together for the baby. It will be okay."

I immediately cried my heart out. My mom had a way of doing that when she got "soft." Things were never the same between Veronica and me, and shortly after that, we fell apart. And not long after that, I was back with Carla.

Beyond any other feelings, I didn't want to regret losing Carla forever. Even though I still felt like I was suffocating many times in the relationship, I was worried that I would be making the biggest mistake of my life by letting her go. She was all I knew. She was familiar, like family, accepting my now 245 pounds of femininity. At the time, it was the closest thing to unconditional love I'd ever experienced.

I struggled desperately over the first couple of years after moving to Atlanta to fight off my attraction towards men. I did not want to be gay. I was taught it was not right, no one would accept me, and more importantly, I would go to hell. Although I did not grow up in a religious household, my mom believed in the Bible, and that meant so did we. She was no Bible beater by any means, but we were Christians, and Jesus was the way and only way. Everyone knew Jesus couldn't stand fags, so I was not going to be one. My dad never said anything about church or God and never attended church with us during the times we went with Mom while she would go through her phases of "getting her life right with God." By the time I reached high school, I would go to church on my own and even read Bible scriptures every night before bed. I was always drawn to a Higher Power. I was determined not to disappoint my family, my friends, Carla, and especially God. I prayed every night that God would make me fall back in love with Carla and take these ungodly feelings away from me. I prayed that He would give me the feelings I was "supposed" to have for her. I prayed hard, very hard, and at times, I thought it worked.

Being in Atlanta exposed me to gay men, as I had never seen before. There were a few boys I knew growing up that I thought was gay, but two of them ended up marrying a woman. I did not have any gay cousins, uncles, or anyone else as examples. Although there was my Dad's old high school classmate, who cut my hair up until the time I got to the 7th grade. Calvin who was a woman's "hair dresser", was about 5'9", medium build, brown skin, and leaned towards the feminine side. He also sported a perm that he tied up in a ponytail. My dad took me to this shop because he said all the regular barbers would not know what to do with my hair, but I wonder if he knew I was sweet just like Calvin and knew I'd fit in better there. Even though I saw a wide variety of gay men in Atlanta, I was still very naïve and never associated with any. It was still very secretive, and I wasn't one to pick up on any hints or come-ons.

DeVry had a lot of older students, and there was one gay man named Kevin Beckford, who was from New York. He was about 25, chocolate, 6'2", and 225 pounds of muscle. He flirted with me often in lab class and once invited me over to his place. I thought he was just friendly at the time, but he made me very curious, and so I went. He never did acknowledge that he was gay or said anything that gave it away, but he liked me. We just chatted a bit in his living room, and I left. Before walking out the door, he hugged me and kissed me on my neck. It was the first time I had ever hugged a man, or a man had ever kissed me in that way. At that moment, I felt the same way I did back in that bathroom at James Island Middle School when Rodrick touched my butt. Kevin made me feel vulnerable and out of control. It was like he had touched my soul. It scared the hell out of me, and I never talked to him again. I even stopped seeing him in the lab, although I'm not sure why. Sometimes I wondered if he was even real.

That was the closest I ever came to talk to or interacting with another gay man until the internet became popular in 1997. AOL Messenger had chat rooms that introduced me to sexual conversations with other men. It was the first time since Kevin, I could openly connect with guys like me, but without the fear of being rejected face-to-face. I was used to rejection from Black boys growing up; why would dating Black men be any different?

I became addicted to logging on to my dial-up network as soon as I got home from work to jump into the chat rooms. The common phrase used when letting someone know you had a pic in exchange for theirs was "PIC4TRADE." There was rarely a day that passed that I didn't go on to look at pics of handsome men. Eventually, chatting and exchanging pics couldn't appease me; I needed more, more than my then virgin girlfriend, Shenika, was giving me at the time, which was nothing. Shenika was an "around the way" girl from Decatur that caught my attention during my last year of college while I was on a long break from Carla. She was a year younger than me and had approached me one night on the dance floor at a party. I knew I was getting close to exploring outside the chat rooms, so I broke up with Shenika because I did not want to cheat on her.

I was twenty years old and curious about what an interaction with a guy would be and how it would feel. Cory was visiting his aunt for the summer from New Orleans. We met in the M4M (men for men) chat room after he posted about having an eight-inch penis. *An eight-inch penis*? That sounded huge! Although I had never measured my dick, it seemed much bigger than mine. Since Veronica had already told me what a big dick I had, I just had to see his! Hell, if it weren't for her, I probably wouldn't have had the balls to show my "small" penis to another man. That would have made me too ashamed.

Corey was not shy about what he wanted. After talking for about a month, I finally agreed to meet him behind his part-time job at a sandwich shop. I drove my car and parked behind the strip mall. We prepared the exact time and location we would meet because this was the era before most people had cell phones. As soon as I parked, I saw this guy walking towards my car. I thought it was strange that he was not coming out of the restaurant since he worked there. Instead, he was walking from an apartment complex that sat behind the strip mall. As he walked towards my car, I started to notice he didn't look anything like the pictures sent and appeared to look younger than 19(the age he gave me).

Nevertheless, I decided to trust the age he told me. He was still cute enough for me to satisfy my curiosity. Although by this time, I had strong doubts. I wasn't going to leave after coming this far, and I had to see this humongous penis he was working with.

The plan was for us to give each other head, and although I was nervous, I couldn't wait. When he entered the passenger side of my new 1997 black Nissan Sentra, he immediately said, "What's up? Pull it out." And I did just that. I pulled my dick out, and less than a minute later, I was coming all over myself, at which time he pulled out his hard, skinny dick. He had lied about having eight inches. It did not matter to me, though; it was still a dick other than mine. I was not going to let it pass—this was my first time having the opportunity to put a dick in my mouth. I put my mouth around his penis and immediately tasted chlorine as if he had just gotten out of the pool. I was a bit thrown off by the taste, but it could have been a lot worse. I had no idea what I was doing, but my whole goal was not to give him any teeth. I'd heard those bad dick-sucking stories before from my friends or in the locker room during gym, and I wasn't going to be one of them.

I must have been doing something right because he came faster than I did. It happened so quickly I didn't even have a chance to take it out of my mouth before cum filled the back of my throat. It was the nastiest experience I'd had up to that point. I loved eating pussy and the taste of it, so I was quite surprised at my reaction. I could not open my car door fast enough to spit his cum out of my mouth.

Less than thirty seconds later, we "dapped" each other up, he got out, and I sped off with feelings of extreme guilt, dirtiness, and disgust. I could not get home fast enough to wash my mouth out with peroxide, mouthwash, and toothpaste. I knew then I was not gay and would never indulge in that act again. I sent him a message informing him that I wasn't gay because I hated the experience. I also told him not to talk to me anymore. I was so excited that God had taken these gay feelings out of me.

Three days passed, and I was back in the AOL M4M chat room. I didn't want to suck any more dick, but I could not stay away from chatting with men. Not surprisingly, Cory popped up again, feeling insulted because I told him I wasn't gay. He typed, "Sorry, I came in your mouth. By the way, I'm only 16."

I thought he was trying to hurt my feelings, so I shot back, "That's okay. By the way, did you mean centimeters when saying you had 8 inches because it definitely wasn't that big!"

"Ours is the same length, yours is just thicker," was the last response I got from him before blocking him. He was clearly delusional.

I was happy that I was disgusted by the experience. I knew I couldn't possibly be gay, but I was so confused because the attraction did not go away. I couldn't understand it, but I moved forward. I went back to dating my girlfriend, Shenika, who was a virgin and made me feel confident. I enjoyed being with her. My weight had also gone down from 246 pounds to just over 200 pounds; I hired a personal trainer the day I went into a gym to purchase a bottle of a new diet pill called Phen Phen. With my new beard coming in, my face started to mature, giving me a bit of sex appeal. Shenika was a little shy, a very girly girl, but she still had the tomboy vibe to her. She was also the opposite of what I was used to, with big titties, thick thighs, and an apple booty. Her physique would typically intimidate me, but the fact that she was a virgin and passive made it feel safer.

I didn't feel as boyish as I used to feel. I was a man. The fact that she was a virgin meant I had the upper hand because, by this time, I had already been with four females. I was also a couple of years older than her, which helped. Just like all my relationships, I fell for Shenika hard and claimed my love for her. It wasn't much longer before Shenika offered me her virginity, and we were having sex regularly. Shortly before I graduated college, I broke up with her because she became too needy, always wanting me to buy her things, drive her around, and tend to her every need, all things I did willingly at the beginning of our courtship. I was learning that I had a way of making people need me and then leaving them when it became too much for me. She was no different.

I was 21 when I graduated from the DeVry Institute of Technology. I remember Momma and Daddy being so proud of me that day. Momma hadn't been that proud since my 7th-grade talent show where I performed "Don't be Cruel" by Bobby Brown. I lost, but that did not stop her from being the loudest cheering me on in the high school cafeteria.

"You're still my winner," she said to me on the way home in her new "talking" 1987 Nissan Maxima after seeing my disappointed look. She stopped by Burger King for a burger, something she rarely ever did, but something she knew would make me feel better after losing the talent show.

I was still coming into my looks and feeling more attractive by the day. I had also been successful in not hooking up with another guy, but that didn't mean my feelings went away. I noticed other guys out in public even more, and I still cruised the chat rooms, although I wouldn't act on any of the conversations. I was no longer grossed out at the thought of being with a guy again.

When I graduated, Carla and I had been broken up for over a year and a half. I heard she moved to New Jersey with her uncle and was doing well for herself. Although I missed Carla, I was not going to repeat my same old pattern.

One weekend, while visiting Charleston, I ended up running into Carla's little sister Nikki at James Island High School's homecoming game. Nikki was the only one in her family that acted as if she liked me. Her older sister couldn't stand me, but after all the back and forth I put Carla through, who could blame her?

"Hey, Nikki, how's Carla doing?" I asked.

She told me Carla was doing well in New Jersey, and I should hit her up. I decided against it, but it wasn't even a week later before Carla called me and said, "I heard you were asking about me." I could tell she missed me, and it was obvious she wanted me back. This time, she was reaching out to me, not the other way around. It had been a year since Carla and I talked, and although things seemed so different, it was just as comfortable as it had always been. A part of me wanted her back. I missed her.

This time it was different. Never mind that she had a boyfriend at the time in New Jersey. Carla sounded different. She was vibrant. She was independent, ambitious, and had a happiness about her I hadn't heard before. She had a sassy new way about her, and suddenly she became very stylish, by her own admittance. She seemingly became a new girl I thought I wanted. In my shallow mind, I believed this was a whole new Carla that would never make me feel suffocated again.

With this new transformation and the fact that she had been on my mind so heavily, I knew I had to have her back, and I was sure it would last forever. My newfound "maturity" revealed that we should never have broken up ever anyway. Those breakups were me being immature, unwilling to endure relationship challenges, and allowing my curiosity to lead me astray. Now, I was assured that we were meant to be together. We had to be; we always ended up back in each other's arms.

Three months after Carla and I rekindled our long-distance relationship, I met this guy named Terence at the gas station. Terence was about 5'11" and brown-skinned with a handsome face. His frame carried about ten extra pounds. He was dressed in a suit, had on a Marriott name tag, confirming he worked right around the corner at Marriott Suites. While I was pumping gas, he continued to stare and smile at me. I smiled and stared back; after all, he was cute. After he completed pumping his gas, he walked over to me and asked what my name was. Me? This guy was trying to pick me up at a gas station in broad daylight?! This had never happened to me and felt unnatural. But I had to do everything in my power not to melt.

"I'm Conner," I said, Conner? *Where did I get that name*? I didn't know, but he sure was not going to get my real name.

After a short conversation, we exchanged numbers, and it wasn't long before Terence ended up naked, straddled over me as I sat on my plaid couch with my pants down to my ankles. He proceeded to jack both of us off until we both came all over ourselves. Again, I immediately felt disgusted and asked him to leave. I felt dirty. Guilty. Like an abomination. I could not shower quick enough to wash off his essence. This was the final confirmation I needed and was so happy about it. There was no way I was gay if I felt so disgusted by the sexual acts. I knew I was no longer confused because I could never see myself with a man again. I could not believe that after all those years of hoping, wishing, begging, and praying to God that my prayers were finally answered. I was normal and could put all those feelings behind me. I had finally prayed the gay away.

I was reassured; I was not gay, and I was supposed to be with Carla. I needed to make this work with her, but not with her living in New Jersey. My Christian values wouldn't allow me to shack up with her. She couldn't afford to move to Atlanta in an apartment by herself, and I knew I wasn't moving anywhere. I had a great career as a computer programmer, and I was not about to give that up. I knew I had to do the right thing. I knew

I would be able to make it over those humps in our relationship and make it back to my longing to be with her, so I knew it was time to ask her to marry me.

6

HUSBAND AND WIFE

I HAD NEVER BEEN to New Jersey, but Carla was consistently asking me to visit her. She loved it up there and couldn't stop talking about the people, her job, and the Dominican hair salon she frequented that was down the street from her house. Carla could not wait to take me to New York City, which was a short train ride from there. After booking my flight, I told Carla I would be coming to visit her for the weekend. She was so excited.

"Make sure you plan a special dinner for us the night I arrive," I requested. How classy of me to ask her to plan a special dinner for us so I could propose. In my 22-year-old mind, it was her city and her house, and I did not have access to make anything happen. This was 1999 before the days of Google.

"Of course, I will. You don't have to tell me that!" she replied.

Carla picked me up from Ronald Reagan Airport around 10 p.m. that Friday night. I could tell she was excited to see me when she met me at the gate as I deplaned, and I was just as excited to see her. Carla looked so sexy and was filling in as a woman with nice thighs and ass. And she was rocking a short new haircut, reminiscent of the one Nia Long wore in *Boyz n the Hood*. Carla was never one to get her hair done much, and when she did, it was always the same wrapped style. For her to cut her hair like that was a big deal. I loved this new Carla.

We arrived at her basement apartment below her uncle's two-story home in a quiet New Jersey neighborhood in the city of Teaneck. It wasn't the Jersey I had pictured in my head; it was much more peaceful and uneventful. A "good" part of town.

I went to settle in and freshen up a bit, while Carla put the finishing touches on her carefully prepared meal. She knew I was a big seafood lover, so she prepared a lobster dinner with potatoes, corn on the cob, and a salad. She had two candles on her small dining room table, set with napkins and plates. I brought my Jessie Powell CD and popped it into her CD changer. I knew I wanted the song "You" to be playing in the background when I started the proposal. It was track #11 on the CD, so I knew we had plenty of time to catch up and get comfortable before it would be time for the big question. After about 45 minutes or so, the track came on, and I reached for Carla's hand. Although nervous, there was still a sense of calm that came over me as I remembered the lines I practiced on the flight from Atlanta. I felt like I had prepared to take the stage or do a class presentation. I looked in her eyes and began to pour out my heart to her:

"Carla, I love you so much, and I know that we have been through a lot over the years. I have taken you through so many ups and downs, and you have always stuck with me. I know that I've made many mistakes, but I am ready to ride this out with you."

Carla's eyes began to water as she realized what I was about to do. Her hands even started to tremble a bit.

"I don't want to break up anymore," I continued. "I want to go through the rough times together. I know that we belong together, and the fact that we can't stay away from each other confirms this for me. That is why I want to spend the rest of my life with you."

I pulled out the one-carat diamond engagement ring I spent the traditional one month's salary on two weeks before and got on one knee. Carla held her hand over her chest and melted.

"Carla, will you marry me?" I asked as I looked up into her glistening eyes.

Carla had her hand over her mouth as she burst into tears. I knew she could not believe I had just asked for her hand in marriage.

"Yes! Yes, Greg! I would love to marry you! I've always wanted to marry you! This is my dream!" she said with utter excitement.

Although all of my words seemed perfect, and it was said with the best intention, something about me was removed from what I had just expressed. I knew it was the right thing to do, but it didn't feel like it. It's like my mind and heart were on two different planes.

Less than ten minutes later, she was on the phone calling her sister. This made me feel like maybe she was as removed as I was. I wondered if we both were doing this because our minds were telling us we were supposed to. Why wouldn't she just want to relish with me a bit more instead of calling her sister?

"Greg just proposed to me wit a ring! He proposed to me wit a ring! Put Nikki on three-way!" She yelled to her older sister, Tonjalah, as I sat on the couch next to her.

I found it strange she said, "With a ring!" like what else would I propose to her with? I'm not sure what they said on the other end, but I wasn't confident they were excited about it.

When she got off the phone, I asked, "Wah dey say?"

"Dey say congratulations, dey been happy!"

I could tell she didn't even believe that.

"Why you tell 'em I proposed to you 'wit a ring'?" I gestured with air quotes.

"Cuz, people always say dey gettin married, but don't get no ring!"

That told me she told her sisters that so they would know I was serious about marrying her. Tonjalah always did give her a hard time about going back to me any and every time I was ready. I'm sure she couldn't possibly believe I was asking her sister to marry me. For all I cared at the time, she could have kissed my yellow ass! I didn't care that she was just trying to be the big sister.

I made it a point not to tell my mother what I was planning on doing before doing it. I knew she would not be excited about the engagement, and deep down, I knew she would be the one to tell me it was a mistake.

I didn't want to hear that. I knew she would be the only one who could talk me out of it, and I had my mind made up. I knew if I phoned her afterward, it would be done, and she couldn't say much about it.

"Hey, Momma! Guess what!" "What, Greg?"

"Me and Carla getting married. I proposed to her, and she said yes!"

"Y'all are what? Getting married? Really? Ha." She burst out into laughter. "Y'all are getting married? You sure you want to do that, Greg?"

"Yes, I'm sure. We always breaking up and getting back together, we might as well stay together. She is going to move to Atlanta in a couple of months."

"When are y'all getting married?"

"I'm not sure yet."

"Well, if that's what y'all want to do, I'm happy for y'all. You know I love me some Carla and always call her my daughter-in-law!"

"Thanks, Momma!" I knew she wasn't happy about it just by the tone of her voice. It was as if she was biting her tongue for the sake of sparing my feelings. I think the only thing that made her hold back was the fact that she really loved Carla. If she hadn't, we probably would have never lasted that long. My mother had a significant influence on me. That need for Mommy's approval still followed me.

My dad was easy; he always just went with the flow of things and let me do what I wanted for the most part. All he said was, "You sure you ready to get married?"

"Yes, I'm ready."

"Okay, as long as you are happy."

Carla moved to Atlanta in December 1999. I was a year out of college and making over $45,000 a year at BellSouth, which wasn't bad for a 22-year-old. I had a three-bedroom apartment in Dunwoody that I shared with Nard, a friend I met in college.

Carla's dad committed to giving us five thousand dollars to put towards a house if we went against spending money on a big wedding, so we settled on doing something small instead. I didn't mind too much because buying a house sounded much more appealing. After settling on the direction of how we would be getting married, it didn't take me long to get the ball rolling to iron out the plans. I know if I waited on Carla, we would never get married, and we'd continue living in sin. She took her time with everything. Besides, I was always the type to do things quickly. It's in my nature. Not to mention, I can be a bit controlling, and I loved planning events.

Within a few weeks, I had planned the entire wedding myself. Granted, it was a small and simple affair for only 25 of our family and friends, but it still took organization and effort. I found a wedding officiant who belonged to the network of Unity Churches that was willing to marry us. Although I had my Christian beliefs and foundation, I did not regularly attend or belong to a church at the time. Like me, Carla didn't grow up in church, but her family had the Christian foundation. Ironically, a month before we got married, Carla introduced me to possibilities outside of religion.

We were sitting on the couch, watching a special on religions when I said to her, "I can't understand how people don't believe in Jesus!"

"I don't know if I believe in Jesus. Not like that. I don't know what I believe. but I know there is a God, though."

I was confused. Wasn't that the same thing?

"How you mean, you don't believe in Jesus, but you believe in God?"

"Like what makes one religion right over the next one? Who is to say that Jesus or Allah or whoever is the right way? I think they were both men just like us. It doesn't really matter; it is still just one God for us all."

When she said the simple words, something resonated within me. I didn't know what at the time, but I knew it was a spark that I wanted to explore. It just made a lot of sense to me. I knew that a large part of asking her to marry me was a part of me wanting to do the Christian thing. I grew up constantly hearing about judgment day and how Jesus was going to come back like a 'thief in the night" and surprise us with his heaven or hell list. I didn't want my soul to burn in hell forever. Never mind the fact that I never understood how a soul, which has no physical feeling, could burn forever and ever in this place called hell, but I was too afraid to find out. I'd do my best to stay in WWJD (What Would Jesus Do) mode. Everybody knows you don't question God or the Bible.

Six weeks before our wedding, our wedding officiant came over to give us a pre-counseling session.

"I don't like marrying people who I don't believe should be getting married. That's what brought me here today. Just to get to know you guys a bit," she said.

She was a very tall, Black lady with a firm demeanor. Although I could tell she was a powerful woman, she was still very pleasant and made me feel comfortable. The way she explained how she felt about life, religion, and God was very similar to the seed Carla planted in my head. Instead of the "man-made law," she was about love and freedom.

"I believe that we are all God's children, and all connected to him. He, or She, is the one and only force that are inside all of us. Jesus was a perfect example of the connections we can all achieve and maintain with God. We can do exactly as he did."

I really took a liking to her and knew I would later check out the Unity churches she said she attended.

During our session, she asked us a variety of basic questions about how we met, how long we've been together, and such, which were all easy to answer. Then, she threw out the hard question, "Why are y'all getting married?"

I was stumped, and Carla was too. Neither one of us had a quick answer. And, what we did say didn't even seem to make much sense. Something like, "Well, because we have been together for so long and work so well together. If she cooks, then I will clean, and we are always there for each other. We used to always break up and get back together, and I know we can't stay away from each other."

"Yes, and we know each other so well," Carla added. "We can always count on one another. We work well together."

I wondered if Carla really meant that. Neither of our basic answers was a great reason why we were getting married, so I am not sure what made Pastor Linda Lo decide to marry us.

I don't even think either one of us said, "Because we love each other." I wondered if Carla was feeling as uneasy about this marriage as I was. It's like I really believed we should be getting married, but I never felt settled in my spirit about it.

Apparently, neither did anyone who attended the wedding. Everyone had looked as if confused and wondering what the hell we were doing. If it wasn't a somber face, then it was a blank uncomfortable one. Our parents and siblings looked like they were attending a funeral. Or maybe I was just projecting my own fears.

While we were on the way there, I remember my sister saying to me, "Man! I can't believe my little brother is getting married!" I didn't think I could believe it either, but here we were. February 26, right after the turn of the millennium, we were pulling up to the venue where I would be marrying my high school sweetheart.

I had chosen to get married at Sylvia's Soul Food Restaurant in their Downtown Atlanta location near Underground. We reserved the loft that sat above the dining room. Not quite the ideal place to get married, but it fit our budget, and I thought I could impress my family by taking them to a famous restaurant, even though I was making them pay for it. I believe it was $25 a person. Ghetto, I know, but I was only 22, and no one thought to tell me any different.

Carla arrived with her older sister, Tonjalah. She was waiting in the bathroom until the ceremony was ready to get started. The seating in the loft enabled us to hear all the restaurant noise during the ceremony, which made for a quite annoying experience. After getting everyone shuffled in and seated, we were ready to begin. Keeping with the simplicity, we decided not to have anyone in our wedding party, so only our parents and Carla would be walking down the aisle. My mom, who was about 5'5", short reddish-brown hair, ivory white skin with maybe a size 16 waist, was escorted by my father who had rich dark skin, square, silver-framed glasses, and a small afro. He was about 6'1" and 175 pounds, nearly 40 pounds less than his normal weight. Over the years, he had lost quite a bit of weight due to his diabetic issues. They both wore blue outfits, my dad, a pin-striped suit, and my mom, a navy-blue dress. They walked in first, followed by Carla's mother, who was escorted by Tonjalah's son, Jake.

Once they reached the top of the aisle, my cousin, Lonnie, pressed play on the boombox sitting in the back of the room. "A Ribbon in the Sky" by Stevie Wonder played as Carla's dad escorted her down the aisle.

Carla was dressed in a simple white wedding dress with her shoulders out, exposing her beautiful skin, something she took pride in, never missing an opportunity to rub herself down with Palmer's Cocoa Butter. Her hair was cut short with a tiara on top. She also had on some simple makeup; her sister helped her with—in the bathroom. Carla looked more beautiful than I had ever seen her before, despite the somber look on her face. I could never tell if she was sad or not because Carla had a face that always rested at sad or mean. Carla was never good at looking anyone in the eye as she spoke—as if she didn't want anyone to see the pain that was inside. She barely made expressions when she talked or even when posing for pictures, which she hated. Most of her family seemed to be that way. They all pretty much fit the same description: short and petite, with a somber or mean expression on their faces. Besides her younger brother, I believe Carla is taller than all of them, even her father.

When they reached the end of the aisle, where I waited alongside Pastor Lo, her father looked at me with his dark red eyes and extended his hand to me. I shook it and took Carla's arm as he sat down. Carla and I faced the pastor without even looking at each other. As Pastor Lo began to recite our vows, I could see my mother in the corner of my eyes, fidgeting around in her purse. She was always a very fidgety and anxious woman, never able to keep still for long.

"Carla and Greg; please face each other and hold hands," Pastor Lo instructed.

Carla and I faced each other and held hands. Now that I was facing her, I could see both of our parents seated just about seven feet behind her, with my mother in clear view. She was holding a tissue in her hand. Was she crying? Oh Lord, she was always a crier.

"Carla, do you take Greg to be your lawfully wedded husband?" Pastor asked.

"I do," Carla responded, and at that moment, I could hear my mother sobbing behind her.

"Greg, do you take Carla to be your lawfully wedded wife?" Pastor asked me.

Before I could muster a word, tears started to roll down my face, with Carla following suit. I was not sure where all my emotion was coming from and what was making me cry, but it was uncontrollable, and so was Carla's. There were so many things going through my heart and mind, and hearing and seeing my mother crying brought them all out of me. I believe what had me most was confusion. My mind was made up that Carla and I were getting married, and anytime I've decided something, I made it happen and felt good about it. I was making this happen, but I didn't feel very good—that confused me. I was sure I was not going to be gay and would not have any issues staying true to being straight, so I don't remember that ever being on my mind. I'd like to say it was to make it all clearer, but that just wasn't the case. At the end of the day, I don't think I really knew what it was supposed to feel like to want to marry someone. I wanted to marry Carla to do the right thing, not because of a strong desire to marry. I had also had my mind made up I would marry and have all my kids by 25. Time was running out, and Carla was always there, so that had to be right. I really thought I was doing good, but my soul was speaking a different language. This did not feel like I thought it should, but maybe it was just me being caught up on the emotions of my mother. I always hated seeing her cry. I'm not sure what it was, but I believe all the forces were trying to tell me to stop.

By the time Pastor said, "Kiss the bride," Carla and I were both boohooing like we were babies, snotty noses, and all. I'm not sure what Carla was feeling, but I thought she had the same feeling that I did. There was no way she could have been feeling anything good, with the energy I was carrying around with me. It took us ten minutes to stop crying after all the picture taking. I felt like with every snap, our tears got worse. Once we sat down and started eating, things got light and fun. Food always makes everyone happy. I was so thankful for my childhood best friends, JT, Nicky, Jerome, and Twan, and my two old college roommates turned best friends Nard and Thomas for being there. They always showed up for me and made everything feel alright that day. Hell, if it weren't for Jerome and Thomas already being married to their wives, I probably wouldn't have run so quick to the altar. We all always influenced each other in that way. I think most close friends do.

After we ate, all our family and friends came back to my apartment and hung out all night. It was the first time I got to hang out and feel comfortable with Carla's parents, which was another telltale sign that it was not the time for us to get married. I should have already gotten to know her parents better. I had spoken to her mom quite often over the phone, and she was always pleasant. "I'm doing just marvelous Greg, just marvelous!" was always her response when I asked before speaking to Carla. Although we had somewhat built a rapport, I had never really been around her. Carla's mom had to be about five feet tall, 85 pounds soaking wet, with the same dark red eyes Carla's father had. Only, her eyes carried a look of sadness, while his seemed mean. Both held years of pain. I could only imagine the life they experienced.

At one point during the evening, while we were in the kitchen, the subject of religion came up. My roommate, Nard, knew about Carla's position on Christianity, so he was instigating the conversation. My mother and Carla were the main debaters. At the time, my mother did not know Carla was not a Christian until Nard opened his big mouth.

"Carla, do you believe in Jesus?" Nard asked.

"No, I don't! Not in the way that you do!" she shot back.

"What! Oh, my God, girl! You don't believe in Jesus!" My non-church going, Bible-believing mother was having a conniption fit while Nard literally rolled around on the floor laughing at the mess he started.

By the time things settled down from the religion conversation, everyone had started to leave and head back to their hotels, so they could travel back to South Carolina that next day. Before leaving, my mother pulled me to the side and gave me a version of the Bible made for people who needed help simplifying it. In it, she had written,

'May God bless your marriage and open both of your hearts to let this good book guide you. Jesus is always here for you and wants you to be saved so that you can go to the kingdom. I will always love the both of you. Love, Momma'

I never opened that book. Instead, the conversation in the kitchen that night was the start of my deliverance and being able to get to know who I really was.

The Smalls family, Gee with dyed hair, Easter Sunday
in front yard, James Island, SC, 1987

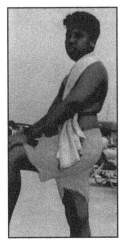

Gee after gaining weight, summer before 7th grade, Myrtle Beach, SC, 1989

Kony, 12th grade, and Gee, 10th grade, 1993

Gee, senior year, 1995

Gee, 20, at his largest, 245 pounds, Six Flags Over Georgia, Atlanta, 1997

Gee, down 20 pounds, and JT at his apartment, headed out for Gee's 21st birthday, 1998

The family at Gee's apartment before attending his college graduation, Atlanta, 1998

Gee at college graduation, World Congress Center, Atlanta, 1998

Wedding: L-R, standing, Thomas, Twan, Gee, Jerome,
and Nard; L-R, kneeling, JT and Nicky, 2000

7

BABY BOY

I PUT DOWN MY coffee and answered the phone. "Gregory Smalls. How can I help you?"

"Greg, I'm pregnant."

Less than two months into our marriage, Carla called me at work from her gynecologist's office, telling me that she was six weeks pregnant. I was surprised that Carla got pregnant so quickly after we decided a month after getting married to stop birth control. I at least thought it would take a few months before she would actually get pregnant. Part of me felt some sort of feeling of accomplishment as if it made me more of a man.

Both Carla and I were anxious to start a family, and all it took was one hint from my mom about wanting another grandchild for me to approach the subject of actively trying. Carla didn't need any convincing; she would have started yesterday if it were up to her. My mother told us how to count the days of when Carla was ovulating to get pregnant, and I'll be damned if she wasn't right on the money. Carla got pregnant right away. The news of becoming a father was a great way to celebrate my 22nd birthday, which had just passed.

By the time Carla was three months pregnant, we were moving into our newly-purchased, newly built home in Decatur near South Dekalb

Mall. Her father never did come through on that $5,000 he promised us, but at least he provided the vision. I'd have to say the first year Carla and I were married, were probably our best times spent together, aside from innocently falling in love as kids back in freshman year of high school. We spent a lot of time together dining out, playing board games, hosting family and friends, working on home projects, or experimenting in the kitchen together. Carla was always great at cooking, even teaching me how to make the best fried chicken, so it was no surprise that she mastered making Asian cuisine and some bomb ass gumbo!

Preparing for the birth of our baby was the best part: shopping for him, painting and decorating his nursery, and following his growth in Carla's belly. I signed up for the automatic emails from Gerber that let me know how the baby was growing from week to week.

Not only were we enjoying our quality time together, we were also having the best sex we had ever had in our lives. During the time Carla was pregnant, there was an energy she carried that made me very attracted to her. We had chemistry we'd never shared before and were connected more than ever. I held compassion inside of me for her and my unborn son; that was foreign to me. I had never experienced this type of compassion before. I was always the type that was unbothered by whatever anyone, including myself, was going through. "Get over it" had always been my attitude when approaching pain or challenges. Now, I even found myself wanting to show her more affection, something that had always been a challenge for me, not only towards her but with anyone, especially family. It was just something we had never done. Even on those occasions where I did feel the urge to be affectionate, I had to force myself.

Once, when Carla was about six months pregnant, I was passing by and saw her at the kitchen counter cutting onions. I got the urge to stand behind her and hold her, but I couldn't bring myself to do it. I literally lingered around and contemplated how I was going to approach her. It was such a huge deal for me, that I decided on a gentle kiss at the nape of her neck instead. It was quick as if I was trying to hurry before having a chance to be rejected or feel stupid, even though I knew Carla would never reject me.

As my lips hit the nape of Carla's neck, I could feel the energy from her body submit to my small gesture of love. She blushed, and I knew that moment meant the world to her. Carla deserved to feel that way.

My life would be changed forever on January 18, 2001. Gregory Virgil Smalls, Jr., who I named and nicknamed "Lil Gee," was born at 5:43 p.m. He was two weeks late, so they had to induce labor, which started at 7:00 a.m. that morning. I couldn't remember being this excited since the days of waiting for Santa to arrive as a kid. I was so anxious to meet my new son and could not wait to see how much he resembled me. I remember wondering if he would have light skin with wavy hair like me, or darker skin with coarse hair like Carla. I wanted him to look like me not only for the typical self-absorbed reason parents do, but I grew up around a family that I did not look like and didn't want that for him. I didn't want that again for me.

When it was finally time for him to come, I had my video camera front and center. Carla had bought it for me when I received my graduate degree from Keller Graduate School in the summer of 2000. I can still see Lil Gee's head popping out of Carla's vessel, and the nurse saying, "Wow, he has so much hair!"

Immediately after his birth, the nurse gave me the scissors to cut the umbilical cord and release him from Carla. The force I had to use to cut it was more than I would have imagined. It was almost as if I were trying to cut a piece of thick white rope with a pair of scissors you would use to trim hair. After cutting the cord, the nurses immediately took Lil Gee from the doctor's hands and took him over to the scale to weigh, measure, and clean him up. Carla had drifted off and was completely out of it.

"He's seven pounds, four ounces, and nineteen inches long. You have a big, healthy boy here, Mr. and Mrs. Smalls! You should be very proud!" the nurse announced, placing Lil Gee into my arms. My son instantly made me feel like more of a man. More than the man I became when I married Carla. This was indescribable.

As I stood there holding him for the first time, it was as if there was no one else in the nursery-like delivery room but him and me. Soothing energy came across my body as our eyes locked. As Lil Gee looked up at me,

I saw a piece of me, a person I helped to create, one that would forever rely on me for guidance, approval, love, and acceptance. At that very moment, in Dekalb Medical Center, I made a promise to him that I would always take care of him, always lead him down the right path, and fight for him. I would do just as my father did for me, and that was to provide and never leave him. I was also determined to do something my father never did for me: I was going to show him emotions and affection. I would not be afraid to say, "I love you" or give him a hug. If he wanted to curl up and cry in my arms, then it would be safe for him to do so. He wouldn't ever have to worry about me looking down on him or seeing him as weak. He was my son and would always be protected. This was my promise to him, and for the first time during his first few minutes of life here on earth, I told my son I loved him while he looked up at me with his mother's cat eyes.

"Let me see him, Greg. Bring him over here," Carla said as she opened her eyes and reached her arms out, ready to hold him.

Caught up in my own world with my newborn son, she broke me out of my daze. I walked over and placed him into Carla's arms, and she held him close to her bosom. Carla looked down at Lil Gee as she caressed his face. "Hey, Mommy's boy, hey. I'm so happy to see you."

Carla was in heaven for about ten minutes before drifting off to sleep. I removed Lil Gee from the tight grip of her arms. I sat with him on the chair next to her bed before he, too, drifted off into a deep slumber. I stared down at him for a while, admiring all of his features. He was such a beautiful baby. Although only a few hours old, he was already looking like his mom with the same eyes, and I could tell he was not going to be light-skinned like me just by looking at his ears and cuticles. I hated at that moment I had succumbed to being concerned with what his skin color was going to be, even if it weren't for the same reasons.

When I looked over at Carla, she was awake, watching me with those piercing eyes. Something seemed different, and I wasn't quite sure what was going through her head. It was as if we were watching each other instead of looking at one another. It felt empty.

8

ON THE DL

EVER SINCE OUR wedding night when my mom discovered Carla's beliefs, I was left a bit confused about everything I had ever been taught. "Who is to say there is one way to get to God or heaven, or who is to say that Jesus is right, and Allah is wrong? What if both are right?" I heard Carla's voice recite this over and over in my head. I really got a yearning to discover more about spirituality and religion, to do some serious soul searching. The first book I picked up deepened my curiosity, so I picked up others to study various eastern religions, African cultures, and spirituality, connecting more directly to God. Discovering that our ancestors were forced to practice Christianity and how it was used to control them was the final confirmation I needed to rebel against the religion. While my third eye started opening, it caused me to question everything I thought about life and myself. I evaluated all the rules I followed to live the "right" life and realized none of it was making me feel good or felt natural. Who made up all of these rules? Who determined what is right and what is wrong? What really is normal?

During that time, I fell into a depression. I was unhappy about where I was in life and felt like my son was the only thing I had going for me. Carla seemed to have fallen into postpartum depression, which caused both of us to withdraw from one another. I felt my new wife questioned whether or not we should be married. One night after coming home from a "Waiting to Exhale" party with some of her female coworkers, she wore a bit of a sour look on her face.

"One of the questions we had to answer tonight was: who has hurt me the most in my past. All of the girls talked about their exes, and it was at that moment that I realized that I was with the man that hurt me the most. It made me feel stupid."

I didn't have a response, but I did feel her words. It hurt, making me feel like a failure of a husband. It reminded me of that time before we got married when she told me that she thought about me just like Lauryn Hill did in the song "Ex-Factor." It was about her lover not providing any reciprocity, and continuously leaving and coming back to her. At the end of the song, Lauryn sings that she finally knows the answer to solve the problem she had with her ex, and that was to leave him forever. I knew Carla had every right to feel the way she did, but I still thought I had given all I could to her, even with my fickleness.

I had taken on the role of "Mr. Mom" in our family. I made sure Lil Gee went to the doctor when he needed to, made sure that we had food and shelter. I took him and picked him up from the daycare that I'd found and researched. And, when it was time for him to get him off the bottle and pacifier, it was the weekends when Carla left town to visit her family that I got it done. It was also the weekend she went to visit her family when I got him to sleep through the night. I refused to pick him up when he cried in the middle of the night, and I didn't allow him to sleep in our bed because, in my mind, that was not a child's place. By the time Lil Gee was three months old, Carla couldn't take it anymore and started sleeping with Lil Gee in his room on the futon. She had that tender, nurturing motherly love that I could not relate to, and all I saw was her giving in and being weak. It was then I began to resent her for being a "bad" wife and abandoning her husband.

I also started to really go deeper into what was going on with me. I couldn't run away anymore. I did not have Carla to distract me now since she was focused on what she was going through and trying her best to be a good mother. And while I was running around attempting to be "Super Dad," I was failing miserably at being a husband. We weren't communicating much anymore, and when we were, it was an argument about who was doing something wrong. I was finding reasons that we were not meant to be married, just like I had done all those times we broke up in the past.

I had also begun to isolate myself even further because of the suppressed attraction I had towards men, which was growing increasingly stronger. I did not know what to do, and the fact that I was losing my desire to be with Carla again was not making it any easier. Those familiar feelings of suffocation consumed me. I hated that I was going through these feelings another time, and so again, I prayed:

"Dear God,

It's me again. I don't know what's wrong with me and why these feelings won't go away. I have done everything in my power to love Carla the way I should and continue to want to be in this marriage, but it's not working. Why isn't it working? Why do I continue to feel this way towards her? And why won't these feelings of mine go away? I asked you for years to take them away, and just when I think you have taken them away, they come back. How can I do the right thing with these feelings? I do not want to be gay. I want to be with my wife and my family. I want to be a great husband and father. I do not want to be one of those holiday and weekend dads who are not really raising their children. It is not how I was raised. Please, God, help me be straight. Please, God, help me fall in love again with Carla.

And so it is!"

I wanted to love her the way I was supposed to, but it was just not in me. Not only was my desire for men getting stronger, but my passion for her was gone. My desire to be married had vanished entirely. Truth is, the day she gave birth to Lil Gee was one of the last times I felt connected to her. I remember during an argument, she yelled at me for not caring about what she was going through that day, only taking pictures and videotaping the birth. She said I was cold. I wondered if she lost it for me that day too.

The very last time I felt connected to her was Lil Gee's first birthday when Carla and I decided to host a party in Charleston at my parents' house on James Island. Carla and I always seemed to fit so well together when we visited home. I'm not sure what it was, but I always said I would be much happier with Carla if we lived in Charleston. I always felt like Carla was threatened by my established life in Atlanta, which made less room for me to have any space away from her. Things would have been different in Charleston.

It had been a while since Carla and I went out, so later that night, my mom agreed to watch Lil Gee while we headed out to Mosquito Beach, pronounced "Skeeta Beach " by us Geechee folks. It's a small strip of clubs and restaurants at the end of Sol e Gre Road that was popular among the locals. Carla had her hair in long cornrows, something that was rare for her to do, but something that made her look really sexy. Coming out of my mom's bathroom dressed in all black, Carla really turned me on. I was also dressed in black and had cornrows, something I did to try and make me and Lil Gee look more alike as he was sporting cornrows too.

When we walked into the small, smoky club, Carla immediately ran off to say hi to her sister, as I walked towards the bar while "Jeeps, Lex Coups, Bimaz & Benz" by the Lost Boyz blared from the four-foot-tall speakers. Before I could make it to the small makeshift bar, I heard a woman with a deep, raspy voice shout, "Boy lookah Greg! You turn out to be a fine yella thing! I thought you was gonna turn out to be a faggot!" I turned slightly to see Bernetta, the girl that bullied me as a kid when my mom made me stay with her when she went out to the clubs. I felt a million things seeing Bernetta after all of these years. She was now a small-framed woman who I had grown to tower over, yet it still made no difference in me feeling like that fearful little boy up in the attic again. I also felt some sort of pride that she didn't see me as faggot anymore, still finding me attractive, nonetheless. I also felt anxious about Carla hearing Bernetta and rushing over to defend me again. There had never been a female that embarrassed me in front of Carla, and I wouldn't know how she would have reacted. I also did not want to cause a scene.

Luckily, after I smiled and nervously said, "Hey, Bernetta, you looking good!" She quickly ran off with her friends to the other side of the club. She probably had no idea the impression she had on me as a kid.

Shortly after ordering a Royal Flush for me and a Shirley Temple for Carla, she made her way back over to me.

"Let's dance!" Carla loved to dance, and so did I, although we rarely danced together or went out.

After hours of dancing, we finally ended the night making passionate love at Old Charlestowne Inn, which was across the street from the Evergreen Motel on Savannah Highway (where we made love so many times before as teenagers). My mom let us have it the next morning, upon our return. She wasn't happy about the diversion of our plans of staying at a hotel instead, without as much as a phone call, but Carla and I needed that night. It reminded us of what was still possible between us.

As time went on, I became even more paranoid of my attraction towards men being exposed, so much so that I held back any thought or feeling that could be construed as soft or weak just as I learned to do as a kid after learning that boys were not supposed to cry. I remember sitting outside on our back patio in the fall, gazing at the midnight sky, trying to let go of the pressure I was feeling about being a young husband and father. I felt trapped in a life that I did not want. I felt all alone in taking care of the house, our son, and my personal struggles. It was all too much for me, and I had nowhere to unload the burden I was feeling. Carla walked out to see what I was doing, and as soon as she mumbled a word, I broke out into tears for what appeared to be no apparent reason.

"What's wrong? Greg, what's wrong?"

I couldn't even get any words out. I was so upset, but Carla knew that things were not good. She knew we were falling apart as a couple and individually. We were both avoiding the obvious.

She sat down on my lap and put her arms around me. "You know I blame myself. You do too much and have too much stress. I am going to start doing better."

I was surprised to hear Carla say that. She always seemed to be stuck in her own little world, but I guess she was a bit aware of what was going on. After crying for another couple of minutes, Carla wiped the tears from my eyes and said, "I'm going back in the house. You stay out here as long as you need. I love you."

"I love you too, Carla." Even though Carla was a part of my stress, and I no longer wanted to be married, I did still love her.

The next day Carla sent me an email at work saying the night before was the closest she ever felt to me, that my tears were a sign of me letting her in. Carla had only ever seen me cry at our wedding.

For the first time, I felt I had let Carla in as well, even though I had never said a word. I had never left any room for intimacy or vulnerability because that would just expose who I really was, what I was struggling with internally. As if the battle between being straight and gay wasn't enough, I was also dealing with the reality of being a father and husband in his early twenties. I was a child, raising a child, married to a child. I had not even given myself a chance to grow up, mature, and figure out what I wanted out of life, much less who I was. The pressure of being married to a woman, who was also dealing with depression and figuring herself out, was too unbearable. Carla and our new baby depended on me. I wasn't ready for any of it. I had thought marrying Carla was the answer, but I quickly felt that marrying her was the biggest mistake of my life. I didn't know what to do.

My only relief from the tension during the time was my new job as an Applications Developer at BellSouth. I loved that job. I worked in a very social department, so we would often have outings away from work just for coworkers. It was my only escape since Carla did not like me doing anything without her or anything that a married man shouldn't do, like drink and party, something I rarely got a chance to explore. She hated it when I went out with my coworkers, and she had a good reason. One of my coworkers was an old friend from college, that I used to date. We never had sex or anything, partly because Issa was a virgin, but we did still like each other. Issa especially liked me. Issa and I would flirt during these outings and maybe sneak away for a kiss here and there, after too many drinks. It made me feel like I was a kid in college again, which was only a couple of years before. I felt a sense of freedom that I hadn't since getting back with Carla a few years earlier.

What also made BellSouth my saving grace was that it required me to travel. I had the opportunity to get away and be alone under the guise of my job, "making me go," not that I really needed a break. It was also during these trips that I became a bit free in expressing my attraction towards men, the secret I'd hidden so well behind my perfect little family, in my perfect three-bedroom and two and a half bath home in Decatur, Georgia. On my very first work trip, I had to go to New Orleans. I had heard that NOLA was a huge party city with lots of street drinking and partying. I had even heard that people made out and have sex on the streets. Having never been, I was extremely excited to go!

One night while touring the hot and sticky sidewalks of Bourbon Street, I ended up in front of a gay club. It was the first time I had seen a gay club besides speeding past Bulldogs on Peachtree Street every now and again. Although curious, I could not bring myself to walk in, so I just stood on the corner and watched. There were lots of men hanging around as if they were looking for a friend. Curious eyes were everywhere. It didn't take long for me to realize they were all "cruising," although I was not familiar with the term at the time.

As I stood there looking curious my damn self, a guy approached me and asked what I was looking for tonight. "Whateva," was all I could muster. I knew I wanted something but didn't quite know what.

"Follow me," he said, and I did. As we were walking, he started to tell me it cost $10 to get head, $25 for him to fuck me, and $50 for me to fuck him. He was a prostitute, and I didn't care. It actually kinda turned me on and made me feel the sense of power I enjoyed.

"I am not paying for you to fuck me! Are you crazy?" I could not believe people actually paid for that. "I'll get some head."

"Okay," he replied, and I continued to follow him into a "bookstore," a code name for a place that sold XXX videos and had booths for viewing porn. The area was tiny and narrow, with a constant flow of men walking in and out. After pulling me into the booth, he pulled my pants down to find my semi-erect penis with pre-cum oozing from the head.

"What is that?" he asked as he wiped it off with a napkin from his pocket.

What did he think it was? I'm guessing some sort of STD or something. I was sure he was used to coming across all types of shit on the street, and this was normal for him. But it still made me feel dirty. The smell from the video booth only contributed to the feeling.

"It's pre-cum. I've been horny and hard all day," I replied, a bit embarrassed. After wiping it clean, he started to suck my dick like it had never been sucked before, and a few moments later, it was over. I was officially on the "down low."

During one of my trips to Jackson, Mississippi, I learned about Club City Lights. I had never been to a gay club before, but I was inquisitive, so I decided to go. When I pulled up to the parking lot of the small abandoned-looking building, I saw a big sign that said, "BYOB" with, "Chasers, beer, wine served." Another first for me at a club, but I figured it was a Mississippi thing. Although nervous, I walked in as confidently as I could and immediately had a seat at the first available stool at the bar, asking the bartender for a Corona with Grenadine in it. That use to be the shit back in the day! It was around 10 p.m., and there were just maybe 10-15 men scattered about the dimly-lit bar. The dance floor was about half the size of a tennis court and adorned with colorful rotating lights and a disco ball. By midnight, the place was filled with a sea of Black men, and I don't know if it was the four beers or not, but for the first time, I felt like I belonged. I felt so comfortable—and drunk—that it was not long before I was on the dance floor, dancing the night away with strangers. It was the most fun I ever had at a club, and it was in Jackson, Mississippi. I had never gotten so much attention from men in my life. For just one night, I could be free without anyone knowing me. I felt liberated.

It was also during this time that I was introduced to Yahoo Chat Rooms. It was far better than AOL because there were more men and rooms just for Black men. "African American Men 4 African American Men" was my favorite room. It was also the room where I met Raheem, in Jacksonville, FL, while working on another project for a local Credit Union. Raheem was everything I could imagine about a man with that name: beautiful brown skin, perfect teeth, a street boy swag with a big dick and a nice ass to match. He was on the DL like me, which made things much more comfortable for me.

Raheem was probably the third guy I had met online while in Jacksonville. He was the only one I ever actually liked. The others were just meet-ups where I may have gotten head, but Raheem and I spent time together. We went out to dinner, watched TV in my hotel room, and hit the straight clubs together. Raheem was also the first man I ever laid against, "grinded" on, and romantically held. Raheem was the best sex I had ever had, although there was never any penetration.

It was also Raheem who caused me to have a significant shift in my marriage. I had to spend a lot of time in Jacksonville, which meant I spent a lot of time with Raheem. I would dread going back to my life in Atlanta. Besides my son, my life was unhappy there. I remember the morning I was going back home, and Raheem had slept over at my hotel for the first time. I was so nervous about it, I had my cell phone and Blackberry two-way off, just in case Carla called. And she did. Although there was no proof of anything going on, her woman's intuition must have been strong. She didn't trust that me having my devices turned off meant nothing. We got into a huge argument over it when I got back home, and nothing I said made her feel better. Even though she never accused me of cheating, she would not let go that I had my devices turned off.

Although it was the worst argument we ever had, it was not strong enough to overpower what was going on inside of me, which kept getting stronger. This made me less resistant to logging on to Yahoo Chat Rooms while I was at work in Atlanta. It became a daily addiction until I eventually met Sam.

Now Sam really shook shit up. Sam was in a five-year relationship with a man at the time. He assured me that my secret was safe with him because he had just as much to lose as I did if anyone ever found out. Although in my mind, he had nothing to lose because everyone knew he was gay. I never even took homosexual relationships seriously. With my frame of mind back in 2002, his gay relationship was not as meaningful as my straight marriage. His boyfriend would get over it. I would be mortified for life.

Sam and I would meet up from time to time in a parking lot, and he would give me head. He loved to give me head, and it was something I loved getting, especially since I rarely got it at home. No one had ever given me head like he did. Sam was my slice of heaven. I would go home to my family and act like nothing happened, although the guilt would be eating me up inside. I was never one to make it a habit of cheating in relationships. Besides me battling my sexuality, the fact that I was unfaithful was destroying me.

One night, Sam invited me over to his house because his boyfriend was out of town. Although afraid, I stopped by after one of my work functions at a local bar. Sam snuck me in his house around 12:30 a.m. while his cousin slept in the other bedroom. After about five minutes, the innocent blow jobs quickly turned into me lying on top of Sam with my pants down, while he lay on his stomach with his pants pulled below his ass. After a little grinding, Sam slipped my bare, married, DL penis inside of him. I was petrified and in ecstasy all at the same time. I stroked a couple of times before taking it out, but Sam quickly put it back in, while saying to me, "I won't let you go too far. I'll tell you when to stop."

Sam knew I was petrified of being inside of him without a condom, and he knew it was my first time. He had been here before and knew with just a few strokes, there would be no turning back. And my strokes didn't stop until I released inside of him. I'd never released that much in my life. I thought, *"this is what an orgasm is supposed to feel like.'*

It felt like the best sex I had ever had. It was quick and simple, but the most pleasure I had ever experienced. It felt so new. If this is what gay sex was like, there was no way I could stop myself from doing it. There was no way I could give this up.

As strong as my passion was for this new sex I was experiencing with men, my guilt had grown off the meter. I did not want to be my cheating parents. It was fine when I was just getting head, at least that's what I told myself, but now I'd fucked a man and with no condom. My first thought was, *Oh, my God, I am going to get HIV and give it to my wife!* I could not be that person who J.L. King, the author of *'On the Down Low,'* talked about on the Oprah show. This was not who I was. Although I still prayed every night that God would make me straight and living as a gay man was something I knew I would never submit myself to, I knew I had to fight this demon alone. I could not stay with my wife while struggling to rid myself of these feelings. I just could not do it. And although she couldn't understand at the time and begged me not to, three months after my 25th birthday, and two and a half years into our marriage, I asked her for a divorce. It was the hardest decision I've ever had to make. I was breaking Carla's heart yet again, just like I did time and time again in high school and college. I never planned for this to happen, but the suffocation had gotten the best of me yet still, and my desire to be free could not be contained any longer. I had even gotten my first tattoo on my left arm, which is of two hands breaking away chains from the Ankh symbol. The Ankh means "life," and with two hands breaking away the chains, it meant being free from society's thoughts and opinions of me. Although it wasn't true for me at the time, I wanted to be that way. I learned about the Ankh and freedom through my favorite artist, Erykah Badu. I loved her music and secretly dedicated "Bag Lady" to Carla, though the bags she was carrying mostly came from the hurt I had caused her. I remember playing it on the way back from a visit to Charleston and singing it loudly. I knew she felt it even though I was not looking at or singing to her directly.

"I'm not taking you back this time, Greg. I'm not," she said to me before playing a song that she asked me to listen to. In "A Song For You," Donny Hathaway sings about loving this woman more than she'll ever know, more than life itself. He tells the woman to remember after his life is over, after their life is over, remember that he feels this way. He was telling her no matter what, he loved her more than anything. It was the first time I had heard the song. It immediately made me feel guilty and afraid. For a quick second, I questioned whether or not I was making the right decision, but I quickly snapped out of it.

Carla was in tears by the time the song was over. My heart was so numb to her displays of emotion. While I hated that she was feeling this way, I couldn't understand why she was not on board with our divorce. I had convinced myself that she couldn't be happy and was only staying with me for the same false sense of security I was holding on to.

"How could you do this to me? I am your wife."

"Only on paper," I responded with the same blank face I had in our therapy sessions. I was always slick in the mouth and good at making people feel dumb. It was my defense mechanism, and what I used to bully others who I knew could not outwit me.

"Wow, you are so cold."

And I was. I hated that I was this way, but it conflicted with what I felt I deserved: happiness and freedom. And I felt like she was the one keeping me from it. But the truth was I had dug my own hole of unhappiness but just couldn't see it.

"Carla, I promise you it's best for us if we divorce. I don't want to be cold, but my mind is made up. I'm leaving."

Music continued to be a form of therapy for me as Lauryn Hill released her *Unplugged* album, which was not very popular among her fans. But this album helped me to even dig deeper into who I was as a spiritual being. Immediately following the massive success of her first album, many believe that Lauryn went crazy because she had disappeared and became completely different from how many saw her. When she released this album, I knew exactly what she was experiencing, although it may have looked a little different. Lauryn talked about how she'd become a prisoner to the industry and what society wanted her to be. She created a false self-image, and when she got to a point where the image held her hostage, she died inside. Lauryn was bound by all of these rules that were made up by someone else. She became a victim of tradition. That was precisely how I felt. At rock bottom, I needed to be happy, and I did not care who stood in my way, Carla included. One of my favorite songs from the album was "I Get Out," which was about her breaking down all the boxes people tried to put her in. The song made me feel powerful and became the strength I needed to leave Carla.

Lil Gee's birth, Dekalb Medical Center, 5:43p.m., January 18, 2001

Gee, 24, after losing 40 pounds, Destin Beach, FL, 2001

Lil Gee, ten months old, and Gee in nursery he decorated
with a Winnie-the-Pooh theme, 2001

Daddy and Lil Gee, late 2001

Gee cooking Sunday dinner just before separation,
Carla and Gee's home, summer 2002

9

BRUTHAFREE

I BACKED MY BURGUNDY Ford F-150 into the driveway of our family home that fall afternoon with my best friend JT in the passenger seat. He had agreed to help me move my stuff out of the house into my new apartment while Carla was at work. I wanted to avoid any dramatic situation with her crying and begging for me to stay. I also did not have the courage to face her. The entire time JT and I were there, I felt afraid that she would show up. I wondered if the neighbors would see me and talk behind our backs. The last thing I wanted was anyone talking about me. I was only taking one of our couches and my old bedroom set that we used as a guest room, so the move was quick. Still, it felt like an eternity. I just knew Carla was going to show up and fight one last time. That didn't happen, but she did call, though.

"Hello"

"You already got your stuff moved out?"

"Yes. I just got done."

"I still can't believe you are doing this to me again, Greg! You are leaving your wife and your son, and I am going to take you for everything you got!" she screamed.

My heart sank. She was trying to use my son against me, acting as if I were leaving him too. She knew how I felt about Lil Gee and knew I would never leave him. She knew how to hurt me.

"I am not leaving my son; I am leaving you!" I shouted back at her. "And you can take whatever you want. I will make more money!"

She hated that I was leaving her and could not understand why. She often argued that things were not that bad, and she could change her ways to make me happy. I complained a lot about how she was irresponsible and lazy. I felt like I had to do everything around the house. Also, she always seemed to put her family before Lil Gee and me. She was more concerned about her mother in Charleston and not her new family. Even if she did fix those things, I knew there was nothing she could do to make me happy. The only thing that eased my guilt of abandoning her was that I felt I was looking out for her. I was putting her first by not making her one of those women who were married to down-low men. I was saving her from me. Only, I was not man enough to tell her that part, so I just gave her the same old reasons I broke up with her in the past: I didn't share the same feelings she had for me, and I didn't think we were meant to be together. Marriage was just not for me. Besides, I was still gonna fight and get over these feelings, just alone this time. I would not drag her along with me and my mess anymore. It was time for me to grow up and be a man and to stop being afraid of being alone.

I moved into a one-bedroom apartment near our family home because I did not want to be far from my son. I still wanted to take him to daycare every morning and read him a bedtime story at night. He was 18 months old, and just like day one, I was determined to always be there for him and hold up to the promise I made to him that day in the delivery room. Nothing was going to stop me, not even the back and forth arguing about me abandoning them that was going on between Carla and me. We agreed to share joint custody with one week of him being with her and the next with me. I would continue to pay the mortgage on the home until we got divorced, and afterward, I would pay her child support, even though we were both taking care of him equally. I was never one to abandon my responsibilities; my dad had taught me better than that. He always put his family and responsibilities first, but unlike him, putting family first meant making sure I was happy so those around me could be happy too, most importantly, Lil Gee. Also, making sure she was taken care of financially helped to relieve my own guilt.

I didn't immediately start seeing men when I left. In fact, I started dating my coworker Issa while still trying to pray the gay away. Issa was so sweet and innocent and still a virgin. Through college, we were always close, but in a platonic way. Issa also leaned on the masculine side, never wearing skirts or makeup, or getting her hair done. She was like Carla in a lot of ways. I really liked Issa but would keep her at a distance. I only wanted to date, not get in a relationship with anyone.

Issa was a very awkward girl. She didn't have many friends and did not really date. Issa did not feel comfortable around men very much and wasn't very comfortable with her sexuality. She hid a very nice body under her baggy jeans and t-shirts. I was one of the few she was semi-comfortable around. Issa was so inexperienced dating that she barely knew how to kiss. Issa craved affection and loved every bit that I gave her. Issa would literally scream with pleasure when I went down on her or put my mouth anywhere else on her body, which I did many times before she finally let me penetrate her. Issa made me feel as if I were the best she ever had, which I was—I was the only one. This fed my confidence.

One night while making out hot and heavy, Issa and I had sex. It was the most passionate sex I had ever had with a woman. It really turned me on. She was a virgin, so she naturally experienced a lot of pain, but she also was very desperate for me not to stop giving her pleasure.

After having a few more sex dates, Issa was becoming way too attached, and I knew I had to let her go. Even though I told her all the time, I did not want a relationship, she still insisted. Taking her virginity wasn't the best idea. I also saw that she had become a part of a pattern I had created in drawing people in and then pushing them away when I started to feel suffocated. I did that with all the women I had ever been with.

Tanya was no different. I had met Tanya on Black Planet a few months after leaving Carla. We clicked immediately after she hit me up on my "EmancipatedGEE" profile. She was another one of those around-the-way girls that were down for whatever and smart as shit. She was a beautiful, chocolate girly girl with a tomboy edge, just like I like them. She was also very aggressive, which I did not love but I was still intrigued. Though not used to this, I welcomed the way she challenged me. On our second date, she really surprised me.

"Have you ever been with men, Gregory?"

"Huh? What?" I stuttered. No one had ever asked me that so respectfully before. Without judgment.

"Have you ever been with men? You're just so animated," she said matter of factly like there was nothing wrong if I had. I knew this was her way of saying I had feminine ways.

"Well, yes, I am attracted, but I do not prefer to be with men sexually. I've had an experience or two and did not like it." I couldn't believe what had just come out of my mouth, but it felt natural.

She was the first person I had ever told this to, and she didn't run away. Although I only told her half the truth, it still gave me a glimmer of hope that I could be myself and not get rejected. I was grateful to her. Tanya then tried to jump my bones.

We went back to her apartment after a great night at Dave & Buster's. In less than an hour, she was straddled on top of me as I lay on my back on her floor while Vivian Green's "Emotional Rollercoaster" played. Holding my hands down to the floor and kissing me passionately, Tanya badly wanted to get in my jeans. Even though I was enjoying the passionate kisses, I was nervous about going any further. My penis kept toggling back and forth from hard to soft as my anxiety increased, and my anticipation heightened at what her next move would be. It reminded me of my first experience with Carla. Finally, before she started taking my clothes off, I mustered my strength up and flipped her over on her back,

"I don't want to have sex with you tonight. I really like you and don't want to ruin it by having sex too soon. I respect you." I kissed her deeply one last time before exiting.

The actual truth was that I was afraid I would go limp, so I stopped it before it could happen. I was not ready for that type of embarrassment.

It was the first time this had happened since my first time with Carla. I wasn't sure if it was her aggression, my new experiences with men, or the fact that she knew I liked men causing this, but I did know I wanted to figure it out. That night scared me off from Tanya a bit. Although we had a fantastic connection, I kept my distance, using my recent separation as an excuse to limit my time with her.

I was still trying to pray the gay away, but I was not very successful at it. I did pray against it less, now that I was battling it alone. I had met a few guys at this point, but still nothing very serious. At most, we would fool around, and I'd get some head. Sam would drop by every so often, and we'd go at it, but it was not nearly enough to satisfy my desire. Then one day, while at work, I logged onto my favorite site, Black Planet, to see a message from this guy named Shawn.

"Sup?" was all he wrote.

Black Planet was not a site known for men to meet men, like BGC, College Club, or Men4Now, and being so naïve, I was not sure of what he meant by "Sup?" I mean, I knew what "Sup" meant, but I did not understand why he was asking me. Who was this dude sending me messages, and why? After viewing his page, I wasn't a hundred percent sure of what his intentions were because he could "pass" as straight, so I did not want to come out of the gate responding in a way that could be interpreted as an intimate interest in him. So, I simply replied, "Not much, sup with you?"

After a few exchanges, Shawn ended up asking me, "You get down?" and although it was the first time I heard those terms, I knew what he meant.

I replied, "Yes," and after he made sure I was DL too, we agreed to meet up at my place later that evening to "smoke and chill," which really meant, "Let's smoke a blunt and mess around."

I was down. I had smoked a few times before and liked it, but it was not something Carla wanted me to do, so I didn't.

As Shawn walked through my door, I was immediately attracted to his medium-brown skin and full lips. I was also very intimidated by his track star body. Although I had lost most of my weight, my body was still not toned, and I carried a deflated belly with lots of excess skin as if I was the one that carried Lil Gee for nine months. Shawn had also already expressed to me that he usually went for darker guys, but there was something special about me. I wasn't quite sure how to feel about that, but I knew it didn't help the insecurities I still had about my light, bright skin and not being Black enough.

Neither one of us was very experienced with men nor very aggressive, but the chemistry we had towards one another was undeniable. After about four hours of smoking and drinking wine, I finally dared to reach over and kiss him on the lips. Then again. And again, until it turned into a full make-out session. Shawn got on top of me, and we grinded with our clothes on. Shawn had gotten me so excited that I ended up ejaculating in my boxers. I was borderline ashamed of so quickly having an orgasm like a high school kid. But that quickly went away after I saw the satisfaction on Shawn's face from being able to make me lose control like that.

Shawn and I started spending a lot of time and smoking a lot of blunts together. It became our thing. On the days I did not have Lil Gee, I was either over his place, or he was at mine. I was very protective of Lil Gee, who was only two and a half years old, and what he knew about my newfound lifestyle. Although my soul searching, and rejection of religion had helped me to reconcile my sexuality with my spirituality. I no longer felt I was going to hell for it. I was still in the closet and did not see myself spending forever with a man...or a woman. Getting married was something I knew I was never going to do again. I could never commit to a woman again, and marrying a man was certainly not an option. Even having a boyfriend was not an option for me because I believed men just didn't share those types of feelings towards each other. We were supposed to be more like homeboys that had sex. Intimacy, affection, compassion, and tenderness was just not something a DL man like Shawn or I would submit to.

After about a year, Shawn started coming over after Lil Gee went to bed at night and leaving before he got up in the morning. I didn't want him to know that Shawn slept over and get suspicious of our relationship, just like my mom used to do with her boyfriends when I was little. The last thing I needed him to do was to go back and tell Carla. Even though it seemed that Carla was accepting our divorce and we were on decent terms by this time, I still knew she was unstable and could go back to hating me in a split second. All she needed was this type of ammunition. Lil Gee never did catch Shawn sleeping over, and I eventually even started taking him out with Shawn and me, or over to his house on Saturdays. Lil Gee started to like Shawn and would look forward to going over to his place, though he had no idea the nature of our relationship.

"We go to Shawn house, Daddy?" he would ask when we jumped in my car.

"Yes, Baby Boy, we goin' to Shawn house."

He responded and said, "I want paaaark." In which I agreed, "Ok babyboy, we will go to the park." He always loved going to the park in Shawn's apartment complex when we visited.

We spent nearly every night together. During the two years we spent together, we would go up and down on an emotional rollercoaster—one day acting like homeboys and the next day acting like we wanted to spend the rest of our lives together. It was nothing for us to hit the straight clubs or sit around at my place playing spades with JT, Nicky, Jonathan, and some of my other straight friends. After a night of whipping ass as spades partners, he would always leave my house when they did, and then turn around and come back once they were out of my apartment complex. We were both very ashamed of our attraction and continued to try and fight our feelings for one another, but it was evident we loved each other in ways two homeboys didn't.

When it came to being intimate, Shawn and I would only get close when we were horny and wanted to "Mudslide." Mudsliding, which was a term coined by Shawn and his best friend Lou, was just another way to say bumping and grinding. Shawn would squeeze lotion all over my erect penis, jump on top of me, and get to work. I wasn't comfortable being on top because of my insecurities with my body. I felt slimmer lying down. Since it was so good, that is all we ever did up until the end of our relationship.

It was very innocent and boyish what we shared. Ultimately, what we offered each other was a safe place to be ourselves, and an understanding of what each of us was trying to make it through. Throughout our relationship, we would often break up because subconsciously, we were both too afraid to own up to what we shared.

And during those breakups, Tanya was always there to share some really great times with me. Concerts, parks, jazz cafés, pretty much anything, Tanya and I did it. I really enjoyed dating her. During one of those breakups, I got especially close to Tanya. I always made sure she knew I did not want to be in a relationship and only date. One one date, we went to Sambuca Jazz Cafe in Buckhead for dinner, before a Musiq Soulchild concert. During the entire concert, we were all over each other, and I knew I could not hold out any longer. She wanted me to make love to her, and quite frankly, I wanted to, but I still felt anxious about it, afraid that I would not be able to perform. I was upset with myself for feeling this way and tried to liquor myself up to relieve the anxiety, but it did not work.

I was great at foreplay and loved every minute of pleasing a woman's body with my tongue, and Tanya was no different. Not being able to get out of my head, I was still not able to keep an erection, so Tanya insisted on helping me with it. Tanya moved to the edge of her bed and asked me to stand in front of her. I knew right then she wanted to go down on me, and I was happy to oblige. Not to mention, I hoped that it would give me the boost that I needed. Before putting my penis in her mouth, I wiped the pre-cum off the head to be polite, something I always did since that day in the bookstore in New Orleans. She swiftly looked up at me and said, "Don't ever do that again!" and then proceeded to give me the best head I had ever had, even better than Sam's. Tanya was a freak, and it was just what I needed to get hard enough to turn her around and prove my manhood.

I knew if I tried to put a condom on, I would lose my erection, so I stroked her raw a few times to keep me excited. As soon as I entered, Tanya urged me to put a condom on but submitted after ensuring her I would after I "opened her up". After I was confident, I would not lose my erection, I slipped the condom on and had some very awkward sex with Tanya. I am not sure if it was as uncomfortable for her as it was for me because she seemed to have climaxed shortly into our session. So did I. That was all I needed to light my blunt and lay back in the bed like I really had rocked her world even though, deep down, I knew that neither one of us was satisfied.

The Monday following our date, I got a call from Tanya,

"I got tested, and I am HIV Negative. You should go get tested too."

Apparently, she was freaked out at the fact that we had about ten seconds of unprotected sex. Even though I knew I was negative because I was not having penetrative sex with anyone since my last test, I still remember at that moment feeling like I was already "damaged goods" because of my attraction towards men. Although I knew it was a trigger because both of her parents died of HIV/AIDS-related complications, I still wondered if had I been straight, would she have rushed to get an HIV test? I also did not fault her for it either because it's the same thoughts I had when entertaining or engaging in sex with men. Those thoughts frightened me and contributed to the negative image I had of Black gay men, and I did not want to be one of them.

It would be two weeks before I saw Tanya again. She showed up at my house after the club one night in heels and a trench coat with yellow lingerie underneath like a scene right out of the movies. It was that night after trying to make love to Tanya for the second time, I knew it would be the last time I had sex with a woman. She was intoxicated beyond measure and seemed to have enjoyed it or faked it very well. My hard then soft, then hard, and then finally soft penis again was not having it. I vowed not to place myself in that position anymore. I finally ended my relationship with Tanya and never dated another woman. And although Tanya fell in love with me, I don't believe she was ready for a relationship either. She was searching to find herself, just as I was. I was there for her to heal wounds, provide a safe space, and help her along the path—like what was done for me. She will always be an essential part of my journey. I loved her too.

While juggling my relationships with Tanya and Shawn, I was also trying to be a great father to Lil Gee. I also needed to get through my divorce with Carla. It appeared she was accepting that we weren't going to be together and wasn't as angry with me anymore. However, I was not prepared to hear what she said to me that day on the phone while I was driving Lil Gee to school.

"My coworkers keep asking me why I'm getting a divorce, and I always tell them I'm not sure or because you just don't want to be married anymore. They said they think it's because you're gay. They said the first time they met you at our house, they thought you were gay. Are you?"

"Whateva!" I felt like my heart had jumped out of my chest; it was beating so hard. "They just messy and want something to say!"

"Well, I had a few other people from James Island, even some of your family members, ask me the same thing. I told them they need to ask you."

Who could be saying that about me in my family? I bet it was my older cousin Deanna. She liked to gossip. Once, when I was a freshman in high school, we were on the deck of my Aunt's rented beach house watching the waves hit the shoreline, when she said to her sister, "You know he gon' be alright once he get his lil dick wet. He'll shake that shit off."

I knew she was talking about me acting like a girl, about how it would take me having sex with a girl to make me act like a man. And for years, I wondered, even hoped for the same thing.

"Well, it's not true," I said to Carla. "People always said that about me. You know that. I guess they just want to start up again." I was trying to stop her from thinking about it because I could tell she may have believed it.

"I guess that's true. T.D. Jakes talked about feminization in men and how it's not their fault. That we need to stand by them and help them through it, not leave them."

Was Carla trying to tell me that it was okay if I told her about my attraction towards men? Was she telling me she would stay with me? *Na, couldn't be*, is what I thought to myself and quickly pushed those thoughts out of my head.

It wasn't before long that my mom called to tell me what Carla had said to me. She and Carla had maintained a close relationship after we separated. They spoke on the phone more often than we did, and they would both come back to me to report something they said to each other. My mother would always say that it was because she felt sorry for Carla and related to her going through postpartum depression. This didn't stop me from resenting my mother for being more supportive of Carla than me.

"Carla told me what her coworkers and our family said. I don't know who would say something like that to Carla. Probably your Aunt Annabel. Is it true?" she asked.

"No, it's not! I don't know why they say that."

"Well, you know you could tell me if it were true, right? I wouldn't tell anyone."

"I know, Momma," I replied. I felt like she knew and was waiting for me to say something. She had to know, right? I mean a mother always knows, and at that moment, I felt like she had my back, like she was there for me after all.

About a month later, my mom, sis, and nephew were visiting my apartment, and Carla came over to see them. While Carla and I were not on bad terms, things still were not peachy keen and could take a turn for the worse at any moment. This night, I guess she felt like being petty. While playing cards, Carla played the song "Bill" by Peggy Scotty-Adams, which is about a woman catching her husband with another man. She kept playing it on repeat and singing it aloud as if she were singing it to me, just like the night in the car on the way back from Charleston when I was singing "Bag Lady" to her. My mom sat there and laughed along with her,

"Girl, you so Crazy! You fool, ya know!"

I felt humiliated and embarrassed. It felt like I did when I was growing up, and the kids were laughing and pointing at me for being different.

A week after they left, my mother and I got into a heated argument about how she carried on with Carla, one that ended in her telling me, "Fuck you, I just won't come to your house anymore!"

I felt hurt that my own mother would say that to me. She had yelled at me plenty before, but never had she cursed at me like that. I immediately responded with, "Fuck you, too, because you're not welcomed!"

I ultimately ended up calling her to apologize for the hurtful things I said, but instantly, our relationship changed. The fact that I would say that to my mother was a telltale sign that she had lost a bit of respect from me. This made me sad.

Those few weeks I spent with Tanya was the longest Shawn, and I had ever been apart. During that time and with my experience walking away from Tanya, it really started to empower me. I was taking control and leaving situations I did not want to be in. I wasn't allowing myself to get trapped anymore. Although I went back to Shawn shortly after breaking things off with Tanya, I started to move in a different direction regarding being comfortable with my sexuality, and Shawn didn't like it. When we would talk about coming out and being ourselves, he would always say something to reel me back in—to his comfort level. He made me feel like no one would ever accept us for who we were, and we could never reveal ourselves. Even though we had been seeing each other for 18 months, Lil Gee and I had already spent Thanksgiving at his parents' house in Alabama and he mine, Shawn was still determined to live a lie.

I know now that what I had already been through with Carla, and trying to please everyone except myself, contributed to the level at which I was maturing in comparison to Shawn. I was tired of lying and hiding from everyone around me. I had already spent way too much energy, maintaining a double life. Also, he had always talked about wanting to have a daughter and getting married one day. Both he and I kept some sort of dating relationship with women. Throughout our back and forth relationship, I knew he wanted to marry the girl he was seeing.

At the end of our second year together, I knew our time was going to be short-lived if Shawn wasn't willing to come out of the closet and be himself. He knew it too. Over the years, I dug deeper into connecting with my spiritual side, which was pushing me to live more authentically. I also started writing anonymously on blogspot.com, under the alias "BruthaFREE." I wrote about my journey, which helped me to release and reflect a lot—although I was still using pronouns, "her" or "she" when I really meant "him."

One day, when reading an interview with Brandy in Vibe magazine, she mentioned a book that had changed her whole life and what it meant to be spiritual: Conversations with God by Neale Donald Walsch. I was so intrigued at how the book was so life-changing for her, I picked it up the next day and finished it two days later.

Conversations with God single-handedly changed my whole perception of what I knew about spirituality and religion. Every word resonated with me and brought about a feeling of freedom I had never known. It was like a light bulb went off in my head. It was like God touched me on the shoulder and said, "You are not a bad person. You are not wrong. You are on the right path." And after those two days, nothing could stop me from freeing myself from all of those rules I was following that never felt natural to me.

What also helped to change my life was Amy. I called her "Grace," and she called me "Will" because we indeed had a "Will & Grace" relationship. I first met her at her home while she hosted her own divorce party. I tagged along with my cousin Nicky who was Grace's personal trainer at the time. A White girl around my age, 5'6" with blonde hair and a bright, bubbly personality, Gracey weighed over 300 pounds but lost over 100 after having weight loss surgery years later. Gracey was agnostic and did not believe there was or wasn't a God, but what she did believe was everyone has a soul that spoke to guide them.

"Talk to soul, dude! Soul has all of the answers!" she'd say when I would often talk to her about my troubles with Shawn, although at the time, I pretended Shawn was a girl. To think that there could be this amazing and positive person who did not believe in God perplexed and intrigued me at the same time. I knew she possibly couldn't go to this imaginary hell being such a great person. She also lived her life so free and unapologetically. She didn't follow any rules. Instead, she lived with passion and by her own instruction. She inspired more freedom in me.

I, of course, was not out to Gracey at first, but that didn't last very long with how safe she made me feel. She was so authentic and loving that one night, I just couldn't lie to her any longer about who Shawn was.

I blurted out, "Shawn is a man, not a woman. I'm tired of holding it in!"

"Dude! That's fucking fantastic, I've always wanted a fabulous Willy! I can't believe you never told me. You know I totally love you and am totally cool! I have a freakin' equality bumper sticker on my car, for crying out loud!"

"I know, I know! It's me. Besides Tanya, I had never told anyone before. I am just now starting to accept it. But now, no more lies!" After that confession, Gracey and I literally shared every detail of our lives.

Shawn saw me growing and tried his best to manipulate me with his emotions, but I wasn't having it. He was very good at trying to make me feel sorry for him with his tears and sad voice. He even started doing all of these nice things, trips included, to get me to fall for him again, but I was over it. It had gotten to the point where I started to lose my attraction for him. Similar to how I would feel when leaving Carla, I stopped caring about his feelings, and it was then I knew I needed to end the relationship and save myself from any more pain. I decided that this break-up would be our very last break-up. When he came over to my house to pick up some of his things, he tried again to manipulate me back into his arms with tears and promises of change—even trying to entice me with the new paycheck from his recent promotion. Material things had never caught or kept my attention, and this was no different. I let him walk out my door in tears, and I knew it would be the last time I saw him.

10

OUT AND IN

SOMETHING DEEPLY SPIRITUAL happened to me when I finally said goodbye to Shawn. I felt as if I was carrying the weight of Shawn's own self-denial along with my own, and I was suddenly freed of it. I didn't realize how unhappy I was with him until I finally had the courage to let him go. I thought I needed him for security, much like I needed Carla, but I didn't. All I needed was the security of my own self-love and acceptance to be okay.

And it didn't hurt that I had the security and love from Gracey encouraging me along the way. I remember writing in my blog after closing the chapters with Tanya and Shawn, and I still wanted to keep referring to men as women, she said to me in classic Gracey fashion, "Dude, it's your blog. If you can't be your authentic self on your blog, then where in the hell can you be? Cut that shit out, man! Those who will love you will love you regardless, and that goes for your family and other friends too. They love you, dude!"

She was right. They did love me, and I knew it. In my next post, I came out, and all of my followers saluted me. It was my most popular post to date. At 27, I wasn't getting any younger and decided that I was ready to start telling everyone. I had tried doing all of the "right" things and had proven that it didn't work for me. I knew my sister would understand and would provide the next safest space for me. She supported me and was always there for me no matter what, even in my most fearful moments.

I remember when I was a little boy, I woke up terrified from a nightmare and ran to my parents' room and knocked on the door to ask my mom if I could sleep with them, "Go jump in the bed with your sister, Greg." And every time after that, when I would have a bad dream, my mom would tell me the same thing until I started going straight to Kony's room. She would never hesitate to pull back her covers and allow me to jump in. I could have told her long ago, and she would have loved me, but I still held fear of rejection. I could never handle that from her, and so I decided I would tell her over email.

Dear Kony,

I've been wanting to tell you this for a long time but was always afraid. There is no easy way for me to say this, so I am just going to say it and hope that you are okay with it. You probably already know, but you need to hear it from me. I am bisexual and am just now starting to accept it. My friend Shawn was actually my boyfriend, but we just broke up. I hope this doesn't change our relationship.

Love,
Greg

Kony responded with love and acceptance. She told me she loved me regardless and wanted nothing but the best for me. She also said she didn't know, which I couldn't believe after her being a first-hand witness to my feminine ways as a child. I even wanted to be like her, sometimes acting like her. I remember when we were younger, and my parents would leave us alone at home, I would put on a big shirt as if I were wearing a dress. I would wet my hair, which would make my big, soft, curly Afro look like a long Jheri curl that would hang past my ears like the DeBarge family.

I would also put on my mother's high heels and walk around the house. During these years, the popular R&B group New Edition was just coming on the scene. I remember my sister always liked Ralph Tresvant, whereas Ronnie DeVoe was my pretend boyfriend. I never correlated this to liking boys but just having fun with my sister. In my mind, these things didn't have to mean I liked boys. I liked girls. I thought of myself as Prince, which some people referred to me as due to my effeminacy, hair, and high yellow skin. Though Prince was not the most masculine man in the world, he still only liked girls, and so did I. And in addition to playing with her dolls, I also played with Hot Wheels and G.I. Joe's caught frogs and jumped ditches, so I guess I can see how she could have thought this.

When I reminded her of this over the phone one day, she said, "I thought you grew out of it."

"Nope, I just realized around middle school that I needed to do my best to act like the other boys, or they would mess with me."

It felt so liberating to be able to share this with my sister. I knew she would be the safest to tell. My sister always protected me growing up, just as big sisters do. However, her job was a lot tougher than many because of who I was: a young feminine Black boy with a White mother, trying to be boy enough and Black enough but failing miserably at both. Even though she and I had the same racial makeup, Kony did not deal with the same torment I did. If anything, it made her more popular. Sure, she had her fair share of girls hating on her for her long hair and light skin, but she never got bullied or tormented for it. My sister saved me many times as a child, always jumping in some boy's face, telling them, "Leave my brotha 'lone!" The fact that so many of the bullies wanted to be with her also helped me. One of those bullies ended up being the father of my nephew.

I still didn't have any immediate plans of coming out to my mom, but I was no longer going to hide it from her if she asked. I still resented her for the way she was siding with Carla during our divorce and didn't feel I owed her anything. I didn't want to give her the pleasure of knowing the intimate details of my life. But as fate would have it, a few days after coming out to my sister, we were on the phone when she casually said to me, "I ran into your Aunt Annabel in the store, and she told me she heard you were gay. I told her it wasn't true and not to believe that stuff. Right?"

"Well, I don't discriminate; I like both."

"You do?"

"Yes, I do," I said firmly.

She could tell there was nothing she could say to move me. Besides being a man at the age of 28, she knew she lost any power when she said, "Fuck you" to me about six months earlier.

"Well, that's okay. You know I love you regardless because you are my son. If someone asks me about it, I'll just ask them why they want to know. I'm not going to tell nobody."

While I was happy, she said she loved me, I was disappointed in her immediately worrying about what other people had to say. "I don't care if anyone knows. Didn't you already have an idea? Are you really surprised?"

"Yes, Greg, I had no idea. I knew you weren't like the other boys, but I just thought you were a little soft."

I was a little disappointed that she didn't know. It made me feel like she was not connected to me and never was. Maybe she never did connect with me because of her postpartum depression right after I was born. How could everyone else in my neighborhood growing up see it but not my own mother? She even knew I liked to play with Barbie dolls and got her friend to make me a knock off Cabbage Patch doll, one year for Christmas.

She must've remembered how I'd always watch her in the mirror while she did her hair and makeup—before going out to the club with her friends. One Friday, when I was in the fourth grade, I begged her to dye a patch of my hair blonde because I wanted highlights in my hair like she had put in hers. "Oh, gawd, your father is going to kill me for doing this!" she said, but she did it anyway, and I loved her for it.

I felt like all of these things were indications that I liked the same sex and didn't understand why she didn't get it. After she tried to convince me she didn't know, she asked the inevitable.

106

"Hmm. Well, okay. Are you going to tell your father? I don't think you should, you know he's sick and can't handle news like that. You don't want to put any stress on him."

With diabetes and his alcohol addiction, my father's health had been declining for the past few years. My mother's nagging of him to attend AA meetings—ever since I was young—never seemed to keep that brandy bottle away from his dark smoker's lips. He would at least hide the liquor bottles under the seat of his red 1985 Jeep Comanche pickup truck, although I'm sure she always knew it was there just like I did. He was losing more weight and couldn't seem to gain it back no matter what he tried. He was always a pretty low-key guy, but he had gotten even more low-key by staying in the house often and being even more quiet than normal. When he found out Carla and I was getting a divorce, he didn't have much to say as usual.

"You sure you want to do that? Is that going to make you happy?"

"Yes, Daddy, I am sure."

And that was that. Just like when I married her and just like any other decision I've had to make, my father would say, "As long as you are happy." While I loved the autonomy and that he never gave me any flack on decisions I made, a part of me wanted him to have more of an opinion on my life. Maybe give me more influence instead of letting me make every decision on my own. But on the other hand, I also loved that he accepted me no matter what. I knew this, but I still did as my mother wished.

"Okay, Momma." Deep down, I knew I only agreed because I was not ready to tell him either. I used her asking me not to say anything as an excuse as to why I hadn't told him. But I knew that wasn't the real reason. Aside from the fear that naturally comes from telling your father such a thing, we really weren't that close. Over the last couple of years, I started to feel the desire to form a deeper relationship with my father. I am not sure if it was due to my new spiritual awakening, the lack of support I felt from my mother, or me just growing up, but I tried to build a closer bond with him. It never seemed reciprocated.

"Hey, Daddy, how you doin'? What's going on?"

"Ooh, not much, just working and doing the same ole same ole. How's that car runnin'?"

"It's running good, Daddy. No problems. How's your...?"

And before I could finish the next sentence, he would rush me off the phone and put my mother on. He was probably just doing what he usually did and did not recognize my efforts. But it still felt like rejection. I would even initiate telling him that I loved him—something he never did. It was tough getting inside of his head, he never seemed interested.

I was so relieved I'd finally told my mother. Although I didn't think it mattered much, at the end of the day, it really was her acceptance I wanted the most. At the time, I felt like I'd gotten it. It made me feel as if I was ready to tell everyone at that point, and I did. Within two weeks, I had even come out to my homeboys. Some of them had a feeling, and some didn't, but everyone accepted me with open arms.

After about six months of that incident while playing cards at my apartment, Carla and I had finally gotten to a place where we were friends again. The divorce was finally over, and we were even close enough to have lunch after our final hearing. This was where she started telling me about a man she was dating at the time.

"I don't really care about these men like that. Just treat me right, give me whatever I want, and I'll be happy. I don't want nothing else. I don't need no man. I'm looking out for myself! I'm done marrying for love!"

I knew it was me who had turned Carla so cold towards men, but I was just happy that she loved me again. I was happy that we could be in each other's lives without having to be married. I loved this new relationship.

"I got something to tell you," I said to Carla over the phone about a week after our divorce.

"What?" I could tell she already knew what was going to come out of my mouth.

"I'm bisexual."

"I know. And though I am not surprised, I am still shocked it is coming out of your mouth. It makes it real. Thanks for telling me."

Carla and I became closer after that, talking on the phone daily, going out to eat together, and exchanging stories about the men we were dating.

We had even become each other's top friend on MySpace, which was a pretty big deal during this time.

I called Carla on the way home from work one day. "You won't believe how these guys go crazy over each other! You would think they were women." Even though I was out, I still was very small-minded when it came to the gay world.

"Why? They are just like everyone else. Men have emotions too," she responded.

"I guess you are right. I guess it's just new to me." It was interesting that she was the one being more open-minded and less stereotypical than me.

After all those years, I finally realized what kept me going back to Carla. I knew that she loved and accepted me. I needed that so much because I did not love and accept myself. Now that I could do that, we could serve another purpose in each other's lives: being great friends and co-parents for our five-year-old son. I knew Lil Gee was too young to tell, so I was not in a rush. I was only concerned about ensuring he had the best life possible and did not want my newfound life of dating men to have an imprint on that. He had grown so quickly—from being a jovial, free-spirited toddler to a quiet, loving little kid.

It was quite normal for him to be playing in his room and yell out, "Daddy! Daddy!"

"Yes, Gee?"

"I love you!"

"Aww, I love you too, son. So much."

11

DESPERATE MEASURES

I REALLY WANTED A boyfriend. Even though Shawn and I spent two years together, I never felt like I had a boyfriend, and I wanted to experience that, especially since I was out of the closet now. I was 28, carrying a new sense of freedom, and was now dating men when I started a new job as a Telecommunications Support Analyst at an IT company called Intercom. It was my responsibility to ensure that the call center phone system was up and running and to fix any issues that arose. This meant I worked closely with the call center, which, as most call centers at the time, was filled with black and brown people—just how I like my eye candy. And they sure did have plenty for me to look at, making my boring IT job into something to look forward to every day!

Among all the eye candy was Raphael, this new hire who really caught my attention, and from the way he acted when I came around, I could tell that I had caught his attention too. It began with the lingering eyes and subtle work-related comments when I went into the call center. It eventually led to outright flirting and him creating "issues" that I would need to come over to his cubicle to help him fix.

After becoming very friendly, Raphael invited me to lunch one day, and the official courtship began. Raphael was unlike any other guy I had ever dealt with, not that there were very many. Physically, he fit the bill: short, semi-muscular, and dark brown. His parents were from Cuba and Jamaica, which made for a very sexy accent and a man full of passion and control, which can sometimes equal crazy. Raphael was all of that, and I liked it. Not to mention, all our coworkers knew he was gay, and that really impressed me. Although I was out to friends and family, I was still not completely comfortable at work. Seeing how comfortable he was and how everyone accepted him influenced me to come more out of my shell.

The first time Raphael came over to my house, he was so aggressive, attentive, and affectionate as soon as he walked through the door. I must have been just that irresistible to him because it did not take long for him to lock lips with mine. The way he held and kissed me made me feel so wanted, so desired, so vulnerable. It was the way Roderick made me feel in our 7th-grade bathroom, and how I felt with Michael from DeVry. I realized that it was their aggression towards me that made the difference in the way it made me feel, not just that they were men. Raphael pursued me in ways I had never been pursued before, and I knew I wanted to explore more of it. He already had me hooked, and we had just begun. Unfortunately, the next day Raphael sent me an email at work, saying he had something to tell me at lunch.

What could my half-Jamaican lover possibly have to tell me?

"Papi, I am still living with my ex Kevin. We were together for seven years and have a house together. We stay in separate rooms and live as roommates. There is nothing going on. He is moving out soon."

"You what? Oh, NO! I could never be with you, Raphael. Not while y'all are living together."

I was devastated because I was really attracted to him. I loved his energy and free spirit. I also liked that he was honest with me, but he could never offer me the security that I needed.

"Please don't leave me, Papi. I promise it'll be over soon."

I knew this would never work for me, but something about Raphael would not allow me to leave him alone. I told Carla about it, and she told me to just "go for mine" and not worry about it.

"His ex ain't got nothing to do with you. As long as he treating you right, that's all that matters." Soft-hearted Carla had gotten so gangsta since our divorce. I don't think she would have given the same advice before I broke her heart.

Despite my reluctance, Raphael and I continued to hang out. We spent time expressing our feelings towards one another, mostly at work or after work at my place. Although I was submitting to my weakness for him, I always let him know that I was not his and that I was dating other people until I found a boyfriend. I really wasn't, but it made me feel better to tell him that.

One night about two months into seeing each other, we were hanging out at Traxx Night Club drunk, dancing, and kissing on the dance floor. This was the first time I'd made a public display of affection towards a man. He made me feel free. Up until this point, Raphael and I hadn't had sex. We hadn't even seen each other naked yet. It wasn't because we didn't want to, but two months before meeting Raphael, I had a tummy tuck to remove all the loose skin left after losing much weight over the years. I was still healing. Though I was more comfortable with my new flat stomach versus the stomach with stretched-out, loose skin, I was less comfortable with the thought of explaining, to a lover, about a huge scar across my body.

Aside from that, Raphael also intimidated me. I knew Raphael was a top because he had asked me more than a million times if I wanted some of his "Jamaican Dick," and he was extremely aggressive. He even would go on to tell me he did not touch or suck dick, nor did he like his ass touched. That confused the hell out of me because I thought all gay men liked dick. I knew that not all wanted to get penetrated, but what was the point of being gay if you didn't at least like to suck or touch dick? I didn't get it.

"Well, I like my dick sucked and touched, so you gonna have to get over that," I told him.

But it really didn't matter at the time because I was very curious about his "Jamaican Dick." Besides Sam, I had only experienced penetration with one other man, and I was the top with him as well. I tried to bottom once or twice, but things always ended before they really got started. I battled with the thought of how being penetrated would make me less of a man, how it would hurt, or if I was honest, I also feared that I would shit on him. These thoughts simply would not allow me to relax. This coupled with the fact that the last time I tried being on top, I experienced the same performance anxiety I had felt when being with women, helped to make oral and bumping bodies more than enough for me sexually. I never experienced anxiety during those moments, and the fact that no penetration meant that I was protected from HIV was a huge bonus.

But Raphael made me feel differently. He could break past those barriers. The way he treated me and the way our energies intertwined made me desire something different. I knew Raphael had years of experience, and I wanted to know what it was like with him. All the alcohol, dancing, sweating, and kissing had me feeling ready, and tonight I was going to submit to what I was feeling.

I had always imagined my first time would be very uncomfortable and painful. I imagined screaming and begging for him to stop. I imagined tears and sweat running down my face as I mourned for the experience to be over, but it was the exact opposite. Not only did my half-Jamaican lover make me feel weak mentally and emotionally, but he made my entire body weak as well.

"You alright, Papi? I got you, Papi. I love you." I replied,

"I love you too, Raphael. I love you too."

Submitting to him was effortless, even though his dick was larger than average. I saw and felt why he kept asking if I wanted some of that "Jamaican Dick." I didn't even try to stop him from going inside me without a condom. Maybe it was the fact that Rafael said he loved me, or perhaps it was the fact that he touched my dick though it wasn't his preference. Whatever it was, I am not sure, but what I do know is that he turned me out repeatedly. In the process, he made me fall in love with him.

Raphael had left before I woke up the next morning, leaving me with the sweet smell of our lovemaking from the night before, along with conflicted thoughts of us having raw sex. What was I thinking? How in the hell could I let him do that? I went right into victim mode after realizing what had happened and called Raphael immediately.

He answered with, "Good Morning, Papi. How are you? I loved every bit of you last night."

"Not good. You went inside of me last night with no condom. Are you clean? Are you HIV negative?"

"Yes, Greg, I will show my paperwork just so you know, but how dare you ask me that like I'm dirty or something? I didn't act by myself, Papi. That's not right."

He was right. Aside from my ignorance of using the term "clean" to describe an HIV status, I also accused him of something, acting as if I didn't have a choice in the matter. It was my fault for not insisting we use a condom, but the truth was that I was caught up in the moment of passion. And I used the negative test results I got back from my HIV test the next day as an excuse to allow him to penetrate me condom-less every time we had sex. He had to be telling the truth if I was negative, right? My ignorance was really showing itself.

I submitted to him in every way possible. However, every other week, I broke up with him due to his living situation—from my illusion of having self-respect. This back and forth game continued for about three more months until I couldn't take it anymore, and one night kicked him out of my house. I was in the last year of my twenties, and it was time for me to grow up and really respect myself like I said I did. I couldn't take not being able to ever go over his house, only seeing him once or twice a week after the club or work, and not ever being able to come around his friends. He was very controlling, getting upset whenever I hung out with my friends or went to the clubs. He would also throw insults at me to make me feel unattractive, or at least it's what I felt.

"There ain't nothing straight about you except the way you dress," he would say, making me feel like a feminine queen and a lame dresser.

"Your body doesn't even bother me that much." Was that supposed to be a compliment?

"Ew, I never really like light skin guys. Must be something special about you." This was starting to become some sort of pattern with the men I dated. I could not get away from not feeling Black enough. I think Raphael was insecure with himself and my own potential, and he did what he could to keep me down and away from anyone else. He wanted me to just stay home and be a Daddy to Lil Gee, instead of getting out more and being more exposed to the community.

Although I never allowed them to meet, he would always buy Lil Gee clothes and video games. It wasn't too hard to keep them apart because I hardly got to see Raphael. He just loved that I had a kid to take care of because he knew that meant I would not be running the streets like he did every night. It would be nothing for him to cuss me out on the phone, hang up on me, and not talk to me for days, even ignoring me at work. He was a pro at mind games, and everything had to be under his control. I had let myself be played long enough, and I had to get myself back.

So, I broke up with him. For good. It was the only time I had ever broken up with someone I still wanted to be with. This is one of the most conflicting emotional times I ever experienced. Nothing is harder than having to let someone go that you always want to be around, not to mention he was the first person I ever let inside of me and do so raw. To me, that was a big deal. Was I dick whipped? Or was this love?

Gracey hated Raphael, and he hated her. She would always tell me to leave him.

"You can do so much better, dude. He doesn't respect you, and you know he's cheating."

I knew she was right, and she was my saving Grace from going back to him.

And unbeknownst to Lil Gee, there were many days and nights that he also got me through rough patches. On those nights, I wanted to call Raphael, I'd remember how weak he made me and how I couldn't put myself back in that dangerous situation. Not only was he breaking my heart, but I had allowed myself to have unprotected sex with him the entire time we were together even though I never trusted him. This was not the way a responsible father was supposed to act.

It was that night at The Cheesecake Factory, Lil Gee's and my favorite restaurant, that I knew I would never go back to Raphael.

Looking across the booth as its dwarfed Lil Gee's six-year-old body and seeing his eyes smile at me while asking, "Can we get cheesecake after this Daddy? A turtle one?"

As I said, "Yes, son, we can get a turtle cheesecake," something took over me. His eyes, his smile, him calling me daddy, and just wanting cheesecake made me feel an insurmountable amount of gratitude. I was grateful for my life, my health, and Lil Gee. I knew I had to always be my best for him, and no man would ever make me fall short of that again. I was going to make sure of it.

12

LOVING ME

I WASN'T HAVING ANY luck meeting anyone of interest, and it was really frustrating. Why didn't anyone want me? Wasn't I cute? Wasn't I sexy? Wasn't I attractive? Didn't I have a good-paying job? Didn't I have a new townhome and a nice car? My credit was damn near perfect, and I had not been a hoe around Atlanta like "they" say everyone else had been. Why didn't anyone want me? Over the years, I started to lose my hair and finally resorted to wearing a bald head. Although I liked it, I stopped looking mixed. All my life, my hair was the one thing that everyone would rave about. Did I lose the one thing that attracted people towards me? I remember wondering in disbelief, almost feeling offended when people acted surprised after I've revealed to them my mom was White. "You're biracial? I would have never guessed! I just thought you were light-skinned!" they'd often say. All of a sudden, being referred to as normal bothered me.

During these next two years, I would sometimes meet two to three guys every week that I met off of Adam4Adam, mostly coffee and parking lot dates, hardly ever sex. I had become a serial dater in search of love. Every guy I met, I wanted to find a way to make him my boyfriend. I was so desperate for love; I was making myself like men I would never go for. I was tired of being out and proud but having no one to love—no one with whom I could have endless sex without the guilt and shame of sleeping around.

There was one guy named Frank that I chatted with online for about two weeks. We seemed to really like each other, and we even spent hours on the phone talking about any and everything. The day when we finally met, it was at this French bistro near his office at Perimeter. When we both walked up to the door at the same time, I was pleasantly surprised that he looked just as good as his pics. By the way he kept smiling and winking at me the entire time we had lunch, he seemed to like what he saw as well. The conversation was just as good as it was over chat and the phone, and by the time the date had ended, I knew I had met my next boyfriend.

"Enjoy the rest of your day. I can't wait to see you again," Frank said as he walked me to my car and kissed me on my cheek. He was such a charmer.

However, I never heard from Frank again. He blocked my profile online and my phone number, so I could not speak to him again. This type of behavior was not uncommon for me to experience with guys. They would lead me on to make me believe they liked me, and then I would get ghosted. Why wasn't I enough? My heart was just a game to them.

Raphael had turned me out and left me desperate for sex, but I was trying my best not to go back to him. He continued to pop up here and there over the years. I still loved Raphael, but I was determined not to take him back in the capacity that he was before. Apparently, my breaking up with him hurt him too. He could not fathom that I couldn't handle him living with his ex until he was able to move out. This made it easier to stay away from him because he was also guarding himself against me. We never made love again.

One Sunday, a few weeks after leaving Raphael, an older gentleman, maybe in his early 40s, approached me in the produce section at Walmart while I was picking out collard greens for Lil Gee and me to eat that evening.

"What's up, Red? Hit me up if you ever need cleaning services," he said to me, staring at me seductively while passing me his business card.

It was apparent he was flirting with me and wanted to offer more than cleaning services. He was so quick and smooth with it that I didn't even have time to laugh at the fact that he was really offering cleaning services. Harold was a very handsome man, 12 years my senior, standing about five feet eight with a medium build, caramel brown skin, and beautiful teeth and lips. He was very blue-collar and rough around the edges in a country boy type of way, which was a turn on for me. I decided to nickname him "Harold" and file him in my thoughts for later. For now, I had to finish shopping and go get Lil Gee for the next two weeks at my house. Carla had been making it a habit lately of going to Charleston for weeks at a time. She started working as a caterer there and was taking care of her mom, who was battling health issues.

"Hey, Carla, how is everything going?" I yelled to her out of my car window while Lil Gee jumped in the back seat.

"Everything's going good. I am catering a lot more weddings and events. I'm going to email you my new logo to check out!"

After Lil Gee and I finished up dinner, we watched "Finding Nemo" for the hundredth time before I put him to bed at 9 p.m. I decided to lay down with him for a while, and he immediately smiled and snuggled next to me. I could see how happy he was lying with me. I sometimes forget how little things like this meant so much to him, and even more, how much they meant to me. I lay there with him for about twenty minutes while we talked about a variety of things. He was in such a talkative mood, and that could be because he was stalling on bedtime, but talkative, nonetheless. When he gets this way, I tend to let him drive the conversation to wherever he wants to take it. Since he was getting older, I tried to talk to him more about different things, random things, just to open his mind to life's possibilities. I look for every opportunity to share with him any knowledge I have that I know he will never get from going to school.

"I want a brother or sister," he said to me out of the blue.

"You do? Do you know how you can get one?" I asked.

"Yes. My mommy would have to get a baby in her stomach."

"I could have another baby, too, you know."

He looked amazed that I just said that, like how in the hell can you have a baby without my mommy?

"If your mommy had a baby, who would be the father?"

"You!" he answered as if it was the only answer there could be.

I just laughed, hugged him, and kissed him on his forehead and then his cheek, "Good night, Baby Boy. I love you."

"I love you too, Daddy. Can you turn my SpongeBob night light on?"

Moments like these reminded me of what's to come. The many questions he will look to me for answers for. I tried to open his mind up as much as I could without forcing anything into his head. I also did my best to make him feel comfortable enough to ask or tell me anything. I knew one day I will have to have a conversation with him about my sexuality.

I ended up calling Harold over for "services" a few days after Lil Gee went back to Carla's. There was something about him that gave me a sense of security during our short time at Walmart. I was usually good at picking up on this type of energy, so I trusted it. It was not long before walking through my door that Harold took me into his arms and was kissing me passionately. The way he held and kissed me made me feel like he could not get close enough. After about an hour of the most passionate lovemaking I'd ever had, he asked me if he could turn the lights on in the dark room.

"Why?" I asked.

"Because I want to see you. I want to look at you."

I reluctantly allowed him to turn on the lamp, as I laid across the bed on my back. Starting with the top of my head and ending at my toes, Harold began to run his fingers all over me. He ran his eyes across my body in awe of what he had just experienced. I felt his appreciation for the energy we just exchanged during our moment of passion. This was the first time I had ever allowed anyone to watch and touch me like this; it was the first time anyone wanted to. Although this made me uncomfortable, I was enjoying being worshipped by him. When Harold got down to my tummy tuck scar, he touched it softly and began kissing it gently from one end of my hip to the next. When he was done, he kissed it one last time and said, "You're beautiful." And for the very first time in my life, I felt it to be true.

Harold was delightful and charming. He loved taking care of me in any way that I needed without me ever having to ask. Harold pampered me and bought things even though I asked him not to. I still loved that he wined and dined me. Harold was crazy over me and wanted me to be his, but I knew I could never be with him. I just did not feel the same way about him that he did about me, although out of desperation, I did try to make it work once.

Harold was also extremely closeted and had no plans of ever coming out. He was old school and was perfectly fine dying in the closet. Not me. I was not having that type of life again, and I stood firm in that knowing. If he was going to have a piece of my love, it was going to be on my terms. I knew what I wanted, and I was grown enough to satisfy myself until it came. While I cared for and respected Harold, we were both clear on his position in my life—to provide "services" when I wasn't dating anyone.

One particular time I put Harold to the side was when I met Aiden at my friend Chris' housewarming party. Aiden was about 5'10", slender, brown-skinned with a very aggressive personality. It didn't take him long to approach me after I walked through the door.

"You're cute. I want to take you out this weekend. Can I?" he asked after walking over to me at the bar. I was stunned but intrigued.

"Sure. I guess you're cute enough," I snapped back.

Truth is, I found his boldness incredibly intoxicating, and I wanted to know more. It didn't hurt that he was cute.

Aiden and I spent the next two weeks together at his place. We vowed not to have sex until we got to know each other better, but we would make out heavy every night. It was both figuratively and literally hard for us to not have sex. Per usual, when I met someone I like, I fell hard for Aiden. I really liked him, although there was something about him that wouldn't let me feel our connection was entirely real. It was almost as if Aiden was too good to be true. He did everything perfectly. He said all of the right things, always sent thoughtful messages throughout the day, and would always want to buy me things. When I went away with my my friends to the largest Black Gay circuit party in the nation, Aiden had roses waiting for me in my hotel room, one for each day we had known each other. My plan to hoe out at Sizzle Miami turned into me spending every moment on the phone I could with Aiden. My two new friends Brenner and Marlon weren't too happy. The two of them agreed with Gracey: they didn't like Aiden. They all said there was something fishy about him.

"Something in the milk ain't clean," Brenner would say to me. This was something I'd tell him about the boys he would meet.

About six weeks into our new relationship, Aiden and I were making out hot and heavy one night until I just couldn't take it anymore. Before I knew it, I was going deep inside of him, making him moan as he felt every inch of me. I had never topped a man that was so aggressive, and it turned me on. Aiden felt amazing wrapped around me, but it did not take long for me to realize that I had entered Aiden without a condom. I hadn't done that since Raphael! I quickly pulled my penis out.

"Damn, boy! Look what you made me do! We said we weren't doing this."

"You're right, but damn it was lookin' so good, I couldn't help it," Aiden replied.

The very next day, Aiden sent me a text message telling me that he had something devastating to tell me, and he hoped that I wouldn't leave him. He said he couldn't bear to tell me face to face and needed to tell me this way. I had an inkling of what it was.

"I went to the doctor today, and he told me that I am HIV Positive." It was as if the words came across my screen before he even typed them. I knew this was what he was going to say.

It was just a feeling I had—a knowing—one that allowed me to stay surprisingly calm at the moment.

Before becoming comfortable with being attracted to men, HIV was something I always feared and felt all Black gay men had. It was one of the reasons I did not want to be gay because I did not want anyone to think that I had HIV just because I was gay. Furthermore, I felt it would be my destiny once I decided to live my life as a gay man. I believed this for quite some time while dating, and it scared the shit out of me at first.

However, it became so common that I became comfortable with the fact that the man I was going to end up with would be HIV-positive. It was no longer a deal-breaker for me, and it helped after getting more education on the virus and learning that people lived healthy and long lives with HIV when they took care of themselves. Most of these men seemed to be a lot healthier than me.

In the text, Aiden went on and on about how he found out, what made him go to the doctor, and so forth, but I believed none of it. He was a liar and that I couldn't live with. I was done with Aiden.

When we first met, I told Aiden that I was negative but was not opposed to dating someone positive. Aiden told me he was negative too, but I had a feeling he was lying. He just didn't believe that I would still date him, so he thought he would get me emotionally involved first and then tell me. It didn't work, although he did try his best over the next two weeks to get me back.

I knew about this drug called PEP (post-exposure prophylaxis) that could be taken up to 72 hours after exposure to prevent contracting HIV, so I immediately went online to find out where I could get it and booked the next appointment. Although I had learned by this time that I only had about a tenth of a chance contracting HIV from Aiden because I was the top, I still wanted to do all I could to lessen my chances. I came out of that situation HIV negative and never talked to Aiden again, but it wasn't my last encounter with HIV. I dated a guy three months later that was openly HIV positive, and we had great chemistry and great protected sex. If it wasn't for the fact that I was his rebound, we might have had a longer courtship.

The only man that remained consistent between 2006 and 2008 was Harold. I thought I was only staying around because of our sexual chemistry and what he had in his pants. Harold surely always delivered, but it was so much more than that. Harold helped to build my self-esteem. Harold was satisfied with any time I gave him, no matter who else I may have been with. But after two years, I knew I had to let Harold go if I wanted to make space for something real. It was not fair that I let him hang around, knowing he wanted more.

He loved me. I felt guilty about spending time with him, knowing I would never feel the same way. I believed that if I continued putting out that energy, I would never get what I really wanted: the love of my life. So, I freed him and little did I know how freeing it would be for me as well. Although my desire for a relationship was still strong, at times even feeling desperate, I always knew what I deserved and wasn't going to settle. I learned this from Harold. There was no way I could settle for anyone that made me feel anything less than he did. He made me see my worth, and this came right after spending time with Raphael, a man who offered me the least security in a relationship that I had ever had.

I was learning a lot about dating men since leaving Carla, like how I was now considered to be masculine by many. After a life when I had always been told I acted like a girl, suddenly, I am considered masculine? This was utterly foreign to me and very off-putting. It did not make me excited like I thought it would; it made me feel uncomfortable with an insurmountable amount of pressure to be masculine, even more than I did before coming out. At least then, I was expected to be feminine. I thought I wanted this label, but I didn't. It still held me hostage, just in a different way. Now it was something for me to try and keep, not capture.

When meeting men online, commonly, I was asked if I was masculine. This always intimidated me because I never quite knew how to answer. "I'm just regular," was my typical response. I felt like if I'd said I was masculine, I would be setting them up for disappointment and me for embarrassment. I knew I wasn't quite the feminine gay guy that wore make-up and heels, so where did I fit in?

Adam4Adam, BGC, and Men4Now was also the first place I had ever seen a box for "Mix" in the race section of the profile. Interestingly, I still always chose Black, although it seemed the "Mix" selection was a very popular one to choose online amongst the Black gay men. Even in our adult years, we were all still trying to be a different kind of Black at the time when the Black we already were was enough.

What was even worse for me was reading online profiles where next to the requests for "No Fems" were those for "No Fats." The masculinity factor I could navigate a little easier, but what about my body? Although

I had lost a lot of weight and had even toned up a bit by going to the gym regularly, I was still very insecure with how I looked. There are just some areas that forever remain flabby after losing a lot of weight, and this was something that really fucked with me. I was also still becoming comfortable with the scar across my waist, one I was sure all the boys would scowl at.

Nearly every profile I clicked seemed to belong to a man who worked out for a living. He'd have six-pack abs, bulging biceps, flaring chest muscles, thunder thighs, and glutes to match. These men were gorgeous. How in the hell was I to compete with all the beautiful, perfectly-shaped men in Atlanta?

The reocurring trait I found amongst these men in my dating pool was hurt. I was still hurting throughout this process too. I thought that just because I was now out of the closet, I would suddenly be free from hurt, but I wasn't. Hidden behind the rainbow flag I now wore on my back, there were still years of pain that weren't going away just because I was not afraid to say that I loved men.

For Black men who love Black men, all of the years of shame and rejection for both the color of our skin and loving men still lie at the core. Until we become aware and work to move the trauma, we will continue to shame and reject those who are just like us. After all, "people who hurt, hurt people," and we are no different. In fact, we are so great at it that we can shame, hurt, and reject others while calling it "reading" or "throwing shade" and still be allowed to be a friend.

I've witnessed this, even amongst my group of gay friends. Once at my friend Brodney's birthday party, there was a "burn book." Something which originated from the movie Mean Girls, where the main character, Regina George, created a book that was full of her high school classmates' pictures with mean notes that she and her group of friends wrote about each of them. We all passed the burn book around and read each other for filth, laughing afterward at all the mean things we had said about each other. I was so into this culture—I'd even earn the nickname "Regina Gee" from my friends because I was such a "Mean Girl." It didn't bother me at the time, but I feel so ashamed looking back at it now.

Luckily, I had my reprieve—Gracey—who eventually moved in with me. I never had to worry about my next read or wonder if someone was throwing shade at me. Gracey always encouraged me no matter what and was ever loving towards me.

In my dating, much of this hurt translates to a lot of rejection. It did not take long for me to notice that men would reject me at any given time. It became evident that dating was a game of who could reject whom first. No one wanted to be the gay looking or feeling stupid; we had been dismissed for far too long for us to allow that to happen. This fear of rejection also prevented us from allowing ourselves to be open to falling in love with one another. We subconsciously found reasons why it wouldn't work out, so we rejected one another before anything even had a chance to get started. And many times, this fear of being rejected wouldn't allow us to approach one another, much less say we liked one another. It's sad, and the fact that there are so many beautiful men in Atlanta to date makes it even easier to skip to the next guy and look for a better thing, only to learn that, although the packaging is different, the contents are the same.

I met many men over those two years and was even fooled into thinking one or two of them were the real thing. But I was dating in hurt. I walked around with blinders on, dealing only with the surface, the superficial, never digging into what's going on internally. I learned a lot from these men, though, and I am thankful for all the experiences. I also believe that I shared love with them. It may not have been the type of love that was meant to be in a relationship, but it was an exchange of love, no matter how temporary it was. We fulfilled a void for one another, and I only hope to have taught them as much about themselves as they taught me about myself.

Over the past two years, I had also become pretty distant from my family and childhood friends, and all things "Greg." I was rebelling against the life I used to live. I was now introducing myself and was requesting that new people I meet call me "Gee" and not "Greg." I ended up despising "Greg," even making my coworkers call me "Gregory." "Greg" was a punk who never lived up to the "big, strong, good looking man" my mom had envisioned the day I was born. But Gee? Gee ain't no punk! Gee was hot shit! Just like my mom had intended when she gave me that name.

With the distance came fewer home visits. Going home made me feel like "Greg" again, and I hated it. Nobody saw the new me. Nobody saw "Gee." Besides, I was having too much fun living my new free life in Atlanta, and not being able to be myself, especially to my dad, was too much for me to bear. It only added insult to injury that his health was continuing to decline.

On his birthday on November 4, 2007, my mother called me in a panic.

"I had to call 911 just now for your father. I went into his room to check on him because he had been sleeping all day, and he was only responding in moans. I noticed he had used the bathroom in the bed, and I could not understand anything he was saying! I thought he had had a stroke, so I called 911. When they got here, they said his sugar levels got too low, and now they are back to normal. They are taking him to the hospital, but I think he will be fine. I will call you back."

I hung up the phone and immediately got scared. I called my sister to talk about what was going on. She told me that she was on her way to see what else she could find out. She was crying hysterically, and it got to me. I absolutely hate to hear my mom and sister cry. It breaks my heart. I worried about my mom and how it was affecting her; I knew she was a worrier. And being 300 miles away in Atlanta, I felt so helpless.

I immediately thought about my father dying. Often when my mom calls me, I get a bit panicky because I fear she is calling to tell me something bad about my father's health. I knew he was in quite a bit of a struggle concerning his health, and for some unexplained reason, I kept expecting him to die. It's sad but the honest truth. I thought about how things would be after he passed, like if I would speak at his funeral and how much it would affect me if he died. I hate to say it, but I never thought it would be that big of a deal for me, that I would be fine, especially since I'm not used to seeing or talking to him much. However, when I got that call from Momma, I got so sad and scared that I wanted to cry.

It also made me think of my own connection with my son. How could I be questioning my reaction to my father's death? I would never want to have the type of relationship with Lil Gee that would make him wonder if my death would affect him much. I wanted a much better relationship with my son, and I was determined to have it.

Lately, he had been getting in trouble at school. On two of the days, it was just him talking in class or not paying attention. However, yesterday I got a call from his teacher telling me that she had to send Lil Gee to the office for fighting with a student. He was going to have to spend three days in in-school suspension. When I arrived to pick him up after school, he walked towards me with his head down.

"What's wrong with you?" I asked as he got into the back seat.

"I'm going to get beat because I got in trouble at school." I hated it when he would say this. I had spanked him a couple of times when he was younger, but that was rare and in the past.

"First of all, I never beat you, so stop saying that all that time. And second, what did you do?"

"I hit a boy at school."

"You did what? What happened?"

"I was sitting down, and Reginald was getting in line, and he asked me what I was looking at. And you know that look in your eyes when they get really dark and really small, like you about to hit somebody?"

Just going along with him at this point, I said, "Oh yeah, I know what you are talking about."

"Well, he was looking like that. So, I jumped up to hit him before he hit me."

It took everything in my being not to laugh at the cute way he sounded. Luckily, he was in the back seat while I was driving so I could hide my face from him. But after I got over the humor in his response, I explained to him that he should never hit anyone first but always protect himself. I also told him to never let someone else's words negatively affect him. Although the situation was funny, I was concerned about it. This was totally out of his character. Occasionally he gets in trouble for talking in class, but it's been a bit extreme this week. The way he was trying to get violent with another child is so unlike him. I wondered if there was something deeper going on that I just didn't know about. Sometimes I wondered if his mom going to Charleston so often was affecting him. Maybe he misses her? Or was there something I was doing that would make him act out like this? Was I not giving him enough attention—leaving him lonely? Did I handle the situation correctly? Maybe he should have hit him first. Lord knows me waiting around to get hit when I was a child didn't work out well for me. Hmm, or maybe, I am blowing this way out of proportion? I just don't know, but I worry. I was starting to feel like my mother.

That's not the only occasion when I can relate to my mother. Like the times when people would question whether or not Lil Gee was my son, because of his skin tone.

"That's your son? He don't even look like you! His mom must be really dark!"

I hate that people can't see our resemblance just because of our different skin tones. It's just like what they said when I was growing up, no matter which of my parents I was with.

Even my mom always says, "I tell everybody Lil Gee just looks like a Black Greg!"

I hate that I get so triggered by both comments.

13

DADDY'S DEAD

IT WAS FEBRUARY 2, 2008, and Lil Gee was outside playing with the neighbor's son while "Just Fine'" by Mary J. Blige blasted across my living room. It was unseasonably warm out for an Atlanta winter, so I lifted all the windows throughout the townhome so I could feel and smell the fresh breeze while mopping the dark wood floors. I could feel my LG flip phone buzzing on my hip, so I turned the music down and saw that it was a call from Kony. My sister didn't call much, so I immediately panicked.

"Hello? Kony? What's up?" I answered.

"Greg, they just had to rush Daddy to the hospital! I think he is dead! He passed out on my couch while I was cooking him lunch, and I couldn't resuscitate him!" my sister yelled.

Although loud, she had a calm in her voice that still expressed fear of the unknown. I think we all had this thing about us, that nothing seemed like a big deal. As a family, we were all nonchalant.

I didn't know how to respond.

Just two weeks before that, I was in Charleston celebrating Lil Gee's birthday. Carla and I wanted to host a party with his cousins at the James Island Skating Rink. During that weekend, we had a few family members over, and my father had cooked shrimp and gravy, one of his best dishes.

He was in good spirits that weekend, despite the issue he had going on with his eyes, but he would be getting that taken care of the following two weeks during his cataract surgery. I had planned to come back to assist him during the week of his recovery. I remember Lil Gee sitting on my lap while I sat on the couch, and my father sitting in his favorite recliner with his feet propped up. I snapped a selfie with him looking over Lil Gee and me while we were watching TV, probably football or reruns of Sanford and Son or M*A*S*H, two of his favorite shows. Dad and I talked about a lot that night, mostly catching up on my life. I felt that my dad was still worried about me since Carla and my separation in 2002. Although I did not come out to him yet, I knew he couldn't have escaped all of the gossips, especially with how much my mother can talk. I had planned to come out when I returned for his surgery. By the time our conversation ended, I had assured my dad that I was happy and life was going very well for me.

"I'm proud of you, son. Keep living your life and being happy."

I couldn't help but feel he knew all about my life.

"Oh my God, you there now?" was all I could muster to say to my sister.

"I bout to head to the hospital. Momma drove down ta Myrtle Beach this morning with Aunt Denise for a Women's Church Conference. I don't know what Momma gonna do!" she exclaimed.

Oh my God, Momma! Out of everyone, our mother was the least nonchalant. She was the drama queen, the worrier. And now, I was worried about her. How would she take this? Would she be able to take it at all?

I admired my sister's strength. She grew accustomed to these types of situations due to working as a nurse. She'd always been the rock of the family. Still, I knew deep down inside my sister was hurting.

And it was one hour later that she called to confirm my father's death. Just like that, he was dead.

While it was a shock to hear that my father passed on, I knew he had been on a slow path to death for the past ten years, one I believe he welcomed. This was the third time I had received a call when my father had gone unconscious.

I was numb to it all at first. The truth was, I had felt disconnected from my father for quite some time. While my father and I never had what I would consider a close bond, we did share a father-son connection, no matter how surface-level it was. And the fact that from 2004 to 2008, I rarely came home due to my love and excitement for my new life, plus the lack of acceptance I felt while visiting did not help. Daddy was the old-school-father type. He showed up as a father the best way he knew how without having had one himself, and that was: always to provide and never abandon his kids like his father did. He would work all day and sleep all night, or work all night and sleep all day, but whatever we'd do, we could not disturb him. Father needed his rest.

Never an unapproachable or mean guy, he was actually a very nice, understanding man who got along with most. I rarely saw my father upset or out of control with his emotions. Anytime I did, it was my mother who brought him to it. Although not clinically diagnosed, my father seemed always to be a very depressed man, and admittedly so during the last couple of years of his life. I'm sure this led him through his battles with alcohol, which ultimately led to that morning phone call from my sister.

After hanging up the phone, I ran upstairs to my room and started rustling through the closets for clothes to pack. I had never taken a flight to Charleston from Atlanta before, but I was feeling way too anxious to make the four and a half-hour drive alone. I wanted to get home as soon as possible, so I could handle business and be there for my mom and sister. It was as if my body was moving, but my mind was not there. I could not keep still until finally I fell to the floor and started weeping.

"DAAAAADDY! DAAAAAADDY!" I yelled. "DAAAAADDY!"

Memories of my father flashed through my head. I could see him picking me up off of the couch and placing me into my bed after he got home from work late at night. I loved it when my dad carried me and would often fake being asleep so that he could. I saw all of the times he took me fishing or heard him say, "Jam Up!" after tasting something my mother cooked. I remembered every year he took me trick or treating, and all the times he told me, "Yes, as long as you don't tell Momma." I regretted not naming Lil Gee after him as he asked me to, that one Saturday night after he'd had one too many drinks. I was around age 14 when he busted through my bedroom door, asking me to promise to name my firstborn after him. "I'll think about it, Daddy." I knew I would never do it; I just wanted him to leave. I hated it when he was drunk. I also hated the name Virgil just like he did when I was born, which is why I only ended up with it as a middle name. But now it seems like the best name in the world. I thought about all the things I learned from him, like how to ride a bike, tie my shoe, swing a bat, shoot both a gun and the bow and arrow he gave me for my 12th birthday. I remembered all the meals we shared, just him and I, that one summer in Virginia. I remember him teaching me how to drive, telling me to hold my hands in front of the air conditioning vent to cool my sweaty palms the day he took me to get my license.

"DAADDY!"

"Will? Are you okay?" It was Gracey knocking at my door. "Come in...my dad died, Gracey. He's gone!"

"Oh no, Will, I am so sorry!" Grace hugged me. And though Gracey and I usually didn't hug, her embrace comforted me.

"What can I do?" she asked.

"Can you go tell Lil Gee to come here? I need to tell him." Gracey left the room as I gathered myself and wiped my tears. I never had to tell Lil Gee anything like this before. I didn't know how. I was afraid.

"Daddy? What's wrong? You cryin'?"

"Yes, Gee, Daddy's been crying. Granddaddy died this morning. We won't be able to see him again."

"Grandaddy Virgil?" he asked with fear in his eyes.

"Yes. My father." Tears rolled down my face as Lil Gee fell into my arms.

He cried, "Granddaddy! I love you, Granddaddy! I want to see you again, Granddaddy!"

"Me too, Gee. Me too. We both do." I held and rubbed his back as we sobbed. I suddenly wanted my daddy back even though I felt he'd been gone long ago.

About an hour later, I knew my mom had made it to the hospital to receive the news, so I picked up the phone to give her a call. She answered immediately.

"Greg, are you getting on your flight?" she asked with tears in her voice.

"Yes, Momma, I'm coming home tonight." And I burst into tears. We had to cry together on the phone for about two minutes before we got ourselves together.

"I'm so upset I wasn't here when he died, Greg. Before I left this morning, I told him I didn't want to go, Greg! He made me go. He knew he was going, Greg. He didn't want me to be here. He told me to go and enjoy myself. That I deserved it. OOH VIIIRRGGIIL!"

"It's okay, Momma."

"He told me that he appreciated me and loved me very much. That he didn't know what he'd do without me. He thanked me for taking care of him for the past couple of years while he was sick. It was the last thing he said to me, Greg. He knew he was going to die."

My mom had been caring for my dad as his health declined, making sure he ate, went to the doctor, and took his meds. There were many times he couldn't make it to the bathroom, and it was my mom who was there to clean up after him. His dependency on her reconnected them. It was then I witnessed the power vulnerability had in connecting two people. I had never seen my parents so close to each other. He did love her despite what I thought I witnessed over the years, and he wanted her to know this before he passed on. He was preparing himself—and her—and he knew she would not be able to handle finding him dead.

On my flight to Charleston, I cried almost the entire way as I listened to Lauryn Hill's "Unplugged" album on my iPod. I had hoped to find the same push that I got listening to this album during my separation with Carla to help get me through this. I hoped to be able to purge all I needed before arriving at my parents' house.

"You gotta be strong for Momma, Greg," had been ringing in my head ever since receiving my sister's text at the departure gate. I knew being strong meant that I could not be the crybaby of the family anymore. It was Momma who deserved to be the weak one, not me.

I asked my cousin, Lonnie, to pick me up from the airport, and as he rolled up in his 1989 Chevy Cavalier, I headed to the trunk to put my bags in. Before I could even lift the trunk, Lonnie was coming to take my bags and asked if I was okay.

"I'm alright, cuz. As good to be expected, ya know." I wasn't sure what it meant to be okay, but I guess if I was still functioning, I could be considered just that.

On the way to my childhood home, we listened to some old school OutKast and smoked a blunt Lonnie brought for me. He knew that would calm my nerves before facing my family.

As the car turned down Water Street, where our family home resided, we could see the long line of cars parked on the side of the street belonging to people paying their respects. My Uncle Randy and Cousin Sheryl were standing outside when we pulled up. The last thing I felt like was giving greetings to everyone, but I knew I couldn't escape the intentions of my family. I walked over to give them both hugs before walking in the house full of people, and the first person to catch my eye was my Aunt Mary.

"Aww, come ya Greg, give Auntie hug," she said, and I ran into her embrace. It was just what I needed.

Aunt Mary was the only blood aunt on my father's side I'd grown up around, and she was my favorite. My other two aunts were in-laws—both married to my dad's brothers—and although my mother's sister did not disown us, we still did not see her very often. Aunt Mary was the mother of eight children and the oldest sibling of my father and eight brothers. She was the only girl amongst the siblings and being the oldest, she naturally fell into a motherly role with all of them, which in turn made her feel as if she were my grandmother. I remember I used to wish she was my grandma, and I would call her that from time to time. Since my maternal grandmother did not accept us, and my paternal grandmother died, my desire to fill that void increasingly grew. I think Aunt Mary knew this. I remember spending every summer with her in Beaufort, SC, about an hour away from where we lived in Charleston. She and her husband, Uncle Barry, always treated me like I was amongst their other ten-plus grandkids. Seeing her first was a welcomed comfort.

"E gon' be okay, Greg. Yo Daddy in a betta place. Momma's in da room." It's almost as if she was giving me instructions to see her, which I had every intention of doing. I wanted to see Momma's arms open for me to hug her.

I turned to face my sister behind me. Without saying anything, I turned around and hugged her tightly as a few tears dropped from my eyes, falling below the shades I had worn since leaving Atlanta. Then I made my way to my mother's room, where she lay on the bed while her three best friends surrounded her. When she saw me, she immediately rose, and I gave her a big hug. A few more tears shed while everyone left the room. We stood back, I removed my hat and glasses, and we just looked at each other with our "everything's going to be okay" faces. I almost felt like my mom was consoling me more than I reassured her. I felt the weakest at this point, and I wanted to be the strongest like Kony said, but overall, we all were doing well considering. As my mother's friends exited the room, my sister entered. We decided that I, along with my uncle Randy, would take care of the arrangements; we wouldn't draw the process out for too long. My sister started rehashing the details of what happened at her house that morning. She talked of my dad being in a weird state. He had called her that morning because he wanted her to pick him up and bring him over there. This was an odd request as he very rarely went over to my sister's house. She mentioned how he talked about hearing my mother's voice, even going as far as picking up the phone to speak with her—he'd thought he heard it ring.

"He been jokin' up, man, like ain't nothin' was goin' on. He ask me to go fry him some chicken, so I gon' in da kitchen and do 'em. Ya know, Daddy had like my chicken now! He used to say dat ting been jam up, man!" my sister said with a smile on her face.

After calling his name from the kitchen a few times with no response, she went in to see what was going on. She found him passed out on the couch with foam coming from his mouth. She immediately called 911 and started trying to bring him back to life by performing CPR.

All the while, I teared up as my sister told the story. She talked about the incident similarly to how she would with a patient, not her father. She was incredibly sharp, and I admired her strength—always did. By this time, my cousin Minnie entered the room and stood in the corner, offering her usual comic relief. She made jokes about how I was the "cry-baby" and my sister being the strong one. I hated hearing her say this.

It made me feel like a little kid again. Crybaby Greg. Like always, I said nothing. I just went along and made fun of myself with them. It was my way of protecting myself.

About 5:30 a.m. in the quiet house, I awoke to my mother crying out for my dad. "Oh Virgil, oh Virgil…"

I heard her over and over again from my childhood bedroom as I rustled back and forth, trying to fall asleep. It broke my heart. I wondered if I should go in there, or leave her to her tears. After a few minutes, I didn't hear it anymore and went to the bathroom, which was right next to her door, and I could hear her sniffling. After washing my hands and leaving the bathroom, I peeked in and asked, "Are you okay, Momma?"

"Yes, I just keep thinking he's here. That he is still here with me, Greg. I can't believe that he is gone. Oh, Virgil…." And she began to weep again.

"I'll lay with you, Momma." I jumped in the bed and put my arm around her. "Did you get any sleep?"

"Yes, a little bit."

I couldn't remember the last time I'd laid in bed with my mom. It had to be during middle school. We lay there for a while until the sniffling stopped, and the room fell silent. And for the very first time in a long time, I felt an extraordinary bond lying there beside her. My arm rested across her back, and I could feel that she felt protected at that very moment. She has been the rock throughout this whole ordeal of taking care of my father, and I wondered how long it had been since someone held her and made her feel protected. I wanted to protect her and make sure she was okay. Make sure she knew just as Daddy would tell her, "Everything's going to be alright." I needed her to know I was going to be strong, and she could depend on me now that Daddy was gone. I was going to step up to the plate and make Daddy proud of me.

The next day, the house filled again quickly. Everyone seemed to be holding up fine except me. I just didn't want to be around anyone. I found myself often going into my room to shed private tears as I listened to all of my family and childhood friends, laughing and talking in the other room. All I could think about was Daddy, and I would find myself getting emotional and feeling like a failure. I felt like I was the man of the family and needed to show everyone how strong I was, even though I felt weak on the inside.

While I looked through all the pictures to find the perfect one for the obituary, I was again reminded of all the good times we had. We had taken so many pictures with my dad when we were little kids, like pictures of me lying around his lap, or him carrying me on his back. They reminded me of Lil Gee and me. I wondered when those times changed because I never remembered those physical affections from him. I wondered if he stopped when he saw I leaned on the feminine side. Maybe he wanted to toughen me up. Perhaps he just wanted me to be strong.

My sister came into the room to ask me to go back to her apartment with her to pick up a few things. It would be the first time she returned since leaving for the hospital behind the ambulance carrying my father's mortal body. As we walked in, we were immediately greeted by the stench of the two day old fried chicken wings that still sat in the grease-filled black iron skillet. The TV was still on playing the five o'clock news, something my father watched daily. His cane rested against the wall, and his Washington Redskins hat sat on the tip of the end table, right next to the couch. Mom and Dad were always the biggest Redskins fans. His favorite jean jacket hung on the back of the kitchen chair, while his "shower" shoes, as he would call his flip flops, were scattered on the floor. I could see the stains from the fluid that came from his mouth crusted on the couch.

As I gathered his things and cleaned off the couch, I played back in my head the events as if I were there when it all happened. I heard the sly jokes he was making, and the laughing about my mother and the phone. My daddy had a way about him, so I knew he was ready to go. It was time for him to transition, transform, start a new existence, and he chose my sister to be there with him. She was a daddy's girl and was the best person to be there to watch him go to rest.

By the end of the week, I had made all the arrangements with my Uncle Randy. I felt very proud that I took the lead for picking out the casket, my dad's suit, the program, and a host of other things for the funeral. I felt a sense of pride, one that I knew my father would feel for me as well. It was the first order of business for me to handle after his transition, something he usually would have done. I was taking charge of my family, stepping into his shoes. I initially decided I was not going to attend the viewing of my father's body the day before the funeral, nor was I going to view his body at the actual funeral the day after. I just did not want that to be my last memory of him. I knew my father had gotten sick. I did not want to see him that way for the last time and to be honest, I've always had a fear of dead people ever since I was a child. I hated to see people in caskets. After seeing someone in a casket, it would haunt me for days to the point I could not sleep at night. Dead bodies were scary to me, and I did not want to be afraid of my father. Even though I was thirty now and had not been to a funeral since I was a kid, I still held the fear.

"You really should, Greg, Daddy looks so good," my mother insisted on the phone while at the viewing. "You would be really proud, Greg, and I think it would bring you peace."

For some reason, I believed her, and some part of me felt I would regret not seeing my dad one last time, even if it were just his lifeless body in a casket. What did I have to be afraid of anyway? Whenever I would tell him I was scared that ghosts or spirits were in my room, one thing my father used to always say was, "It's da livin ya need to fear, not the dead. Dey can't hurt ya."

"Okay, Momma, I will come by," I responded. Something felt good about my decision; it was as if it were the push I needed to do it.

My father looked great. He looked like his old self again, and I immediately broke into tears when I saw his face. Although I was sad, I was pleased to see my father looking handsome and at peace. The pained face I was so used to seeing over the past two years had suddenly disappeared. He looked happy and no longer broken. He finally was healed, and this gave me joy despite my sorrow.

Seeing him made the next day a little easier as there was a burden off of my chest going into the funeral. It was noon when the long black limo arrived to pick us up and head to First Baptist Church for the funeral services. I asked Carla to ride along with us so she could be there for Lil Gee in the case that I needed to be there for my mom. It felt good having Carla ride with us and being by my side. The church was as packed as any funeral on James Island would be. I decided not to speak but instead wrote a dedication to my father to include in the program. I was too afraid I would embarrass myself and not be able to hold up in front of everyone. It was weird hearing everyone else speak about my father.

"Virgil was a very soft-spoken man. He didn't say much. He was cool, and nobody ever disliked him. He once saved the entire Naval Shipyard during hurricane Hugo after an electrical circuit blew. Virgil would never tell you that, though, because he was a very humble man."

I never thought of my father as soft-spoken, but I guess it made sense. It made me reflect on the time his friends teased me and called me Boy George. He didn't say anything to defend me. Maybe he was afraid to shoot back. Perhaps he felt just like me around his peers: powerless.

My father's open casket was placed in the foyer so that everyone exiting the church could see him one last time before heading to the gravesite. As I walked out, I took one last look at my father and kissed him on his forehead. He was stiff. He was cold. That wasn't Daddy anymore.

As the black limo pulled up to the gravesite, I could see Gracey, Brenner, Marlon, and Raphael standing on the outskirts of the gathering of people. My eyes began to well up from the love and appreciation I had at that very moment. I was shocked and happy to see Raphael. We hadn't spoken in months, and he was the last person I expected to be there. Later that evening, when everyone gathered at my mother's house, all of my new gay friends and Gracey were now laughing and talking with my family and straight childhood friends. I would have never thought that these two worlds would converge. For the very first time, I felt comfortable and accepted in Charleston.

Lil Gee, almost 2, and Gee, Christmas 2002

Gee and Lil Gee before preschool graduation, 2005

Gee at his first house after divorce, Lithonia, GA, 2006

Gee, 30 and dating, with friend Gracey, 2007

Gee and Gracey at Brenner's house, Snellville, GA, December holidays 2007

Nephew Jakeem, Kony, Mom, Gee, and Lil Gee after Dad's funeral, February 2008

Last pic of Gee's father before his passing, 2007

14

HEAD OVER TIMBS

AFTER ABOUT FOUR months of being back in Atlanta, my emotions had settled down a bit as things got back into a routine. Although I still thought of him, I did not feel like I was mourning my father anymore. I carried around a bit of guilt and regretted him not knowing about my attraction for men. The fact that he died right before the week of his cataract surgery, the very time I had chosen to come out to him, made me feel some sort of way. I couldn't quite figure it out. I think, somehow, I managed to numb that guilt and regret at his passing.

Life, for me, was good. Lil Gee was growing up to be a great kid, and Carla and I were the best of friends. I had built a new gay social circle, and we all were living the life in Atlanta. I had just turned 31, was feeling confident, and coming into my looks as a grown man. I felt free from all of the challenges I experienced over the past thirty years and more comfortable with being a sexual and spiritual being. I loved the new "Gee." The spiritual connection I'd been nurturing over the years allowed me to release any guilt I was harboring in many areas of my life, including sex. It was not something I felt judged by anymore just because I was not in a relationship. I had discovered a newfound liberation, and I loved my new single life.

A week after returning from another year at Sizzle Miami, my good friend, Brenner, and I was sitting at Einstein's eating dinner and reminiscing about our great and wild time. Brenner could not believe that I fucked this boy under the DJ booth on the dance floor at Club Space. Hell, I couldn't believe it either! I had never done anything like that before, but I was excited to be able to tell the story. After wrapping up our dinner, we got a text from another friend, who was a few doors down at Joe's on Juniper, and he asked us to join him and a group of our other friends. I was tired and ready to go home, but I reluctantly tagged along.

"Who knows? Maybe I will meet my husband tonight," I told Brenner. "Fine. Let's go!"

I had never referred to myself as meeting "a husband" before; in fact, it was never something I ever thought possible, nor did I desire it. Although I wanted a committed relationship one day, men just didn't and could not marry men, so it was never something I aspired to do. Besides, after my marriage experience with Carla, I never wanted to feel restricted again.

Shortly after joining our other four friends on the patio, in walked a smooth, dark brown-skinned, sexy man with full dark lips, a gorgeous smile, gleaming perfect teeth, wearing a white tee that hugged his biceps perfectly. He and five friends sat down at a table, on the opposite end of the patio across from ours. It didn't take me long to point out to my crew that I thought he was hot! The slight Nelly resemblance he had took me over the edge. I always thought Nelly was sexy! The fact that he was seated directly, in my view, gave me ample opportunity to get eye contact to assess if there was mutual interest.

Not long after he was seated, I looked up to see this Nelly-ish-looking man watching me, and I then knew I would have a chance of knowing him. I could be aggressive in getting the attention of someone I wanted. I made it clear to him I was interested, and it appeared he was doing the same. After a few beers and two shots later, our bill was ready to be paid. I knew I had to make my move quickly, or I would miss the opportunity to connect with him. As my friends engulfed in chatter, I stood up and made my way to his table.

"Greetings everyone, my name is Gee. How are you all?" I said as I stood over the table.

I had never done anything quite this bold in my life. This was not the same as approaching a guy at a club.

"I'm Katie, and you are beautiful!" said the obnoxiously drunk, twenty-something-year-old White girl.

Although I could immediately tell she was the annoying one of the bunch, I appreciated her complimenting me and validating my approach to their table. There was an empty chair sitting at the table behind the man of my dreams. After everyone said hi, I excused myself, took the chair, and placed it directly between him and his friend (so I could be close enough to have a private conversation).

"What's your name?" I asked, staring directly into his glowing eyes.

"Juan."

"Very nice to meet you, Juan, I am Gee. I think you are so attractive, and I just had to come over to meet you. Now that I am even closer, I am so glad that I did. We've been staring at each other all night, and I couldn't leave without speaking."

"Oh, wow!" Juan said, blushing even more. "Thank you so much for that, but I was actually looking at your friend in the white V-neck sitting next to you, not you."

I was dazed and confused, to say the least, because I knew Juan was looking at me. However, since he said he was talking about my friend, Kyle, I had to go with it and let my good humor and charm get me out of it.

"Oh really? So, I walked allllllll the way over here for you to tell me you want my friend? Okay, okay, that is cool. Well, my friends are all hot, so I don't blame you. Good thing, a brotha got confidence, because you just crushed me! I'll go give him the message that you want to hook up with him."

I made my way back to our table, surprisingly confident and not the slightest bit embarrassed. I shared with everyone that Juan wanted Kyle and not me. Kyle was surprised because we both saw Juan looking at me.

Kyle mentioned he hadn't found him attractive from the time he walked in, so I knew a hookup would not take place, but I called Juan over anyway. I introduced the two of them, and they began to share small talk. All the while, Juan's leg is touching mine as he stood there talking to Kyle.

Now, what is this man doing? Does he want me or not, or is he just playing games?

I slid my chair over so we weren't touching anymore, but as I moved over, so did he. After his small talk with Kyle, they discovered some commonalities that gave them a reason to exchange numbers, and so they did. Afterward, Juan began to tell me his friend was interested in me, and I should come over to say hi. I kind of brushed it off and gave the "no thanks" look, so he said goodbye and went back to his table.

After he left, Kyle and I just talked about how weird that was, since it was so obvious Juan was looking at me. And as I looked over, of course, Juan is looking at me again. This time, he gives me the "come here" finger. I gave him a look like, *Naw muthafucka, you come over here! I've already come to you!* But, after he insisted, with his cute, puppy dog face, I went over anyway.

I sat next to him as the White chick continued to rave about how beautiful I was and how stupid Juan was for passing me up.

"I know, I know," Juan responded with regret.

Oh, he knows? I thought, but I wasn't trying to set myself up to be rejected again, no matter how cute he was.

Well, apparently, I did not have to, because Juan soon went into how things went down at his table upon their arrival. He went on to explain that his friend, Donovan, had called "dibs" on me first, so he did not want to overstep. Juan also went on to tell me that he had no interest in Kyle, but was just having fun with the rest of his friends while "claiming" him. Donovan kept nodding in agreement the whole time while Juan told me he wants me to put his number in my phone. I told him that I would just get it from Kyle since he already gave it to him, but he insisted on me taking it myself. It did not take much for me to concede. I did as requested and put his number in my phone. I also gave him mine, and by the time we all had made it to Blake's on the Park, Juan was texting me, letting me know he made it home. It made me excited that he was already hitting me up. All I could do was think about him the whole time since he gave me his number.

The next morning, I woke to a "Good Morning" text from Juan. There is nothing like a man who is not afraid to show interest, and he was doing just that.

Since he had shared that he was going to Alabama for work, I replied, "Good Morning, make it to Mobile?"

Juan texted back, "No, I missed my flight; the next one isn't until 2:30."

It was 11 a.m., so I suggested that I meet him at the airport for a lunch date before he left since I lived so close. He agreed, but not before warning me he had dressed hastily that morning. I wasn't sure what that meant, but I said okay.

I met Juan at the airport at noon, dressed in khaki shorts, white V-neck, brown belt, brown & green boxers, brown flip flops, and a green fitted cap. Now at this point in my life, I felt I had just learned how gays dressed and thought I had it down to a tee. In hindsight, I was a mess. At any rate, I tried to ensure I was cute and sexy, but like it was accidental, not purposeful. Again, in hindsight, I failed miserably.

As I approached Juan near ticketing, where he asked me to meet him, I automatically felt like I was looking at a superstar. He was dressed in a long-sleeved white and gray ECKŌ shirt, some jeans, and white and gray hi-top Pumas. I thought he looked cute, maybe a little hot for June, though, especially to be flying south. Juan was as attractive, if not more than I'd imagined. I worried that my liquor the night before was making him more dreamier-looking in my head. But nope, he was even dreamier.

Although I wanted to give him a full-on hug, I played it safe and greeted him with a dap and one arm embrace before we made our way to Houlihan's. I sat across from him at the booth and couldn't get over his flawless skin and beautiful smile. He asked me if he thought he could "benefit" from a nose job, and I just could not stop laughing. He had such a way with words. Since he brought up plastic surgery, I used the opportunity to tell him I had gotten a tummy tuck a few years ago. This was my way of giving him all my "ugly," so he could be prepared. He was curious without judgment or rejection. I felt safe, Juan felt safe, and our chemistry was intense. I was so into him that I immediately fell for him. At this point, I had been the aggressor, which is not all too uncommon for my sometimes overbearing personality. I was turning up the charm, and Juan was feeling it. He could not stop blushing and smiling at me. His face looked like a cross between vulnerability, peace, and joy.

It was approaching 2 p.m. now, and we knew our time was ending. When paying for the check, I immediately pulled out my card, and he did as well. I liked that he didn't expect me to pay but also allowed me to when I insisted without much challenge. This let me know that he could take care of himself but enjoyed being cared for. This was important to me.

Walking out of the restaurant and being met with the flight monitor showing that his flight had been delayed another two hours was no mistake. I suggested we go back to my house since I lived less than ten minutes away. He agreed, and we were on our way.

A part of me was happy that his flight got delayed because I got to show him my fancy Infiniti G35 and brand new townhome. I knew this would make me a better catch; at least, that's what I believed at the time. Of course, the other part of me wanted to spend as much time with him as possible. I'm not sure if this was because I wanted to be with him, or I wanted to show him how great I was before he left town so that he could think about me all week.

We spent our time talking while the TV watched us. He was almost as flirtatious as me but in a coy way. I guess it's the Aries in him as it is in me. I could tell by his vulnerable disposition that he was feeling the way I was courting him. I could also tell it was something he was not used to, but he welcomed and very much enjoyed it. My subtle touches electrified him as much as it did me. I remember being wrapped up in wondering if he was a top, bottom, or versatile. I knew from my little experience in the gay world; this was something I needed to find out quickly, even to see if I would be compatible with the person. If we weren't sexually compatible, there would never be a chance. At this point, I had had enough sexual experiences to consider myself "versatile."

We ended up spending an additional four hours at my home, getting to know each other. Thanks to Delta and two-additional flight delays, we got to know a lot about each other. I even took the time to show him my tummy tuck scar, to which he replied, "Wow! That's a belt!" I could have easily gotten offended by it or felt ashamed, especially since I was still becoming secure with having it, but Juan made me feel comfortable. I had also learned that his stomach was the part of the body that he was most insecure with after I attempted to place my hand on it. I've always liked to rub the stomach of the person I was seeing, even when I was dating women. I'm not sure if it was because when I was a teenager, my cousin, Minny, would always rave about how she loved when her then-boyfriend used to rub her stomach, or because how it made me feel when my mom would rub my tummy to check my temperature when I was sick. It could have been because I envied flat stomachs because mine always hung well over my belt, but for whatever the reason, I liked it.

I also learned that he spent part of his life in foster care due to his mom's battle with drugs, he had never had a relationship that lasted past three months, had terrible credit and he was arrested a couple of times, which led to a suspended license and repossessed car. That meant he was on MARTA, and in the gay community; that was not SMARTA! But it didn't matter to me...neither did his age. My 31-year-old self had vowed never to date anyone who did not have a car, was under thirty or did not have experience in relationships. Those were three things on my list that were deal-breakers, but at this moment, at that time, none of it mattered. It was like he was telling me he was a millionaire with a private jet, a yacht, ten cars, and a dozen properties across the globe. I felt I had hit the lottery!

The topic of sex finally came up, and I nervously asked Juan the ultimate question. "Are you a top, bottom, or versatile?"

I am not quite sure why I was nervous, because nothing he could have said would have been a deal-breaker for me. I was willing to be whatever he needed me to be. I had finally found love, and the endorphins would allow me to adjust to anything.

"I'm a top, but in a relationship, I will do anything to make my man happy," he responded.

"That's what's up. I am verse and know you would love to get up in this, because I know I would love to get up in that!" I excitedly answered with the sexiest voice and eyes I could muster.

"I told you I'm a top!" he retorted almost defensively.

"Okay, that's cool. I didn't mean to offend you," I apologized.

"It's not that. It's just people always trying to call me a bottom, and I'm not."

I could tell he was insecure about being called a bottom. It was fine with me, and it even relieved some pressure of having to please him as a top.

It was about time for us to leave, and I just couldn't help but pull him in by the waist and kiss his beautiful mouth. I needed to know what my thick red lips felt like up against his thick dark ones, to exchange breaths with one another, to introduce our tongues and feel his body submit to my secure embrace. I wanted it. And it was better than I had imagined since I met him the night before.

His kisses filled me up. It instantly created a bond that would take us through the next week until he returned.

Juan's trip ended early, which meant we would have our second date sooner than later. Before he returned to Atlanta, we spent hours throughout the day talking on the phone and nearly all day chatting on Yahoo Messenger, where I would join him in listening to his favorite genre of music: show tunes. I tried to like it, and I really thought I did, but it turned out to be just the newness of love. I had learned a lot about Juan in those first few days. We would damn near fall asleep on the phone together, not wanting to be the first to say goodbye.

"You hang up."

"No, you hang up!"

Yes, we played that game, and it was fun.

We couldn't wait to see each other, so we scheduled the date for the same day he returned. Because he didn't drive, we decided that I would pick him up from his apartment complex. Buzzing through the gate allowed him to know that I was pulling up. As I parked, I saw him walking down the stairs wearing a green Polo shirt, baggy blue jeans, classic Timberland boots, and a NY fitted cap. He was giving me the character Pookie from one of my favorite books, B-Boy Blues by James Earl Hardy, something I ultimately didn't expect but appreciated. I always loved a man in Timbs.

He was just as, if not more, attractive than he was the first two times I saw him. We headed over to Nikiemoto's in Gay Midtown, where he taught me how to use chopsticks. I never liked using them. Forks were always the way to go for me, but he thought it was a sin to eat Asian food without chopsticks. I thought that was cute.

After dinner, we headed back to his place and talked on the couch for hours. We played a card game called "dirty hearts," which is usually played in a group with shots. Anytime either of us pulled a heart, he would have to answer a question, commit to a dare, or take a shot. The twist for us was no shots allowed. We had to answer the question. We thought it was a good chance for us to ask each other any questions we wanted to know without things being awkward or uncomfortable. And best believe, neither of us held back!

We found out so many things about each other, from our coming-out stories, our exes, the last time we had sex, STD's we ever had, our last checkup, our biggest physical insecurities, to the way we felt about each other and what our intentions were. I had expected Juan to be HIV positive because of my past experiences, and I felt so strongly for him that I knew this had to be the case. When he pulled the next heart, and it was my turn to ask, I decided to go for it.

"I have a feeling I know the answer, and it really does not matter what the answer is, but I have to ask what is your HIV status?"

"Negative as of March. How about you?"

"Did I pull a heart?" We both busted out in laughter.

"No, really, I am negative, too," I said. "I was last checked in April."

"That's good to know. Is that what you thought I was going to say?" he asked.

"No, I thought you were going to say you were positive. I've been feeling like the man I ended up with would be positive for some odd reason. It just seems like it's all around me, in everyone I meet and in everything I see. Black gay men and HIV seem to go hand and hand."

"OMG! Me too! I just knew you were going to be HIV+. The last guy I dated when I first moved here suddenly stopped dating me because he found out he was positive a few months after we met. That's crazy; we both thought that and were both wrong."

I suspected many Black same-gender-loving men felt this way, mainly because of how mainstream society portrays us, and even how we represent ourselves. Hell, Juan and I were doing it! It was refreshing just to have an honest conversation with someone I liked. During our game of "dirty hearts," I also found out that most of his relationships usually ended because he got bored. This was a bit scary to me. If he always got bored, would I bore him as well?

We both shared that we were really into each other and wanted to see where things would lead. We were both ready for a serious relationship and were willing to leave ourselves open with one another to explore if we were the ones for each other. It sure felt like it. In our openness during a game of dirty hearts, we decided we would not jump into sex. We wanted to wait.

Juan shared, "Sex is probably the least important thing for me in a relationship. I've had plenty of sex, and it does not interest me. I've been to sex parties, had threesomes, and done the promiscuous lifestyle. Sex is just recreation for me. I can probably go the rest of my life without having sex and be fine with it. When I have sex with a person too early when meeting them, I lose interest."

I never could understand why men thought this way. It seems a bit heteronormative, in my opinion. We are both men, so if you believe something about me after having sex, what is it that you think of yourself? I didn't express this to him, but it crossed my mind. It also intimidated me a bit that Juan had had so much explorative sex in his 26 years. I was still relatively new to sex with men, and the most exciting thing I had ever done was have sex in the club that one night and had one threesome. I was just starting to feel comfortable with who I was sexually. I also always felt like sex was something you took advantage of within a relationship. It was when you had the most sex! I believe this came from growing up with my "no sex before marriage" religious thinking.

"I am the opposite. I would die if I couldn't have sex again for the rest of my life. I am a very sexual person, and I can definitely get into casual sex, but sex also creates a deeper connection for me. A sexual connection is necessary to experience another soul fully. Mentally, emotionally, spiritually, and physically is how you fully connect with someone."

Juan looked confused. I could tell he was not feeling what I was saying like it was something he had never heard before and couldn't believe that I experienced sex that way. I was looking at him just as crazy. It was awkward for a few seconds, and then Juan was back to pulling the next card.

After answering a few more questions, I kissed him. Then, I kissed him again. A few kisses later, I laid on top of him while my tongue ran all over his neck, lips, and mouth. This lasted for hours. Making out with him without the intention of it leading to sex was refreshing. It allowed me to fully be in the moment without anticipating what was coming next. It felt good. Natural. It made me want him even more. It reminded me of those days I made out with Carla on her great grandmother's couch.

I reluctantly got up to make my way home. It was getting late, and we both had to go to corporate jobs in the morning. After a few more kisses and hugs, we said goodnight. I couldn't stop thinking about him on the way home—how I wanted to spend the night with and hold him all night. I was smitten and couldn't wait to know more.

Over the next month, we saw each other every day. By the fourth date, we were spending every night at each other's houses, which was comfortable with Lil Gee being away for the summer with his mom in Charleston. My friends were now feeling the sudden absence of their ringleader—me. They thought I was damn near crazy for the way I flipped my life upside down for this new man. They never hesitated to let me know that I had dumped them and was acting "brand new." Brenner didn't like that our nightly phone calls had ended. Aside from my roommate and closest friend, Gracey, I hadn't brought him around yet because I wanted to be sure this was real. And although it felt real, I didn't know when Juan would stop feeling this way about me. I had to make sure it wasn't just a fling—a nonsexual one at that. It had happened way too often to me in the past.

I must admit I was feeling some type of way about him not showing any sexual interest in me. I knew we had decided to wait, but for him, waiting seemed too easy. He never talked about it, made suggestive advances, or got aroused. Not even when we cuddled or spooned. I couldn't figure out why he wouldn't be turned on while spooning me, because I, sure as hell, was. I know I don't have much ass, but damn! I remember one morning, he was standing over me on the bed while pulling the string on the ceiling fan, and I reached my hand under his basketball shorts and grabbed his penis. He seemed embarrassed, and it immediately made me uncomfortable, almost like I had violated him.

He quickly snapped out of it and said, "Don't touch it unless you gonna do something with it."

"Oh, I can definitely do something with it," I bragged.

We were both trying to come off as confident and sexy, but neither of us succeeded. It was impossible amidst the awkward energy that had taken over the room. I immediately regretted doing it and felt like he wasn't attracted to me sexually. I felt rejected.

That night while getting ready to get in the shower, I turned to Juan as he lay on the bed and said, "Why don't you join me? An innocent shower, no sex." I thought this would have been an excellent way to break the ice of what happened earlier that morning. A year before meeting Juan, I had dated this guy that invited me to do the same: take a shower without having sex. It was such a vulnerable moment, and I wanted to share it with Juan.

"Okay."

I could tell he was a bit reluctant.

After about two minutes of being in the shower, Juan stepped in behind me. A few seconds passed before I turned around to see Juan's naked brown body for the first time, as he watched me. His penis stood erect. I wondered if he fluffed before entering the shower or if he was really turned on by me.

"Sorry. It's been a while." He said as he saw my eyes get lusty while staring at his erection.

"You don't have to apologize." And I hugged and kissed Juan. We were both excited but again restrained from sex. I was so relieved that he was turned on by me. I wanted to have him badly but refused to be the first to take the next step. After all, it was him that wanted to abstain the most. At least it seemed that way since he was so easy for him.

While drying off, Juan looked at me in the mirror and said, "In Miami at the club, did you use a condom with that guy?"

I was stunned. Had it been on his mind since the night we played dirty hearts, and I told him this story when asked, "where was the wildest place you had sex ?"

"Yes," I answered immediately. It was a lie. How could I have? We were drunk dancing, which soon led to drunk kissing, which later led to me pulling his pants down, pulling my dick out, and drunk fucking him. It literally happened that fast.

"Okay. Just asking."

I could tell he didn't believe me. I hated that I lied to him. The guilt was immediately eating at me. By the time I lotioned my body and put my basketball shorts on for bed, I confessed to Juan.

"I was lying. I did not use a condom with that boy in Miami. I was ashamed to tell you the truth. I am sorry and hope it doesn't change anything."

"It's okay. I knew you were lying. How could you have used a condom on the dance floor at the club? He was a whore."

And we cuddled up in bed and watched Weeds before falling asleep. It was so easy to confess to him.

Thirty days after the day we met, things were still going strong. I had even put him as my top friend on Myspace, moving Carla down one notch. We saw each other every day and every night, talking on the phone and chatting via Yahoo! all day while at work. I continued to fall deeper for him. At this point, I was ready to bring him around my friends, so I did that night at Midtown Bowl, and it was a blast. Juan was electrifying and magnetic. Everyone he encountered seemed to love him like I knew they would.

On the way home, Juan could not keep his hands off me. Although he was always very affectionate, his touches were a bit different tonight. They were suggestive and aggressive, and it was turning me on. He had never been this aggressive with me, and it was even making me blush. I felt vulnerable. Yes, we both agreed to not having sex with one another, but who was I kidding? I wanted to rip his clothes off on our first date.

Besides, I wanted to uphold our commitment unless he showed me he was having just a hard time as I was.

When we walked through the door of my townhome, he immediately started kissing me aggressively. We began to tear off each other's clothes, and before we knew it, we were butt-ass naked in my living room, our threads spread across the floor. I hurried up the stairs as Juan followed me closely, smacking me on the ass, and hugging my waist from behind. Our tongues swirled as our hands caressed, touched, and grabbed body parts. Pushing me on the bed, holding my arms down by my wrists, Juan kissed and nibbled me all over my body. Flipping me over and tasting me from behind, his tongue was unapologetic. His touch was forceful, his demeanor was stern. It was nothing like I imagined our first time would be. It wasn't romantic or sensual. Although I enjoyed the feel of his body and mouth all over me, it felt unnatural to me, like it was a scene out of a movie: acted. Not connected and like a performance, it didn't feel like our lovemaking made us into "one."

After about 15 minutes of us having some of the least rhythmic sex I had ever had in my life, he said to me, "Let me see you cum." And, so I did, even though I wanted him to cum first. I came, and he laid next to me.

"You're not going to cum?" I asked.

"No. I rarely cum during sex," he replied nonchalantly.

I had never heard of such a thing, but I did not ask any questions or make any comments. I heard that many women do not orgasm during sex, but it was the first time I had ever heard about a man who didn't. It made me feel insecure and unwanted, like I didn't have any sexual power with him. I felt defeated, and it showed.

"Don't worry. We'll find our groove," Juan said in a comforting tone.

I guess he felt just as awkward as I did, or at least picked up on my sense of anxiety about it. Although a little disappointed in our first lovemaking experience, I was still ecstatic that we had crossed that bridge. Even though it was not the experience I had dreamed of, I did feel closer to him. And besides, I knew sex could always get better with time.

"Hey, baby." Juan turned and looked me in the eyes. "I love you. I was holding back telling you because I didn't want you to think it was just about the sex, but I can't help myself. I have fallen in love with you."

All the insecurities and fear I had just felt moments ago during our lovemaking experience disappeared. My heart melted. It didn't matter that we just had the most awkward sex I had ever had or that I was not able to bring him to climax. He still loved me, and I loved him too. I loved him since the day I picked him up from Hartsfield-Jackson International Airport.

"I love you too, Juan," I assured him as I nestled into his arms, and we slept the night away.

15

LOVE AND LOSSES

THE SUMMER OF 2008 was the summer of falling deeply in love with Juan. We spent every day and every night together, and life felt like a dream. We talked and cuddled every moment we had together. We cooked together, cleaned together, and wore each other's clothes as if they were our own. Juan had also become really close to my circle of friends, fitting in perfectly. I had even gotten a chance to meet his family and friends, which whom I was terrified to meet—especially his mother.

About six weeks after Juan and I met, he was on speakerphone with his mother when he said to her, "So, I got a boyfriend, Mama."

"YOU GOT A WHAT?!" she screamed. "What the FUCK you mean you got a boyfriend? Didn't you tell me you would never have a boyfriend?"

Juan had warned me as to how boisterous she was, but I was not ready for this.

"I know Mama, but I met someone I really like, so I had a change of heart."

"Well, what he look like? He don't wear no makeup or have no arched eyebrows, does he? Don't be bringing no flaming queen around here! You know I don't put up with that shit!"

I gasped, and she heard me.

"Mama! He ain't like that!"

"Is he listening? You got me on speakerphone? I don't give a fuck if he heard me, I meant what I said!" and she hung up the phone.

Juan saw the terror in my eyes.

"Don't worry about her. I told you she was crazy as hell. She likes to talk shit. And besides, it does not matter what my family thinks, you are first. If they don't accept you, then they don't ever have to see me again." My heart melted. *Would he really give up his family for me? Did he love me that much? Or did he really not care for his family that much?*

Could he leave me so easily?

Juan had a work trip planned to his hometown of L.A. and asked that I meet him there for an extended weekend. I was ecstatic to go to L.A. for the first time and even more ecstatic to get to know more about Juan. I was not so excited to meet his family, especially his mother.

"I'm so nervous to meet his mother. I hope she likes me." I said to my mother over the phone while lying in the hotel bed. Juan had run out to get some breakfast.

"Why? Just be yourself. She will love you. Everybody loves you!" she responded. Despite her tough exterior, my mother did always know how to make me feel better.

"Well, I hope so. Anyways, I'll let you know how it goes. Juan is on his way back in."

"Okay. Tell Juan I said to take care of my son!
Love ya." "Love ya too. Bye."

We had planned to meet at the Santa Monica Pier for lunch at Bubba Gump Shrimp with her and his older sister. It was early August, and the weather was hot, but the breeze from the beach was a welcoming delight from the sun's rays. We waited outside of the restaurant for about ten minutes before Juan pointed out his mother Sara and his sister Coco heading toward us. Sara was about 5'5", brown skin, with a medium-sized waist, maybe a size 10, and big breasts that she was clearly not ashamed to show off. She had on a youthful wig that complimented her round face. His tall, beautiful, seven-months pregnant, brown-skinned sister smiled widely as she approached Juan and me. Juan looked just like both of them.

"Heeey, Juan!" She hugged him tightly and didn't seem to want to let go. His mother followed suit. I immediately admired their natural display of love and affection. This was not the mother who I imagined in my head.

"Is this Gee? GotDAMN HE IS FIIIINE!" his mother screamed and give me a big ole hug. We connected immediately.

Juan gave me an "I told you so" look, and we walked in to have lunch.

My mom was right. She loved me.

Although things were going great between Juan and me, there were a couple of things that made me a little insecure. One thing was that, just like Shawn and Raphael, Juan would always make it a point to let people know light-skinned guys weren't his type, but they were the only guys that would approach him. Even in the summers, when I got darker while working on my tan, he would barely even notice. This would take me back to childhood with never feeling Black enough. Hearing this would make me feel like he wasn't really attracted to me and was only lying about it. On the other hand, he mentioned that sex wasn't important to him, so I could see him being with me. But then again, it didn't help when he'd talk about love for small, uncut penises, and guys with a gut. My not-so-small, circumcized dick and relatively new flat tummy would never fit those desires. Was I good enough for him? Did he really want me?

I don't think my new roommate of four months, Gracey, loved my new relationship at the time. Who could blame her? After all, Juan did take her place in many ways.

All the relationships around me started to change. My codependent friendships were not surviving this new intimate relationship. These friends were beginning to feel replaced, forgotten as if they had lost their value because space they once occupied, was given to Juan. With all the time I spent with Juan, not many of them were able to handle it, nor understand.

Although Gracey was frequently dating, I do not think she was able to be happy with my new relationship with Juan. She and I used to spend countless nights together, Starbucks Caramel Macchiatos in one hand with a blunt in the other. We would dream about the day we would meet our soul mates. I'd show her my next date's *Adam4Adam* profile, while she showed me her date's profile from Yahoo Personals. I was her shoulder to cry on when the boys broke her heart. She was my sounding board when the boys would frustrate me to no end. Then I found my dream, Juan, and shit changed like a muthafucka. When we fell in love with each other hard and quickly, it left little room for much else. I admit I was one of those men that fully absorbed myself in my new relationship. Juan got most of me. By the end of the summer, Gracey and I had faced challenges within our relationship, which eventually led to a big argument and her moving out. We did come to peace before she left, but things were never the same. We tried making an effort to spend time together, but I think we both realized our relationship was over.

At the end of the summer, Carla decided she wanted to stay in Charleston and pursue a catering career. I was at work one day when she called me on my cell phone to tell me.

"Say wah?" I said to Carla after her breaking the news that she was not coming back to Atlanta and wanted to take Lil Gee with her.

"I want to stay here. My catering career here is really picking up, and I want to establish myself more here. Not Atlanta."

A knot started to form in the back of my throat as I tried to hold in the emotion I felt at hearing the news that my son would be moving four and a half hours away from me. I could not get any words out as tears dropped from my eyes. Carla could hear me on the other end of the phone as I failed at hiding my heartbreak.

"I'm sorry, Greg. I'm not trying to hurt you, and you know you can see Lil Gee anytime you want, but I have to do this for me. My life can't stop."

Carla always had a passion for food, and she also never really felt at home in any other place besides Charleston. I knew these two things, so I shouldn't have been at all that shocked, but when she was persistent about keeping Lil Gee with her as well, it brought about my biggest fear: that I would not get to be an active part of his life. Ever since Lil Gee was born, he had been the center of my life. As he got older, I made sure we did homework together, watched movies, ate together at home, or even went out to eat just like my mom used to do with me. I was determined that just because I divorced his mother, it did not mean I would not continue to be "Super Dad." My pride would not allow me to become one of those "weekend fathers," as it was not the father I was raised to be. And I certainly was not taught to be one of those "deadbeat dads" that the media often portrayed Black men to be. Furthermore, I wouldn't give anyone the chance to say that I left my wife and kid to be gay. I refused.

For the five years following our separation, Carla and I shared joint custody across the board. I would have him five days one week; she'd get the remaining two days, and then we would switch. This is what we had become accustomed to, and I did not want it to change.

While I had my own personal feelings about this, I also knew the reality was that we were divorced, and that meant life could take us in separate ways and maybe to separate cities. For me, the fact that she was moving to my hometown, where my family was as well, made it a little better. However, Carla was not established in Charleston, and this bothered me a lot. I challenged her to see my side of things. I felt she should allow Lil Gee to stay here in Atlanta, where he was already established at home and in school until she was able to get established in Charleston. At the time, she was living with her mother, father, and brother in their old, small home "down the island" that was not well taken care of. This was the same home she grew up in, and while I did not feel the house was unsafe, it was not how or where I wanted my son to grow up.

We all want our kids to have a better life than we did, and in my opinion, this was not it. I felt like my seven-year-old son shouldn't have to live in those conditions, especially to share a bed with his mom in her old childhood room. To make matters worse, much like my father, her mother was battling health issues and alcoholism, and I knew she would be often responsible for watching Lil Gee while Carla worked. And "down the island" hadn't changed much, still being the breeding ground for drug dealers and addicts. It was an all-around unhealthy environment, one I did not want my son to be a part of. How could I feel good about myself while my son lived in those conditions, and I was living much differently? It just didn't seem right. I expressed all of this to her, and she still held on to the fact that it would be fine, and she wouldn't be there long. I reluctantly agreed for her to keep our son there with her, but only if he continued to do well in school and didn't show any signs of regression. If he did, he would need to come back with me until she got on her feet. She agreed.

Before starting school in Charleston, I went to pick Lil Gee up to spend some time with him for a couple of weeks. He seemed to be okay with the idea of moving, which hurt my feelings a little bit. But how could his life, with me, in Atlanta compare to being able to hang out with cousins, who were around his age? All he saw was fun. All I saw was the possibility of his life going in a direction I did not want, but this was happening.

One thing I knew about most people in Charleston, not to mention Carla and her family, was that they did not completely agree with the way I lived my life. Hell, some of my family didn't either. I knew there would be people in Lil Gee's ear about me being a faggot and what they thought of that. I knew I had to be the first person to tell him about me, so I could set the standard and example of what it meant to be a man who loved men. But how was I to tell this to a seven-year-old? I knew his mom would not agree with me coming out to him, so I decided I wouldn't get her permission first. I would just tell her after I've told him and deal with it.

Lil Gee and I were watching SpongeBob, his favorite cartoon, and I just decided to spring it on him.

"Do you remember the last time Daddy had a girlfriend?" I asked.

"Yes. Tonya," he quickly replied.

"You remember her? Wow!" I was surprised. "Well, Daddy probably won't ever have another girlfriend."

"Why not?" he asked curiously.

"Because Daddy is gay. Do you know what that means?" "No."

"That means I like guys. You know how boys like girls? Well, I 'like-like' guys. That makes me gay."

"Oh. Okay," he replied as if I had just told him I don't like vegetables. He continued watching SpongeBob.

"Do you have any questions or anything about me being gay?"

"No," he replied matter-of-factly, eyes still on the TV.

And that was the extent of my coming out to my seven-year-old son. I was not at all shocked at his reaction. I knew kids only made a big deal about things that parents made a big deal about, and after all, it was not all that complicated. Had I waited until he was a teenager—his mom once suggested I wait until he was 18—it would have been a completely different story. I was so thankful for my coworker and friend, Tricia, for sharing her story of how she told her daughter what it meant to be gay. It was so simple, so I used the same approach.

So far, in 2008, I lost my father, met the man of my dreams, broke up with my closest friend, Gracey, and was on the way to losing my son as his mom moved him several hundred miles away. I was starting to feel like God was playing games with me: by giving me the man I'd been asking for but taking four close relationships—Dad, Gracey, Carla, and Lil Gee—away from me. It had already been a quite emotional year for me, and now, it was time for me to introduce Lil Gee to Juan.

When telling my son about me being gay, I did not want it to be about anything or anyone else except me. I did not want to present him with, "Your dad is gay, and here is my gay boyfriend." I felt like this approach would potentially cause my son to hold something against Juan. I did not want to do that. I wanted to ensure they met before Lil Gee moved away, so they would at least be familiar with one another. We decided that Juan would come over to have dinner with us one evening, and I would introduce them.

I was not nervous at all because Lil Gee was a laid-back kid who liked everyone. He was polite and well-mannered and didn't make much noise, so I didn't see any reason why Juan wouldn't like him.

When Juan walked through the door after getting off of the Marta bus, I could tell he was anxious. Lil Gee was upstairs playing his video game while I cooked dinner.

"Hey, Boo...so good to see you. Don't be nervous! My son is very laid back."

"I'm not nervous!"

I could tell he was lying. I yelled, "Dinner's Ready" to Lil Gee, and a short few seconds later, he was racing down the stairs.

"What's for dinner, Daddy?"

Juan was already sitting at the table, but Lil Gee hadn't seen him yet.

"Your favorite. Chicken and gravy, rice, and green beans. Look behind you, we have a visitor who is eating with us tonight."

Lil Gee turned around.

"His name is Juan. Juan, this is my son Lil Gee."

Gee walked over to the table and sat down. Juan extended his hand.

"Hi, Lil Gee, it's nice to meet you."

"Nice to meet you too!" Lil Gee shook his hand and dug into his plate. After a few moments of silence, we all started talking about summer coming to an end and all the things that we did. It felt so natural for the three of us to sit and eat together. I wondered how many more times we would be sitting at this table sharing a meal.

16

FIGHTING TO FATHER

THOSE TWO WEEKS came and went quicker than either of us would have imagined. Just like that, the life I had known for the past five years had suddenly changed.

How could I have let him go that easily?

Was this really the right decision?

Will he be okay growing up in that environment?

Will he be influenced by a life full of alcohol, drugs, and dealing?

I wasn't quite sure what to do with the newfound freedom of not having the daily duties of fatherhood. What was once me taking care of my son every day became once-a-month visits and extended stays during school breaks. I tried to be a part of his life as much as I could, but there was nothing that could have prepared me for the loss I felt with Lil Gee not being here with me. More importantly, nothing would prepare me for the guilt that came along with the separation.

Will he be fooled into thinking that his daddy is less than a man because I am gay?

Will he grow up expecting lack in his life?

Will he see the possibilities of what his life could be like?

Will his being away from me strengthen the possibility of him hating me?

While I felt insecure about my position as a father, my new role as a boyfriend was becoming fuller every day. When we were not at work, we were spending every waking moment together, taking advantage of every opportunity to love one another a little more and learn about one another on an even deeper level. Our connection grew stronger by the day, and it was like no love I had ever experienced. Juan was such a breath of fresh air and the exact force I needed amid the significant life changes taking place without any of my control.

Eight months after we met, Juan got a call with a great offer while I was at work. He called to share the news.

"Hey, Boo, what are you up to?"

"Just working. Can't wait to get home to you."

"Me too! Guess what! I got a call today from Rob, my old boss! He offered me a six-month gig as a stage manager on a 24 city tour! It starts next month, and it's making double what I am making now for half the year!"

My heart sank. I fell silent for about five seconds that seemed like an eternity. I had to say something.

"For real?! That's awesome!" I lied.

I mean, it was awesome, but I didn't feel awesome. If he took this job, this would surely be the end of our eight-month relationship. There is no way I could survive a long-distance relationship being so new with me being so insecure. He would be sure to cheat on me, and even if he didn't, I would drive myself crazy thinking he was. I remember when dating Shawn, he was in a play that required him to be gone every night for eight weeks, and it drove me mad! I was so jealous of all the time he was spending with all of these handsome, sexy men who shared something in common with him that I did not have. I think I was also jealous that he was acting, something that was still buried deep inside of me. I couldn't go through this with Juan. I couldn't take it.

I knew he heard the fear and sadness in my voice.

"I am not sure if I am going to take it. I am going to give it some thought. It is a great opportunity, but I also know that our relationship is new, and you are important to me. I know you do not want me to leave."

My heart smiled. My hopes rose. I felt a little bit of relief, but I was still worried. *And what did he mean by "I" did not want him to leave? Would he only be staying for me? Does he want to go? I don't want him staying if it's only for me.*

"You know that I love you and want to be with you every chance I get. I would be afraid for our relationship, but I will support you either way." Although inside I knew I would be angry and resent him for leaving, I felt I had to say the "right" thing, so I did.

Later that evening, I got a text from Juan on my way home from work.

"Hey, do you mind if Parker comes over?"

How could he be asking me for his friend to come over at a time like this? Couldn't he tell I was devastated and worried all day about losing the best relationship of my life? Why didn't he care?

Well, I wasn't going to hold my tongue this time.

"To be honest with you, I don't really feel like having company. I am really having a hard time with the news today. I am so afraid. I am still supportive of whatever decision you make, but I am not feeling good right now. I prefer that he didn't come over."

I was super dramatic, but I was honestly very emotional. And passive-aggressive. However, I needed to make it clear I did not want Juan to go.

"I've decided not to go, Boo. I was going to tell you when I got home, but why wait? I love you, and do not want to risk our relationship!"

I felt the biggest sigh of relief when reading that text. He did care. He did love me, and he loved us enough to not take the chance of risking our relationship, even if he knew it was only me who was insecure about it. While on the one hand, I wanted him to feel just as anxious as I did about being apart, the other hand was grateful for his sacrifice and show of commitment to me.

While my relationship with Juan was well on its way to building a great foundation, the transition of Lil Gee moving to Charleston was very challenging. It was not only a challenge for me having him be away, but it also became a challenge for him in school. Although he wasn't attending school in Atlanta, I kept in touch with his teachers via conference calls and emails. I had learned that he was falling asleep in class, not turning in homework, and failing his tests. His mother was never the type to offer much structure or be very involved in his day-to-day, so it didn't entirely surprise me that Lil Gee started slipping at school. She would also work late nights catering events and leave him home with her mother, who I did not feel was in the best condition to look after him. I knew he was not being taken care of to the standard which he was used to. Carla promised me she was getting her own place by January, but of course, that did not happen. Lil Gee also complained to me about how he hated sleeping with his mom and that he wished she had never moved to Charleston. It crushed me. *I am here and able to give full attention to him; why can't she see that?*

Up until the time Carla went to Charleston for the summer, and I met Juan, we would talk every day. We literally became best friends again a couple of years after we separated. After Carla and Lil Gee moved, we talked less and less. I chalked it up to her being preoccupied with her family, but I also felt like Carla was intentionally separating herself from me. I can't say for sure it was because of my new relationship with Juan, but I would not be surprised if it had everything to do with it. Gracey would always tell me that Carla was still in love with me and couldn't stand to see me with Juan. I don't think that's so farfetched. Even if she wasn't in love with me at the time of her moving, I could still understand her need to separate herself from me in the way she held space in my life. We were close.

In late fall, on one of my visits to see Lil Gee, I decided to meet with his teacher to discuss his progress or lack thereof. I scheduled a meeting after school at 3:30 p.m., and Carla was to meet me there. She wasn't there when it was time for the meeting, so I left Juan in the car and headed to the conference. After leaving the conference, I headed to my car, and Carla was approaching, apologizing for being late and missing the meeting. This was also the first time she had ever seen Juan, so I introduced them.

"Carla, this is Juan. Juan, this is Carla," I said.

"Hi, Carla, nice to meet you," Juan replied. I could tell he was a little nervous by the way his voice trembled a bit.

"Hey, you too, hun, I heard a lot about ya!" Carla politely replied, barely even looking in his direction.

"Alrighty, well, let me get out of here. I got a gig I need to hurry to. See you, Greg. Nice to meet you, Juan!"

And just like that, she sped off in her Blue Toyota Camry. Based on her demeanor and anxiousness, I could tell she was uncomfortable. She couldn't have had anywhere to go, seeing as she had just gotten there and planned to make part of the meeting, so I knew it had to be much more than that.

Shortly after that meeting, Juan broke the lease on his apartment and moved in with me. I always told myself I would at least date a man for a year before living together, but this love made me break all the rules. We shared everything together. We double dated, went on trips, talked about everything under the sun, and even finally found our sexual groove. I could be completely comfortable and free with him. He never judged me and always offered unsurmountable, unconditional love. I was afraid, though, my mom would not approve of him moving in. She hadn't even met him yet.

"Juan is moving in with me. His lease is up," I lied, "and he is always over here anyways, so we gonna save money and just have him move in. Especially now that Gracey has moved out, I can use the extra money." I was making up reasons why he should move in, other than the fact that we just wanted to be together.

My mom laughed. She saw right through me, "Oh, really? Y'all can save money, huh? Well, that's good."

She was very lighthearted about it. Nothing like I had imagined.

"Well, I do hope to meet him soon."

"Well, that's what I was going to ask. Do you mind if he comes with us to Disney World for Thanksgiving? He won't have anywhere to go, and I don't want him being alone."

It was the first Thanksgiving after my dad had passed, and we decided to break tradition and do something different. I don't think any of us was ready to spend my dad's favorite holiday without him yet.

"Sure, that's no problem. I'll get an extra resort bracelet for him, and he can stay with us since I rented an apartment. You and he can sleep in the living area, and me, Tawny and my two grandboys can sleep in the bedroom with the two beds."

I was excited for them to meet. I knew they would love each other. My mom was always the cool mom and got along with everyone.

When pulling up to the rented condo, my mom, sis, nephew, and Lil Gee had just pulled up in the van that they rented in Charleston. It was my year to have Lil Gee for Thanksgiving, so Carla dropped him off at my mom's house for the ride to Orlando.

We all exited the vehicles at the same time, and I gave all of them a big hug, well, as big of a hug as our family gave. Nothing like Juan's family.

"This is Juan, Momma."

Everyone else had already met him.

"Hi, Juan! I heard so much about you. So nice to finally meet you." And she gave him a big hug, bigger than the one she gave me.

"Nice to meet you, too, finally. Thank you for letting me come."

"You're welcome. I wouldn't want you to be by yourself, and besides Greg can't stop talking about you. I had to meet you! You didn't drive here, did you?"

We all busted out in laughter. My mom was taking a dig at him because she knew he didn't have a license. It was all of our first time at Disney World, and we all had a blast. Juan and my mom hit it off, just like I knew they would.

That following spring Lil Gee was visiting Atlanta on his spring break, and we were all hanging out at our community's pool when Lil Gee said, "Hey, Juan, why you not in the pool?"

I started chuckling because I knew Juan was terrified of the pool.

"I can't swim."

"You can't swim? How you mean? Your daddy never taught you?"

Lil Gee and I spent nearly every weekend at the pool since he was 4, so I had taught him how to swim a long time ago. I thought it was cute how he assumed all daddies teach their sons to swim. However, I knew Juan didn't grow up with his father, so it made me a little sad.

"No, he didn't. I wasn't lucky to have a father like yours growing up."
Lil Gee replied, "I can teach you."

My heart melted.

Lil Gee liked him. He was just as nonchalant as the day I told him I
was gay when I told him Juan was my boyfriend and moving in with us.
Even though Lil Gee lived with Carla most of the time, I still considered
my home to be his home. I remember Carla suggesting Juan and I live as
"roommates," so he wouldn't know I was gay. I refused.

"He wouldn't understand or like it. It would confuse him. I don't want
him to hate you." These were a few of the reasons she gave me for coming up
with this conclusion, but I refused to live a lie in front of my son. My living
a lie would only perpetuate the idea that it is wrong to be who I am. I had
lived my life for others, in the closet, for too long. I refused to do it again.

By the end of the school year, Lil Gee was about to fail the third grade.
I didn't feel like Carla was showing enough concern for his schoolwork
or for visits to the doctor or dentist, nor did I feel like she was spending
enough time with him. Whenever I would call to speak to him, he'd be
with someone else, mainly her sister. I'm not sure if she was too wrapped
up in her new career as a caterer, or caring for her mother and family like
she had done since we were married. Her irresponsible ways contributed
to issues in our marriage. We just grew up differently. We cared about
different things. I remember coming home from work one day and our
gas being cut off because she forgot to pay the bill. No heat in the middle
of winter with a baby at home! I was furious!

It was also months past her promised time of finding a home for the
two of them. I was already not comfortable with his living arrangements,
the neighborhood, and her new relationship with my childhood friend
Tank, who was now in jail for selling drugs.

"Me and Tank can't wait to be together when he gets his early release.
He said that he cannot wait to be in Lil Gee's life, and I can't wait to be
in his daughter's life," Carla said to me over the phone one day while
driving home from work.

I wondered why she was telling me this, in this way. Was she trying
to make me jealous? Or was I projecting on to her my own feelings of

jealousy? What right did I have to be jealous? I am gay, and it should not matter who she dates, even if it's my childhood friend, right? On the other side of my jealousy was happiness that she was moving on, and it made me feel less guilty about leaving her. I had very mixed feelings about it.

All these things were enough for me to decide it was time Lil Gee come back with me until she got herself more settled in her new life. I did not think it was fair that our son had to be in the middle of her mental and emotional rollercoaster. He deserved stability and the best chance at life, and I felt like that was here with me. It was time for her to hold up her end of the bargain and relinquish custody to me.

"No," she replied, very sternly. I looked at my Blackberry in disbelief.

"What do you mean, no?" I shot back. I was confused by her harshness as if there was nothing to discuss.

"No. He is staying here with me. A child needs to be with his mother unless she is unfit, and I am not an unfit mother. He is staying here with me."

I was shocked at her response and tone. I could tell she had already contemplated this conversation and probably got counsel from her family. Our relationship had become a bit strained, over the past year, because of our disagreements with how things were going with Lil Gee. But I did not expect her to act as if I had no rights as a father.

"You agreed that he would come back here with me if you hadn't gotten your own place, proved not to be adjusting well, or doing bad in school, and that has happened. You can't just tell me no. We have equal rights. You cannot go back on your decision," I said.

"Look, a son needs to be with his mother, and that is that! When you chose to leave your family, you took a chance of not being with your son every day. That is the choice you made!" she screamed.

I could not believe the words that were coming out of her mouth. I thought she was over our divorce, but this language told me otherwise. "Carla, I have rights. I don't want to have to take you to court. I would prefer we work this out together like we've always done," I yelled.

She laughed hysterically. "Court? Take me to court?! You think a judge gonna take my son away from me and give him to his gay father? You must be crazy! Gone take me to court!" she shot back.

"Okay, Carla, bye!" I hung up the phone.

Carla thought that just because I was gay, I had no chance of winning custody of our son in court. And to be honest? I was afraid she was right. What judge in the state of South Carolina would take a child away from his mother and see it fit that his gay dad was better suited? Who was I kidding to think I could win this case? I never in a million years had even thought that it would come to this, and I did not want it to happen. We always worked so well together when we co-parented Lil Gee. I guess that was up until the time I decided to be gay out loud and not just in the closet or amongst private conversations. Or maybe it was because I now had a partner.

What was I going to do? Was I really going to take her to court? Was she not going to allow Lil Gee to come back with me, at least until she got more settled? I really couldn't understand why she was acting this way. It was never an issue when she would leave him here with me for weeks at a time. How was I supposed to be okay with not having shared custody anymore? How was I supposed to be okay with him being raised in an environment I felt was unhealthy—just because I was not with his mother?

Denying my rights as a father and as if she had ultimate control over his destiny? That really punched me in my ego and made me ready to fight. Not only that, how could I live with myself being less of a dad to my son than my dad was to me? That was not how it's supposed to work. I also was not going down as the gay dad who left his wife and abandoned his son. I refused.

But then I felt guilty. I knew I put Carla through a lot. I knew it wasn't easy on her dealing with having a gay boyfriend, then fiancé, husband, and now ex-husband and baby daddy. I knew she didn't want a divorce and wanted to spend the rest of her life with me. I knew she didn't plan for this. And she was a great girl. This weighed on me. Although I did not plan for this either, it was still my choice of not being with her that brought us to this place. Was I now also to take her to court for custody of our son? How could I do this to her?

But then there was the guilt of not providing my son his best possible life. Not only materialistically, but what would he dream for? What would he think was possible? I remember when I arrived in Atlanta at 18, amazed to see all the Black people driving luxury cars because they had great careers and were thriving. What if that had been my reality all of my life? How much farther in my life would I be? How much farther than me could Lil Gee go if I showed him more than I saw as a kid? I couldn't risk it, but I didn't want to hurt her anymore. What could I do? I was so confused.

So, I tried again. And again. And again.

"How about he just comes back here to finish elementary school while you get settled, and he can come back there for middle school?"

Carla refused.

I even gave it one last try through email, but she would not budge.

"Greg, I'm not having this conversation again. Gee is staying with me, and if you don't like it, take me to court!" she demanded.

She was not going to let up. I couldn't believe how irrational she was being. In one last attempt to settle things, I sent her a letter asking if we could go to mediation. One week later, I got another email declining my offer.

And so, as hard as it was, I hired a lawyer and prepared to serve her the papers. I couldn't believe we had gotten to this place. It felt like I had to exchange one love, Juan, for the other, Lil Gee. It did not help that the lawyer I found online suggested Juan move out temporarily until after the court date. This burned me up, especially since the reason I chose him was that his website listed that he specialized in LGBT family cases.

"It will look better if your partner moved out. If you really want your son, you should take my advice. I will represent you either way, but it's what I suggest," he said to me over the phone at work one day.

After hanging up the phone with him, I could not scream like I really wanted to because I was at work. Not that I'm a screamer, but how could he say this to me? I felt like I was being tested, and I had no one to call to vent to. I wouldn't dare tell Juan. I would never want to make him feel like he was standing between my son and me. I also refused to allow anyone to make us feel as if our union wasn't real. I would typically call Gracey or Brenner, but I didn't feel either of them would be in full support because of how things got rocky with our friendships after meeting Juan. And then there's Carla. She was a person I used to call. I really missed our relationship. I missed my friend. I missed the way we came together and co-parented. If I could have the ideal situation, it would be to make things the way they were when she was here in Atlanta because I honestly did not want the responsibility of full custody.

However, my desire for him to have a sound, stable, positive life with endless opportunities was more significant than my lack of desire for full custody or my want for joint custody. If I wanted what was best or more desirable for me, we would not be going through this. My wish was never to be a full-time single parent. I realized what's best for me is what's best for him, so I must keep fighting for what's best for us.

But does that have to be Juan moving out? Is what's best for Lil Gee and I not having Juan in our lives? I mean, finally, I have found "the one," and now I am being asked to give him up? I feel extremely lucky to experience the relationship and love I have for Juan. He is the best man that I could ever ask to be in my life. He is loving, supportive, respectful, secure, encouraging, trustworthy, loyal, and beautiful—inside and out. His creativity inspires me to think outside of the corporate box I live in. I learn so much from him, and that is not something I have experienced so thoroughly in a relationship before. I feel there is an equal balance between Juan and I. Yes, I'm a lot more mature in this relationship, my ego is not as big, and it makes me more open to learning from others. It also has a lot to do with the fact that I feel completely comfortable being vulnerable in our relationship. I truly believe vulnerability is an opportunity for learning.

I love that Juan always makes me feel a part of what is going on in his life. He makes me the priority, even if the selfish side of him does not want to. He recognizes, respects, and nurtures my role in his life, and he solicits my advice and shows its worth by taking it into account, not just letting it go in one ear and out the other.

I thought of the other day when I stood in the bathroom, brushing my teeth, and he suggested we get our ring fingers tattooed.

"But that's permanent!" I said.

"Exactly!"

His words made my body weak. Tattoos on our ring finger, just like we were married.

Who would have known that a year ago when I met him at Joe's on Juniper that we would be here today building a life together? It seems like only yesterday we were sitting on the floor of his apartment watching the show Weeds on his laptop, and here we are sharing a home together. There is no way I could tell him what my lawyer said. It would break his heart.

As I sat in front of my computer, I buried my face in the palms of my hands and silently said a prayer.

God, please continue to strengthen me and surround me with positive, supportive friends through this trying time. Please continue to bring Juan and me closer together. This would only be a thought without all of them, and I am forever thankful and appreciative. I know the right outcome will happen for Lil Gee. And so, it is!

"You fight for your son!" Juan said to me one day while we were taking a shower together, something that had quickly become a routine of ours. "You can't let her just have her way just because she is the mother. You don't want your son asking you one day why you didn't fight for him. That is the worst feeling. Take it from me."

I don't think I would have ever made it to that courthouse without his support. I would have surely punched out and let Carla have control. I would have submitted to my own fear of confrontation, but Juan wouldn't let me. Coming from a childhood of having no father, he was determined to ensure I did all I could do to be there the best way I could for Lil Gee.

The lawyer said I needed to be aggressive in my approach because it was already May, and I wanted him back by August to start school. He helped me to build a strong case against her, containing emails from the teacher, Lil Gee's school records including several absences and tardiness, news stories on the violence that takes place in her neighborhood, and proof the club located at the end of their street that her father owned was known for drugs and violence. He even included a screenshot of Carla's *Myspace* status that read, *"Free Tank! I love you, baby, and can't wait until you come home."* This proved her relationship with him.

"We need to prove she is an unfit mother and unable to provide for him," my lawyer said.

"But she isn't exactly unfit. She is just a bit unstable right now, and I am able to provide the stability he needs."

"It doesn't work that way. The only way you will win this is if the judge feels you have proved she is unfit, and I believe all the facts we have here will help the judge to side with us, but I can't promise anything. You definitely offer a much more stable environment, but of course, there's the obvious that's not quite in your favor."

Of course, he was talking about my relationship with Juan.

I hoped that the judge would see that living with me was the best fit for Lil Gee. I had a stable nine-to-five job—making good money with excellent benefits, a home that he had already been comfortable in, a proven track record of being engaged with the school, and my 25 character letters from friends and colleagues vouching for me as a father. All she had against me was that I was a gay man living with his partner. I knew this alone could be enough to take me down, but I couldn't let it stop me from fighting.

She was furious when she was served the papers. She thought I was bluffing and wouldn't go through with it.

"I can't believe you are trying to take my child away from me! You leave me to be gay, and I was nothing but nice to you! I could have dogged your gay ass out and dragged your ass in court, but I was very forgiving and even became your friend! I can't believe you would betray me like this! I will see you in court!"

I couldn't get a word in before she hung up the phone. I couldn't believe her mentality and the words coming out of her mouth. *Taking her child away from her?* She really felt as if I had no rights as a father, and she had all the rights as a mother. Her narrow-minded thinking was really showing. I knew she had a lot of people in her ear by the way she was talking, people who didn't know any better than she did.

But, I also had people in my ear. Alongside Juan continuously holding me up, Kony always had my back, and now was no different. My mother was also in my ear, ensuring I did not let Carla take advantage of the situation. With the way she seemed to have taken her side during our divorce, I was surprised that she seemed to be on my side now. They all were just pulling out of me what I knew I had to do. Aside from my ego being vested into not letting Carla control me, my heart knew the best place for Lil Gee was with me, and I couldn't let that go, no matter how much I feared her wrath.

She was served the papers in May, and by July, we had not spoken at all. When I would go visit Lil Gee, she would drop him off at my mom's house so we wouldn't have to see each other. My mom would always take Lil Gee outside to the backyard so he could play with the dogs until I got there. She's always loved her dogs, and so did Lil Gee. They always bonded over this.

We were still waiting on our court date when my lawyer called to inform me that we wouldn't be able to go to trial until October because of his schedule. I demanded we go before August because I did not want Lil Gee starting school in Charleston, so he assigned my case to a colleague, and we were given a court date of July 30, 2009, for the temporary hearing. After the temporary hearing, whoever lost had a chance to prove the judge wrong, and then at which time a permanent hearing would be set to determine the final custody outcome.

About two weeks before court, Carla called me to ask me if I was "sure" I wanted to do this because this was my last chance before I wasted both of our time. She asked if I was "sure" I wanted to take my son through all this unnecessary drama. I couldn't believe she was asking me this. After all the times I tried to work with her, and she demanded I take her to court, she now asked me this? If I didn't know any better, I'd guess she was getting scared.

"Yes, I am sure. You've left me no other options," I answered.

I'm usually pretty good at being nonchalant about anything bad that may be going on in my life, but this custody battle was really taking a major toll on me. It was one of the hardest struggles I've ever had to go through, even worse than my battle with my sexuality or the death of my father. Even though I knew I should not do that to myself, I kept playing all of the things Carla had said to me over and over in my head, like *"You left your wife and son when you chose to be gay!"*

And as much as I acted like what she did or said never affected me, it did. After hanging up the phone, I sat on my bed and stared out the window in disbelief. How did we get here?

I didn't like what she was feeling or experiencing through this ordeal, no more or less than I liked what it was doing to me. I just hated that we couldn't agree or feel the same way about what was best for Lil Gee. Sometimes I wished I didn't care so much. I wished I could just let her raise him the way she wanted to, send my monthly check, visit him every other weekend, and be done with it. I sometimes wished I didn't want to be so involved in his upbringing. I wished I was not so concerned about what he was exposed to or learning, or even how he was doing in school. I sometimes wished I was not so worried about how he turned out.

Wouldn't that make things better for everyone? Yeah, me and Carla maybe, but not Lil Gee. Although I sometimes wished those things, the truth of the matter was I cared. I did want what's best for him. I did want to be involved in his upbringing, and I did care about how he turned out. I kept reminding myself that I was going through this for him, and I must forfeit my feelings and keep going. I felt sure he would appreciate and understand it one day. I just couldn't deny the horrible way it made me feel. It was almost giving me a feeling of emptiness. I couldn't explain it. I longed for the days that things were so much easier when Carla lived here.

I kept wondering what it would be like after the court hearing. What if I was granted temporary custody? How would Carla handle that? I was almost afraid to see how that would affect her. I wasn't sure she would be able to stand a judge telling her that her son should stay with her "punk" ex-husband and lover than to stay with her. In fact, I knew she would not be able to handle that.

Or what would happen if she was granted temporary custody? If that happened, I would feel like it's over for me. What more could I do to prove that he needs to be with me? What would happen from this temporary hearing to the next hearing that would prove he needs to be in my primary care? The sad part about that outcome is that I felt my main issue, besides my son not being with me, was that it would almost validate the way Carla felt about our son growing up around me and my lifestyle. It would make her feel like she was right about it all, and that burned me up.

I had to believe and have faith that, however, this turned out, it was the way it was meant to be. I was going to try not to worry about what I could not control.

17

PARENT OR PARAMOUR?

J UAN AND I headed down to Charleston early that Tuesday morning and met up with my sister for breakfast at IHOP around 11 a.m. My mom decided not to come because she didn't want to get "in-between" me and Carla. I guess she still wanted to stay on Carla's good side, although she was in my ear rooting me on. I wouldn't be surprised if she was doing the same with Carla.

After breakfast, we headed over to meet my "fill-in" lawyer, so I could sign the affidavit, and we could head over to court together to make our 1:30 p.m. hearing. It made me nervous that a new lawyer was stepping in who was not familiar with my case.

As we walked in, I saw this short, White, forty-something-year-old boyish-looking woman, dressed in a navy-blue pantsuit. She turned around and smiled as we walked in, extending her hand. I immediately felt at ease with her.

"Mr. Smalls?" she asked.

"Yes, that is me."

"Hi, I am Lara, and I'll be representing you today. Jim has told me all about your case, and I have prepared an affidavit for you to review. It is important you look at it carefully because this will be a bonded court document. Please follow me into my office. Your family is welcome to come as well," she instructed. "Have a seat. You are seeking full physical custody and joint legal custody, correct?"

Juan and I sat across from her desk, and my sister sat on the couch behind us. As I began to review the document, it finally hit me that I was about to head to court to fight for custody of my son. I never in a million years thought I would be here. My heart was pounding out of my chest. My palms got sweaty, and my armpits were dripping wet. I was afraid. I was soon to meet that 14-year-old girl I met all those years ago in College Preparatory English in court to fight for our son.

Am I doing the right thing?

Should I have just let Carla do what she wanted?

Should I cancel before it's too late?

There was no turning back now. I had to stand firm and not be bullied like I was so many times all of my life. I had to stand up to Carla and fight for my son. I had to get over my fear and stop being weak. It was time for me to MAN UP!

"Yes, that is correct," I answered. She handed me the document.

With all the facts and information I presented to my lawyer, my case looked strong on paper. On the last page of the document, she attached a newspaper article about a shooting that took place at her father's club that I did not know about. It also included a picture of the club.

"This is not the picture of his club," I told Lara.

"It's not? Are you sure? It's what pulled up for the address you gave me," she responded.

"Yes, I am pretty sure. This is not it, but everything else is accurate," I answered.

"Okay, no problem. I will remove the picture, and you can sign the document. I will warn you that the judge assigned to this case is a pretty conservative, older southern judge. I suspect his views are conservative as well, if you know what I mean. I don't think we should include that you two are living together. Let's let him bring that up if he wants."

As the four of us approached the outside of Court Room A, I could see Carla, her older sister, Tonjalah, and Lil Gee at the end of the hall.

What in the world did she bring Lil Gee here for? He does not need to be here to see all of this. I did not want this memory for my eight-year-old son, but it was too late.

He spotted me, ran and hugged my thighs, screaming, "Daddy!" "Hey, Gee, how are you? I am happy to see you!" I said.

Shortly after, Tonjalah approached and said, "Hey, Greg. I gon' take Gee while y'all go in. Com' hea, Gee."

"Thanks, Tonjalah. Go wit Auntie, and I'll see you later, okay?" I said.

"Okay, Daddy," he said joyously. He had no idea what was going on.

Carla and I didn't even look at each other. We couldn't. We were both too pissed at each other, her more than me.

My lawyer and I followed Carla and her lawyer into the courtroom, which had enough seating for a hundred people. The space seemed even bigger as there were only ten of us in attendance. The freezing cold air added to my extreme anxiousness as I sat at the table next to my lawyer. I just wanted this to be over with.

"All rise as The Honorable Judge Ronald Wilson takes the bench," the bailiff announced.

In walked this older, white-haired man, maybe six feet tall, in his early seventies with reading glasses on.

"You may be seated," he said.

His looks and Jim Crow-sounding southern accent was all I needed to confirm I was going to lose this case. As a Black gay man, there was no way this man was going to award me custody of my son.

"I understand that Gregory V. Smalls, the father of Gregory Virgil Smalls, Jr., is filing for full primary physical custody and joint legal custody of his son, against the mother, Carla D. Smalls. Is this correct?" the judge asked Lara.

"Yes, that is correct, Your Honor," she responded.

"On what grounds does Mr. Smalls feel he has the right to come and take this child away from his mother? Is she unfit? Is she on drugs? What is going on?" he demanded.

Clearly, the judge must feel the same way Carla does. Regardless of who can offer the best home and environment, the child belongs with his mother.

"Well, Your Honor, there are a number of reasons why we feel that the child should be in the home with his father. The parents separated while living in Atlanta, Georgia, when Gregory Jr. was 18 months old. While living together, Mr. Smalls had always been very active in his son's life, tending to his day to day needs and growth. Some of those things included dropping him off and picking him up from daycare, taking him to all of his doctor's appointments..."

Lara went out to plead my case, giving the judge a full recap of my involvement in Lil Gee's life, including the complete details of our agreement when Carla moved.

"When the two separated, Mr. Smalls still remained just as active in his son's life. The parents shared joint custody of their son, with the child staying with Ms. Smalls half of the time, and with Mr. Smalls the other half. My client was still taking his son to all of his doctor's appointments and got involved when Gregory Jr. started grade school. As you can see from the documents, Gregory Jr. always did very well in school, and his father was always very active, which is proven from the email communications. This lasted until last year when Ms. Smalls decided she wanted to move to South Carolina to pursue her career as a caterer.

"Mr. Smalls was very against her moving but conceded on the condition that their son would go back to Georgia with him if she agreed to get her own home within six months, or if he appeared to not be adjusting well and/or started to fail in school. While he luckily did not fail this year,"

She went on to fill him in on my back and forth with Lil Gee's teachers and how he was falling asleep in class and getting to school late.

"In addition to the fact Ms. Smalls and her son still live at home with her parents and share a room, Ms. Smalls is also in a relationship with her childhood friend who is serving time for selling drugs in a school zone."

Hearing my testimony out loud from the mouth of another was a bit surreal. It was almost as if I were listening to a lawyer talking about someone else. I tried to get a feel for what the judge thought of my testimony, but he was hard to read. In the corner of my eye, I could see Kony and Juan rustling in their chairs as they waited for the lawyer to continue. I was even more anxious than they were. The lawyer then went on to talk about me, which lightened the air just a bit.

"Mr. Smalls is in a stable career that he has been in for years, he owns a home that his son is accustomed to, and he has the time that his son needs to flourish. He went to graduate school, gives back to his community, and is loved by his friends and colleagues. As you can see, there's over 25 letters vouching for his character as a person and father to their son. Your honor, my client can clearly offer their son the best chance at life, and it is only fair that he is returned to Georgia under the primary care of his father. Thank you, Your Honor."

"Well, Ms. Summers, you said a mouthful. Mr. Smalls, is everything your counsel stated true to the best of your knowledge?" he asked.

I stood to my feet. "Yes, Your Honor," I responded.

"Is there anything you would like to add?" he asked again.

"No, Your Honor. That is all," I answered.

"Thank you, you may be seated. Mr. Brown, I understand you are here representing the defendant?"

This was my first time paying attention to her lawyer. When I turned to him, I saw an older Black man, maybe in his sixties, with a worn-out, ill-fitting, brown pinstripe suit, an unattended scruffy beard, and a jitteriness about his whole being that was unsettling. It was like when he stood, he couldn't keep still.

"Yeah, yes, Your Honor. I am representing Ms. Smalls," he answered.

After seeing him gather his documents and stumbling over his words, I instantly knew he was not prepared to take this case.

"Go ahead and give your response and statement to the plaintiff's statement, Mr. Brown," Judge Wilson instructed.

"Yes, Your Honor. You see, Your Honor, we believe the child should remain in the home of the mother. She is not an unfit parent, Your Honor. She does not do drugs or alcohol. Mr. Smalls drinks a lot and was arrested for a DUI last year, Your Honor. He likes to party."

I regretted using her as one of my references when I got locked up that night, but we were close then. I was surprised he didn't mention the weed.

"My client does have a late-night job, but she stays with her mother, who is reliable. Ms. Smalls does not keep her son away from his father. She told him he can see him anytime he wants," Mr. Brown said.

"How can he see his son anytime he wants when his mother has uprooted him to another state?" the judge interrupted, seemingly annoyed.

"Well, Your Honor, my client has agreed to meet Mr. Smalls halfway sometimes, so he can see him more often, and—"

"Mr. Brown, he cannot see his son anytime he wants to if he lives in another state! Do you care to make another argument?" the judge reprimanded.

"Ok, Your Honor, yes. Their son is in a great school system, one that was good enough for even Mr. Smalls to attend when he was growing up. And, Your Honor, I was just hired to take this case on Sunday..."

I could not believe he just said that. Carla must really have thought I was not going to go through with this. She really underestimated what I was willing to go through for our son.

"What does that have to do with her uprooting him from his home in Georgia, where he was doing perfectly fine? When he moved here, we can see he was not doing well. Barely making it to school and getting there late when he did. Why did he move to Charleston?" the judge yelled.

"Well, sir, my client moved here to take care of her sick mother. She had to come home and take care of her. It would not have been right to stay in Georgia while her mother was on her deathbed. That is what families do!" Mr. Brown shot back.

I could not believe he just said that. Her dying mother? Her mother is on her deathbed now? Granted, her mother was sick, but she's been ill ever since I met her 18 years ago. She never mentioned moving here for her mother; she said it was to focus on her career. And didn't he just say her mother was a reliable caregiver? He was making this easy.

"Mr. Brown, she did not have to uproot their son from Georgia to help out her dying mother. This little boy had a stable home in Georgia already with his dad," the judge said.

Wow, is he on my side?

"Your Honor, Mr. Smalls, is also gay and lives in the house with his lover. We feel the best place is with his mother."

He threw the last bone. Of course, she would throw the gay card out, why wouldn't she? It was her best shot.

"Thank you for that information, Mr. Brown. Does this conclude your response and statement?"

"Yes, Your Honor," he said, sounding defeated.

"Ms. Smalls, is there anything you would like to say or add to this?" the judge asked Carla.

Carla slowly stood up with her head down. "No, sir," she answered.

Judge Wilson addressed us. "Would the plaintiff like to respond or add anything before we conclude?"

"Yes, Your Honor. I'd just like to make it clear that while my client was wrongly arrested for driving under the influence of alcohol, he is currently fighting that in court with the City of Atlanta and fully expects to be exonerated of all charges. We firmly believe that it is the best interest of this child to return to his home in Georgia with his father. Thank you, Your Honor," my lawyer said.

"Thanks to the both of you. I'll be in touch with my decision. This court is adjourned." The judge hit his gavel, we all rose, and he left the courtroom.

I was confused. *Do we not get the decision today? When will he make his decision?*

My lawyer must have read my mind because she immediately whispered in my ear and said, "He will probably call both of us in a few days. You just have to hang tight, but I think things went well. We did the best we could. Stay strong, and I'll be in touch, Gregory. Good luck." She leaned in and offered a hug.

"Thanks. I appreciate all you have done," I replied.

As we were walking out, Carla stared at me as if she wanted to stab me on sight. Her eyes pierced me. She always could turn those sexy slanted eyes into the look of the devil in a heartbeat. She had the look of a woman scorned. There was some sort of control Carla had over me that I could not deny. She could totally control my emotions.

I knew this was not going to be easy, but this was the hardest thing I had ever done. The complexity of my emotions overtook me. I felt angry that my rights were being denied, and I felt angry that she was being selfish and only thinking about herself. But on the other hand, I was feeling sorry for her and hated seeing her upset.

On the way back to Atlanta, I decided to give Lil Gee a call since I wanted to say bye. This meant I had to call Carla, a call I did not want to make.

"What?!" she answered the phone abruptly.

"May I speak to Gee, please?" I asked nervously.

"Here, Gee! Your Daddy wants to talk to you!" she said.

She was fuming. I could hear her in the background, bitching to her family about the hearing. All I could think about was how she called this upon herself. I had to do what I had to do. And how could she be saying all of this in front of Lil Gee?

"Hi, Daddy! Where you at?" Lil Gee asked.

"I am on my way back to Atlanta. Daddy had to go and rush back, but I will see you soon, okay? I just wanted to call to let you know I was on the road and will give you a call tomorrow. Does that sound okay?" I asked him.

"Yes. Love you, bye!" he hung up the phone. He never did have a problem hanging up quickly when he was with his cousins.

The rest of the way home, Juan and I pretty much rode in silence, holding hands every so often. I think both of us were emotionally drained. I knew this had to be taking a toll on him as well. What an awkward position for him to be in.

On Friday morning, I had just had my first cup of coffee and was sitting in my cubicle at Intercom, reading through my emails when my phone rang. It was a South Carolina number, so I knew it was probably my lawyer, Lara. Luckily, I worked in an office full of employees who showed up after 10 a.m., and it was just after 9, so it was nice and quiet, which made it easy for me to talk freely.

"Hello?" I answered.

"Hi, Mr. Smalls? This is Jim Schooler with Schooler & Associates. I am calling about your custody case. The judge made a decision," he said.

"Yes, this is Mr. Smalls. Thanks for calling. So, what's the outcome?" I asked nervously.

"Mr. Smalls, the judge has awarded you temporary full physical and legal custody of your son. This means that his mother has no rights and only visitation. You have been awarded 'full' everything. Temporary means that she has up to one year to prove that your son should be back with her, but that rarely ever happens. She is also ordered to pay you $375 in child support monthly," he told me.

"Oh, wow! Really?! I was never expecting nor asking for all of that! Wow!" I was in total shock. The judge had not only given me full physical custody, but he had also ripped every right away from her that she had. She ultimately lost all the power she tried to hold over my head. She was also ordered to pay child support, which was something I never made her do when Gee was in my custody, even though I always gave her child support when he was in hers. I thought it was unfair, but it was just something I offered to do to ease the impact of the divorce. While I was ecstatic that Lil Gee would be coming home with us, I was not happy about the major blow this was to her. The judge awarded a Black gay man full custody of his son. I could not believe it.

"There is one condition, Mr. Smalls. The judge has listed in your order that your son can remain in full custody with you as long as you were not living with anyone that could be considered a paramour," he said.

"A paramour? I cannot live with a paramour?" I was confused. *What was that?*

"Yes. Basically, an illicit lover. Someone you are not married to. If you are serious about having your son, your partner has to move out," he said matter-of-factly.

"Juan has to leave? What?! This is his home! I just can't ask him to leave! He is not an illicit lover; he is my life partner!" I responded frantically.

How could the judge do this to us? It was not legal for us to get married; he knew this would tear us apart. How could he deny that we were a family just because we did not have papers to say that we were? There were only a handful of states where it was legal. What was I to do? How could I ask him to leave? How could I not take my son because Juan lived with me? This was not fair! I should be able to father my son and be in love. I deserve to be a father and a partner!

"The judge does not see it that way. Unless you are willing to risk your son, he needs to move out. The only thing I can say is to go to one of the four states where it is legal and get married. That way, if it came back on you, you could say that you have done all that you can, even though it's not legal where you are. It's a risk, but it's the best I can offer. It's up to you, but congratulations! Have a great day!" He hung up the phone.

I felt so confused. I didn't know whether to be happy or to be sad. I was ecstatic that the judge sided with me but horrified that he was demanding that Juan move out. *How do I tell Juan this? How would he respond?* I did not know what to do. The judge was making me choose between my son and my man, and I didn't want to give up either of them.

The verdict and its added condition, looped within my mind that cloudy, rainy morning at Intercom. I ignored my emails and trouble tickets, and I didn't make any of my meetings. During lunch, I sat in my car and listened to Lauryn Hill's Unplugged CD again. It had helped me through my divorce with Carla, and I was hoping it would bring me through this. I felt so conflicted. I was excited that I could bring Gee back home to Georgia, but I felt guilty for taking him away from Carla and devastated at the news of Juan having to move out. I wanted to call him to share the news, but I just couldn't bring myself to do it yet.

I'll just wait until I get home.

I also felt afraid. I was afraid of the backlash I would get from Carla. I knew she was devastated and probably angrier than she had ever been. There was something about Carla's words that had a way of piercing me to the soul. She knew exactly what to say to hurt me, and I knew she was out to hurt me now. And just as I wondered what she was thinking, I got an email from her.

Greg,

I want you to know that you are the scum of the earth. I considered you a close friend. I trusted you. I cannot believe you sat up there and lied in court. That was not my daddy's club someone got shot at, it was the club next door! And how dare you bring up Tank? He has never met Gee, and I told you I would not be with him if he sold drugs when he got out! And he has ten years! Gee will be grown when he gets out! I can't believe you took Gee away from me! How could you care anything about us? I wish I never met you! Nothing good has come from loving you but my son, and now you have taken him away. 18 years isn't enough, when are you going to stop hurting me? I have been good to you despite all the things you have put me through. I had no intention of keeping you away from your son, and you know that. I know you are gay. I am fine with you being gay. However, I don't want my son to be in that environment. You talk about my people like they are less than you. You made me look bad. You talk about alcoholics and drug users, you should look in the mirror—you are not far from being BOTH! I could have been a real bitch a long time ago, but how could anything good come from evil? Gee was planned. Do you remember? I waited until I was married to have a child for stability. I believe in family. That's why I haven't had another one. I didn't want this for Gee, and I thought I was doing the right thing when I made you his father, but you are gay! You knew you were gay before you married me! The best for Gee would have been living in a family structure. You could never give Gee the best having a man for a wife! I am 32 years old. I still want a family, and time is running out!

FUCK YOU!

Carla

It hurt to read her final words just as much as it hurt when my mother said the same words to me after that weekend she visited me at my apartment. It hurt so much it even had me continuously questioning myself about taking her to court. Lies? She was delusional. She really couldn't handle the truth. Yes, I admit that the shooting which took place was at the club next to her father's, not at her father's club, but I only found out the day after the custody hearing. But does she really think that is why she got her son taken away from her? I didn't question myself for long before I snapped to my senses. She was not going to suck me into her delusion. So, I, of course, responded with my own verbal lashing and took the opportunity to throw it all back in her face, including her decision to just take my rights away, and me repeatedly trying to work things out with her. I clearly stated that she caused us to get here. But I also made it clear that the door was still open for us to work things out. I still wanted us to have joint custody, as I always did.

I didn't even re-read it before I hit "send." I hoped Carla understood it. And although I did throw a few reads in there and got a little petty, I spoke the truth. I was tired of her trying to manipulate me because of her own selfish ways. She really could not see beyond her hurt and emotion, but I couldn't let it get to me. I had to press forward, and so I did. And now, after an emotional day of receiving the court news and dealing with Carla, all I wanted to do was run to Juan's arms and have him hold me. This was just too much.

18

HUSBAND AND HUSBAND

WHEN I PULLED in the driveway, I got a little nervous about going in. "What will Juan say about this? What will we do?" I said to myself. It was making me sad all over again.

"Hey, Boo! How was your day?" Juan asked.

I threw my keys on the counter and ran into his arms.

"It was so…great and horrible at the same time!" I wept.

"What happened?" he asked curiously.

"Well, my lawyer called with the judge's decision," I responded.

"What! Really?! Oh my God, Gee, what happened? Did she win?" He looked terrified.

"No! I did! The judge granted me full physical and primary custody, and she is ordered to pay child support. I'm picking him up from my sister tomorrow," I said.

"Oh my God, Gee, that is great news! I am so happy for you and Lil Gee. I know he will be happy to be back! Why don't you look happier, though? What else happened? Ugh. Was it Carla? Did you let her get to you, Gee?" he asked, annoyed.

"Yes. She did get to me today. She emailed me after finding out the news and said all kinds of hurtful things. Nothing new. But I shot back this time. I wasn't going to let her get the best of me, and I know I did what is best for Lil Gee. She will just have to get over it now," I said.

"Good. I know she is hurt, but it's about Lil Gee. So, what's wrong, Boo?" he asked.

"Well. Here's the fucked-up part. The judge said that Gee can stay with me as long as I wasn't living with a paramour," I told him.

"A paramour? What the fuck is a paramour?" He looked confused, and then it was like a light bulb hit him. His face immediately turned to a look of worthlessness. "Wait, am I the paramour? Isn't that like a person that is seeing a married man or something?"

"It basically means that I cannot live with anyone who is my lover, with someone I am not married to. He is basically saying if I want my son, I can't have you." I burst into tears and fell back into his arms. "This is not fair! How can they do this to us? How can they say our love is not valid? It's not even legal for us to get married! They are trying to break us up!" I cried.

"It's going to be okay, Gee. It's going to be okay. We will figure something out," he said confidently and hugged me.

I couldn't believe he didn't seem bothered. This had to be too much for him. *Did he not care that we couldn't live together? Why wasn't he upset? Did he really love me? Did he not want to be pushed into a ready-made family? Was he rejecting us?* I thought this must be what he wanted. Maybe he was just trying to be there for me while I was going through this, but he never planned on staying if I won custody. Perhaps this is his out.

"How? How will we figure this out? What will we do? Are you not worried? Do you want to leave?" I asked.

"No, I don't want to leave! Don't even think that. I want to be with you forever, just like we said," he assured me.

And I believed him. I felt his sincerity, and my face softened. "I am so glad to hear that. I asked my lawyer how the judge could do this, especially since it's not even legal for us to get married, so it's like we have no options. He said we could go get married in one of the legal states, that way we would have done all that we could, in case it came back on us. He was a real asshole about it, saying, 'Look, if you really want your son, your boyfriend has to go.' I can't understand how this could happen to us…"

"Let's go get married," he said casually as a matter of fact.

"Huh? Really?" I never expected that to be his response. "You want to get married? Just like that?"

"Yes. Why not? We already said we were going to be together forever, right? You still want to be with me, right?"

"Of course, I do! I wouldn't have it any other way! Let's do it!"

I pulled Juan in and hugged him tightly around his waist as he wrapped his arms around my shoulders. I held my fiancé for the very first time. We sunk into each other's arms.

"I love you so much, Juan."

"I love you too, Gee. I always will."

I was getting married again. Who would have ever thought that I would have a second chance at being a husband? I surely did not.

Since school started the following Thursday, I got Lil Gee to Atlanta, settled in, and registered for class, and then it was time to put the plans in place for our marriage. Just as I planned my first bootleg, super ghetto wedding that took place at Sylvia's Soul Food Restaurant, I put the wheels in motion to plan this one as well. We decided to elope. And I still could not believe I was getting married.

At the time in 2009, there were only four states that allowed same-sex marriage: Rhode Island, Connecticut, New Hampshire, and Idaho. None of the states sounded very appealing, but since Connecticut was close to New York, we decided to get married there. We would spend our time there in NYC but make a day out of getting married in Connecticut.

Just like when I told her Juan was moving in, I was nervous about telling my mother I was getting married. This whole gay thing was still a few years new to me and new to her as well.

Me getting married to a man? Was she ready for that? Am I completely comfortable with it?

When I told her we were getting married, she said, "Y'all are just getting married because of what the lawyer said, right?"

"Well, we do love each other too, Mother, but this does help secure Gee's place with me," I responded. She immediately triggered the side of me that was insecure about our upcoming nuptials. I could tell this wouldn't be the traditional, "I'm so glad you're getting married" affair, and that was fine with me. I also knew that it was probably her own shame that would create such a response. Though she had accepted me living as a gay man, me having a husband was a bit much for her.

I found a justice of the peace that would pick us up from the train station, take us to the courthouse to file the papers, and to the beach to perform our ceremony. The only issue was that it wouldn't be until late October, two months from now. This meant there would be two months that we would be living together unmarried. This would be the perfect opportunity for Carla to try and expose me for not making Juan move out. In true elopement fashion, we decided we weren't going to tell many people. I did tell Gracey, and she was so excited for me. She even wanted to come.

"Really? You want to come?" I asked.

"Yes, silly! Why wouldn't I?"

I didn't really want Gracey to come, so I did not respond to her. It was going to be just as we planned it: Juan and I. That was a part of it, but the truth is I was not completely comfortable being celebrated for our marriage. In hindsight, I felt a lot of shame around it. While I was madly in love and looking forward to spending the rest of my life with Juan, I was not entirely comfortable at the time marrying a man.

But why wasn't I? By this time, I had been out of the closet for five years. Juan and I had been together for 16 months. I loved my new-found gayness! But gays didn't get married. Who did I think I was? What would people say about me being married to a man? Would this be too much for my family? Would they accept me? I know the fact that I did not feel like my mother was completely accepting of us getting married had a bearing on me. No matter how old I got, she still had control over me that I didn't want her to have. I knew she was thinking I was doing too much. This felt the same way it did the first time I got married. That time, it was because she probably thought I was getting married too young.

This time though, it's because she still hadn't quite accepted me as a gay man, no matter how much she may have wanted to. Deep down inside, I shared the same feelings in both marriages.

I can imagine what my mother experienced with me coming out of the closet. Now that I was marrying the man I love, it wasn't much different than what her mother endured after finding out she had a baby with a Black man in the mid-seventies. Back then, interracial love was just as forbidden as same-sex love is today. How ironic is it that my mother now had the same experience as her mother, and I was having the same experience as she did. I obviously was not experiencing it to the same degree that she did, with being rejected and disowned by her own flesh and blood. However, shame is shame no matter to what degree, and it still has the same effect, especially when the shame is from a parent to a child. She did, however, do better than her mother by not rejecting me. She loved and accepted me the best way she knew how.

I flashed back to when I first came out to her, and she said to me, "Well, we don't have to tell anyone. It could just be between us. If someone asks me, I'll just say, 'Well, why do you want to know?' and keep it moving." I now realized that after I came out, that's probably when I started to distance myself from home.

But that was my mother. She was so used to living her life in secret that it was natural for her to want to hide the things she knew people would see as "ugly." For years, my mother hid the fact that she had a Black husband and Black kids from her employers because she was afraid they would start treating her differently or fire her. Sadly, it had happened to her before, so I get it, but at the end of the day, it was still shame and insecurity that led her to hide her family from certain people.

While it did not feel good that she wanted to hide a part of who I was because that meant she was ashamed of it, I also knew my mother thought she was protecting me. She was trying her best to be a mother without even realizing that it was her own feelings that she was protecting. I had held my sexuality in shame and secret for so long, and by the time I came out to her, I was over the shame. I was over what people thought of me. Well, at least I thought I was, but this marriage was starting to challenge that.

But she definitely wasn't. This was new to her. Even though the rumors circulated for years, she still hadn't had a chance to fully accept it until I owned it as my truth just five years before. She was still going through her "coming out" process, and she wasn't there yet, especially to the point of feeling utterly joyful about my marriage.

But was I? If I was genuinely joyful about our marriage, then why wouldn't I want to shout it from the mountaintop? Were we keeping it a secret because we wanted to have the eloping experience, or was it because we weren't comfortable with it ourselves? Or maybe, I was just too afraid of Carla finding out. I was not ready for her to know.

Was the way we decided to get married playing a factor in my insecurities as well? Because we did not have the traditional proposal, and if it wasn't for the fact that the judge ordered Juan to move out, we would not be getting married. Was it causing shame? It damn sure was. It's almost like we had a "shotgun" wedding. And at this moment, I realized, just like my father, I got married for "the kids." Wow! If it weren't for Lil Gee, Juan and I would not have gotten married! At least, not at that time.

Two months had quickly come and gone, and it was nearing time for us to head to NYC for the extended weekend to get married. The month prior, we had just moved into our new three-story loft in West Midtown. Not only did we want to get a fresh start in a new place that had both of our names on the lease, but we also needed to get in a better school district for Lil Gee, so we decided to rent out my townhome and move. Our new home was a two-bedroom with an office, and our bedroom was on the top level with Lil Gee's on the bottom. The common areas were on the middle level, which meant there was no reason for him ever to come up to the top level. In my townhome, his room was right across from ours, which partly made me uncomfortable, so this gave me a bit more security.

I always tried to protect Lil Gee from my relationship. Without realizing it, I was so paranoid about him seeing anything "gay" and running back to tell his mother, that I created an imaginary wall between my relationship and Lil Gee. Although the custody was more secure now, those fears still did not subside. It's almost as if I was trying my best to keep both separate while living under the same roof. I was not trying to create this "two dads and a kid" family, and subconsciously, I was doing all that I could to not make it appear that way, although that's what it was. This again was fear of judgment and my insecurities.

I also held onto what his mother, Carla, was going through. I thought about her every day, most of the day. She still consumed me. While I knew my life was not wrong by any means, I also could not forget that while I was seemingly living out the fairytale of marriage and a happy family, she was suffering the loss of her marriage and her child to the man she felt caused it all. I knew she was dying with just the thought of me, Lil Gee, and our lives with Juan, and that did not make me feel good. So, in a way, I thought I was trying to lessen the blow, although I know in her eyes it wasn't successful.

A few days before we were to leave, I sat Lil Gee down to tell him that we were getting married.

"Hey, Gee, come here. Daddy wants to tell you something. Sit down." He sat next to me on the ivory leather sectional we had just purchased a week ago from Rooms To Go. He looked up at me with an eight-year-old's curiosity.

"So, you remember Daddy telling you before that I was gay and what that meant?" I always felt the need to check in with him on that. It never really came up, and I guess I never wanted him to forget. He just looked at me with a slightly blank stare.

"Remember that I 'like-like' guys, and Juan is my boyfriend?" I asked.

"Oh, yes, I remember," he replied.

"Well, Daddy and Juan are flying up to New York to get married this weekend! That means Juan will be my husband," I told him with slight nervousness.

"Oh! Does that mean Juan will be my stepdaddy?" he asked.

I hadn't even thought about that. Juan will be his stepdaddy. I was so busy trying to ensure my relationship with Juan did not influence Lil Gee, it hadn't dawned on me that Juan would now become Gee's stepfather.

"Yes. He will be your stepfather," I answered. Damn. It felt crazy for those words to come out of my mouth. Lil Gee was going to have a stepfather, and it was because of me, not his mother.

"Okay. I going?" he asked.

I immediately felt terrible. I wanted Lil Gee to go, but I knew his mother would just die if I took him with us to see her ex-husband take a man as his "wife" in front of her son. Again, in me lessening the blow, I decided he wouldn't come but would stay here with his Aunt Nikki, Carla's younger sister, who had moved here about five years ago.

"No, you are going over your Aunt Nikki's this weekend. Just Juan and I are going to go, but we are going to have a celebration next year with family and friends, and you will definitely be there!" I told him.

"Okay," he said.

"Did you have any questions about what this all means?" I asked.

"No," he replied and went off to play. I wish things were that simple with everyone.

We decided that we would get to New York early Thursday morning, 24 hours before we were scheduled to get married. It was the second time visiting the Big Apple for both of us. Coincidentally, the first time was with Carla the weekend I proposed to her during her quick stint in New Jersey, and we went to NYC to sightsee for the day. And here I was again in NYC, making a commitment to marriage. Both were rushed weddings, one rushed because I didn't want to "shack up" due to my then religious beliefs and now because of a custody case. I couldn't help but recognize the similarities.

After checking in, Juan and I immediately walked to Macy's to buy clothes to get married in. We didn't fit the gay stereotype of loving to shop; in fact, we both hated it. After rummaging through some racks, we ended up with matching gray pinstripe pants, matching black shirts, and matching vests that had a velvety material on the front and paisley on the back. My vest was purple, and Juan's was turquoise with corresponding ties to match. Then we picked up some black dress shoes from Payless Shoe Store. Yes, Payless Shoe Store!

Looking back, the outfits were a complete mess, but we felt like a million bucks the next morning while we were all dressed up.

The JP had sent us a full itinerary of how things would happen that Friday morning.

- 10:00 a.m. Arrive to Grand Central Train Station
- 10:30 a.m. Take the A-train to Darien, CT Station
- 11:48 a.m. I will pick you up outside of the station. I will be wearing a rainbow hat. You can't miss me!
- 12:20 a.m. We will arrive at Darien County Courthouse to file the papers
- 1:00 p.m. I will take you down to the seashore to perform your ceremony
- 1:30 p.m. We will head back to the courthouse and file the marriage certificate
- 2:00 p.m. I will drop you off at Darien, CT train Station
- 3:15 p.m. Arrive back to Grand Central Train Station

In the cab to the train station, we held hands as we looked out of our windows. I didn't feel nervous or anxious, which was rare, nor did I feel afraid. I didn't feel excited, overjoyed, or ecstatic. I just felt peaceful and calm. It didn't feel like what we were doing was a big deal at all. It did not come along with those grand feelings I imagined most people would have when getting married or when they were on the way to their wedding ceremony. I didn't feel the sense of pride I imagined one felt when courageous enough to enter a same-sex marriage. It's just like it was a part of the process. A part of my joy. A part of our journey. It just felt right.

Neither of us had ever ridden a train besides MARTA or the New York subways. The way the seats were set up felt like a scene out of an old movie from the seventies. We sat across from each other and talked about the most random stuff, not saying anything significant. Before we knew it, we arrived in Darien, Connecticut, a place that's as country as it sounds and yet a place that was progressive enough to validate our love.

The station was tiny, so within a couple of minutes, we were headed out the front door. Our JP Lina Bean wasn't playing when she said she would be wearing a rainbow hat. It was reminiscent of the hat Dr. Seuss'

The Cat in the Hat' wore. She was a short, pudgy, masculine-ish lesbian that stood about 5'1" with the most pleasant voice and warmest energy.

"Juan and Gregory! It's me, Lina!" She ran up to us and gave us big hugs. "I am so excited to see you guys. You both are so handsome!"

"Hi, Lina! Thanks so much for having us! We are so excited!" I said. "Yes, it is so nice to meet you!" Juan added.

"You two as well! Let's go do this!" she said excitedly.

Lina had gotten me a bit excited, and now the impact of her energy was starting to make me nervous. When we arrived at the courthouse, it was as small as a small-town courthouse could be. I couldn't believe that it was this little town we had to come to get gay married.

Lina had a camera with her and stopped us to take photos almost every thirty seconds. "Over here under the Darien County sign. Now kiss each other!" she demanded. I could tell she had created these moments a time or two. She did say she had performed over one hundred same-sex weddings.

The people in the courthouse were courteous and friendly. They were definitely familiar with Lina; I imagined she was there often. As promised, we were in and out of there in a heartbeat, walking to the seashore where we would exchange vows as the wind mildly blew. It was overcast and about 70 degrees.

"Over here! This is a good spot," Lina said as she walked towards a clear area with the ocean in the background, boom box in hand.

"I am going to go ahead and play a little background music as I perform your ceremony. Are both of you ready?"

"Yes," we both said in unison as we looked in each other's eyes.

"Great, then let's proceed." She pressed play on the CD player, and "Halo" by Beyoncé began softly playing in the background.

No, she didn't just play Beyoncé!

Juan and I both chuckled a bit and squeezed each other's hands.

"Awesome, you both are already holding hands! You are making this easy already!" she said, ditching the ridiculous hat and beginning the ceremony we had chosen from several she shared during planning. This one fits us best.

"We are gathered here to celebrate one of life's greatest relationships—marriage. Marriage is a Promise of Love. Marriage is a commitment to life, to the best that two people can find and bring out of each other. It offers opportunities for sharing and growth no other human relationship can equal, a physical and emotional joining that is promised for a lifetime."

As she continued, I got lost in the moment as Juan, and I stood on the beach. Although joggers jogged by, kids threw seashells in the ocean, and Lina stood right in front of us, I only saw Juan. I could feel Juan's soul staring at mine as Lina continued reciting the words.

"Marriage understands and forgives the mistakes life is unable to avoid. It encourages new experiences and new ways of expressing love through the seasons of life. When two people pledge to love and care for each other in marriage, they create a spirit unique to themselves, which binds them closer than any spoken or written words. Marriage is a promise, a potential, made in the hearts of two people who love, which takes a lifetime to fulfill."

We could hear the waves hitting the large rocks that lined the beach as seagulls flew above our heads, almost as if they were blessing our union.

"As we join Juan and Gregory in this marriage, let us search our hearts for the wisdom of this covenant, which has from ancient times been expressed with those ideas that come from the heart. Ideas like love, loyalty, trust, fidelity, and forgiveness. Let us also decide to share our knowledge of these things with them as they start this journey together. Juan and Gregory, I would ask that you both remember to treat yourself and each other with respect, and remind yourself often of what brought you together today."

For a split second, I thought of Lil Gee and how he brought us here today. He should have been here. My energy began to get low before Lina's words quickly made me snap out of it.

"Juan, will you take Gregory to be your lawful husband? Will you love him, honor and keep him in sickness and in health, and forsaking all others, keep only unto him for so long as you both shall live?" she asked.

"I will," Juan replied with a sparkle in his eye. He caressed my hand with his thumb.

"Gregory, will you take Juan to be your lawful husband? Will you love him, honor and keep him in sickness and in health, and forsaking all others, keep only unto him for so long as you both shall live?"

"I will," I smiled widely and tightened my grip on Juan's hand.

"Will you please face each other and join both hands? May I please have the rings?" Lina asked.

I pulled the small blue Tiffany bag out of my pocket and emptied the two silver bands into her hands that Juan and I picked up just a month prior. Payless shoes and Tiffany rings, quite the combo.

Lina said, "Juan, will you repeat after me? I, Juan, take you, Gregory, to be my lawful husband..."

"I, Juan, take you, Gregory, to be my lawful husband..."

Juan was looking intently into my eyes as I looked intently into his as they watered with love.

Lina continued, and Juan repeated after her, "Gregory, wear this ring as a symbol of my never-ending commitment and devotion. As it encircles your finger this day, let it be a reminder that my love encircles our lives together forever."

"Gregory, will you repeat after me? I, Gregory, take you, Juan, to be my lawful husband..." she directed, saying the entire vows for me to repeat.

"Dang, you just gonna give me the whole paragraph at once, huh?" I laughed heartily. "It's okay, I think I got it. I, Gregory, take you, Juan, to be my lawful husband..."

I concluded with, "Juan, wear this ring as a symbol of my never-ending commitment and devotion. As it encircles your finger this day, let it be a reminder that my love encircles our lives together forever."

As I said the last word, it hit me that I was saying these words to the man I would forever call my husband. My husband! My chest filled with emotion as I let out a deep exhale as if I were letting go of all of my fears.

"Juan and Gregory, as the two of you, come into this marriage, and as you, this day, affirm your faith and love for one another - I would ask that you always remember to cherish each other as special and unique individuals. That you respect the thoughts, ideas, and suggestions of one another. Be able to forgive, do not hold grudges, and live each day that you may share it from this day forward, you shall be each other's home, comfort, and refuge, your marriage strengthened by your love and respect for each other. Juan and Gregory, in so much as the two of you, have agreed to live together in matrimony, have promised your love for each other by these vows, the joining of your hands, and the giving of these rings, in accordance with the law of Connecticut and by the authority vested in me by the law of Connecticut, I do pronounce you legally married and partners in life and in love! Congratulations! You may kiss!"

I pulled Juan's face into mine and kissed him passionately for the very first time as husbands. We were married. We were married! We were married, and our journey together was just beginning. With no idea the twists and turns our marriage might take us on, we were excited about our future. The only thing missing on this 23rd day of October 2009 on the seashore of Darien, CT, was the very person that brought us to the decision of exchanging vows on this day: Lil Gee. I wished at that moment that one day we would exchange vows again so he could be there.

Gee and Juan, second date and already falling in love, Atlanta, June 2008

Mom's first meeting with Juan, Disney World, Orlando, FL, Thanksgiving 2008

Gee and Lil Gee during his Christmas visit, Atlanta, 2008

Gee's 32nd birthday with Juan at Divan, Atlanta, 2009

Gee and Juan after exchanging vows at the shore,
Darien, CT, October 23, 2009

19

THE NEW NORMAL

ALTHOUGH MY FAMILY was secure on paper, I was still feeling very anxious about my new life as a husband with a husband, raising a young Black boy. Being that our marriage was only valid in four states, it almost seemed as if we weren't really married. The whole situation seemed surreal. And even though we were now married, I still maintained an invisible wall between my marriage and my son. It's like I was still trying to protect Carla. Although in her mind I had just turned her world upside down, I knew how she felt about Lil Gee growing up around Juan and me. So, I built this wall to keep him from witnessing anything too gay between us. I made sure he did not see us show affection towards one another, nor would he ever see us lying in bed together. Although I knew that I could not make my son gay, I was doing everything in my power to ensure he did not go down that road. The last thing I wanted was for him to turn out gay and for everyone to say it was my fault, especially Carla. I hated myself for knowing better while still conforming to the opinions of others. I was not strong enough, and thoughts of Carla were triggering all these insecurities.

She still hated my guts. We hadn't spoken since the email exchanges shortly after the court case. Whenever she would need to speak with Lil

Gee, she would text and ask me to have him call her. Following the court hearing, she was coming to Georgia every Monday thru Wednesday to see him. I gladly let him go with her whenever she came, just as I never had a problem with that when she lived here. For a while, it seemed as if we were going back to how things were, minus our friendship. We were sharing custody again, which is what I always wanted. I still felt guilty about Carla having all of her rights taken away from her. I knew it crushed her, and that is not what I set out to do. I only wanted the judge to see that Lil Gee should be with me until she became stable enough to allow us to share custody again. I hoped that Carla was thinking about moving back here permanently.

One Sunday, while we attended the Atlanta Unity Church, I got a text from Carla asking me to have Lil Gee call her. I responded that I would, after church. Carla texted back, "You need to be in church repenting after the way you made me look in court," so I responded, "You need to be in Church with the way you manipulated me."

I was still angry with Carla for the way she dismissed me as a father and tried to deny me my rights, and I also realized that I had always resented her for taking Lil Gee with her the first time. I hated myself for being so passive about it back in the summer of '08.

Juan and I were adjusting to married life and having Lil Gee at home with us. For me, it felt normal, but for Juan, it was new. I was doing my best to make the new adjustment have as little impact on Juan as possible, which was insane for me to even think I could do that. I ensured that all responsibilities relating to Lil Gee were still mine. I had no expectations for Juan to suddenly jump into this stepparent role; besides, I was not prepared for that. I had always maintained that I was never looking for another parent for Lil Gee, and Juan was clear that he was not trying to be one. "Lil Gee has a mother and a father, and I am not trying to come in between that. He doesn't need another parent," was something he would frequently say.

While Juan would do anything, I asked him to do related to Lil Gee, by no means did any responsibility fall on him. We would spend a lot of family time together playing Uno or board games like Sorry and Trouble every night after dinner, going bowling or to the movies, and out to dinner. Every once in a while, Lil Gee would sleep over at one of his basketball teammates' houses, but, for the most part, the three of us spent our free time together. This would often make me feel guilty because I felt like I was holding Juan back from going out and being social. He would go out sometimes with his friends, but I would often get jealous, and I knew it would leave him feeling guilty about leaving us at home.

One night, on the way home from seeing a movie and eating at the Cheesecake Factory, Lil Gee was in the back seat asleep when Juan said to me, "Want to go to a party? Parker invited us." On occasion, Juan and I would go out after Lil Gee went to sleep at night.

"Nah. I'm going to stay at home with Lil Gee. You go ahead." I was being passive-aggressive. I did not want him to go, and I knew Lil Gee would be asleep. I did sometimes feel guilty about going out after he went to bed, and tonight was one of those nights. I would often feel like I was doing the same as my mom did with my sister and me, leaving us while she partied. I vowed to never leave my son in a place he was unfamiliar with or did not enjoy being, and I am proud to say I've kept that promise.

Juan ended up going to the party with Parker and may have gotten home around 4 a.m. or so. Juan always seemed to stay out really late when he hung out without me. It made me feel that I was either always making him end his nights early, or he really enjoyed himself when he was away from me. The next morning, he was excited to tell me about his night.

"We had such a good time. I ended up meeting Whitney Houston's assistant! His name is Kenneth. I am going to try and see if he can connect me with some industry vets." Juan's songwriting team had some songs they were trying to sell, so I knew meeting this person excited him. I immediately felt awkward about Kenneth. I wasn't sure if it was just me being insecure about Juan meeting someone new, or if there was something more to what he was telling me about Kenneth.

"Oh, that's cool! Sounds like you had a great time."

"Yea. Kenneth invited us over to a party tonight. You want to go?"

"Sure. Lil Gee is going to his friend's house today, so that will be cool."
I wanted to meet this Kenneth.

When we arrived at Kenneth's loft, I was immediately taken aback
at how comfortable he and Juan were together. It seemed as if they had
known each other for years instead of just meeting the night before.

"You and these tattoos. Boy, I tell you, you need to stop." Kenneth
said as he was touching Juan's exposed tatted arm. "Let's play spades."

There were about five or six other guys there, two of whom Juan and
I sat down to play with.

"You know I love me some spades. You ready to whip some ass, Boo?"
Juan said to me.

"Let's do it!" I responded.

As my spades partner, Juan sat directly across from me, and Kenneth,
who was not playing, was standing next to Juan. As Juan and I talked shit,
Kenneth got in the middle of it and sided with our opponents.

"Why are you so concerned with this game? Seems you sure are
invested in our demise," I said to Kenneth. I was not feeling his aggression, nor his level of comfort with Juan.

"Juan, get your little boyfriend from over here."

"Husband," I said firmly to Kenneth.

"Get your husband or whatever he is from over here," Kenneth said
jokingly. Juan laughed, but I didn't find anything funny. There was something fishy about Kenneth that I did not trust. I could also tell that there
was something special about Kenneth that Juan liked.

In the car on the way home, I said to Juan, "I don't like Kenneth very
much. I felt like he was a little disrespectful to me when referring to me
as your boyfriend and being dismissive when I corrected him. It also
seems like you two are very comfortable."

"What do you mean? You tripping! I'm going to need you not to get
jealous over my friends. He was just trying to be funny. It's okay for me
to have friends, right?"

I immediately felt like I was just insecure and jealous. I know I brought
baggage into our relationship when it came to my trust due to the fact

that I grew up with cheating parents. I also think Raphael had me so paranoid from the way he used to be in the streets so much while living with his ex that I was making Juan suffer for it. Juan had allowed me to be insecure throughout our relationship, even putting up with me going through his text and Facebook messages from time to time. Once I read this message from some guy in L.A., Juan's hometown, who was asking him to meet up for lunch. Juan had responded that they could, and the guy's next message was, "We gonna fuck?" And Juan replied, "No." I was livid when I read that text, and when I approached Juan about it, he acted as if it were not a big deal.

"He was just talking! Yeah, we use to fuck, but it ain't like that. It's nothing."

"Then why are you still talking to him? What is the point of y'all keeping in touch?"

"There is no point, Boo. I'm going to block his number now and never talk to him again."

Juan blocked his number immediately. I knew nothing was going on, and it was mostly just me being insecure, but I still felt it was inappropriate. I was happy that Juan obliged me without any pushback.

By the spring of 2010, I had not heard anything from my lawyer or the courts about the permanent hearing. My lawyer had already told me that there was little to no chance that a judge would overturn his temporary ruling unless something dramatic was proven. I knew Carla had nothing on me, and she needed me. And even though I knew I had all the power, I still wanted to make things right between us. I sent her emails apologizing, again, for what I put her through with the divorce and how things turned out. I even offered her joint custody again. Carla never responded.

One day on my way to pick up Lil Gee from basketball practice, I got a call on my Blackberry. It was from Carla.

"Hello?" I couldn't believe she was calling. Maybe she was calling to finally apologize to me for trying to deny me my rights, which led us to court.

"Hey. I wanted to know if you would be willing to sit down and come up with a custody agreement for Lil Gee. I talked to my lawyer, and she said it was best if we tried to work this out together because she said this thing could get real ugly if we go back to court."

Was she kidding me? This thing had gotten ugly a very long time ago, and it was something I was trying to avoid from the very beginning. I could not believe she was approaching me with this as if she was saying something brand new. This further validated that she knew she had no chances of getting our son back by trying to take me back to court.

"Of course, I would. That is what I've wanted all along, Carla. I want to work something out with you." I was overjoyed. Finally, this was a chance for Carla and me to get back on track with co-parenting and maybe even build a friendship again. I was willing to do whatever it took to get things back to where they were and end this emotionally draining situation. We decided to meet that Saturday at Starbucks in the Edgewood shopping center.

Before arriving, I already knew what I would and would not agree to. I would allow for Lil Gee to go back to her and finish out the next two years of elementary school if: she moved into a new place where Lil Gee gets his own room, or if he could finish out elementary school with me and live with her when in middle school in a couple of years(again if she had a new place where Lil Gee had his own room). Either way, I would pay child support when she had him, but she would not have to pay me when he was with me. I would also maintain health insurance for him. I never believed in making Carla pay me child support for Lil Gee. In my mind, he would always be my responsibility, and anything she did would be a plus. I also think my pride did not allow me to enforce child support on her. I was a man who did not need anyone else to help take care of his child.

I was already sitting down in the corner of the coffee shop when Carla arrived wearing white sneakers, white jeans, and a white jacket. I could tell she had just gotten her hair done, and she was wearing gold hoop earrings and lip gloss. She looked good. It reminded me of the day she picked me up from the airport when I went to New Jersey to propose, only this was a different kind of proposal. I wondered if she was doing one of those "Look at what you're missing" charades, but I dismissed that thought as I knew she was over me.

"Hey. We don't need to be here long, let's just go ahead and get things worked out. Don't you agree?" she asked. Her face was stern and unfriendly.

"Yes, I agree." And I proceeded to tell Carla what I was willing to agree to.

"That is fine, I'd like to take Lil Gee for the next school year. Also, I need to stay in my parents' house to look after my mom, so I won't be moving out anytime soon. However, I am doing some renovations to my mom's house and getting a room together for him. I am putting a lot of money into it, so I ask that I take him for the next three years, not two."

"Okay. And when it's time for him to go to high school, he should be able to decide where he wants to go." I just wanted to come to an agreement and make things go back to the way they were between us. I was tired of fighting. I wanted Carla back in my life.

"Okay. I will get my lawyer to draw up the papers and have you sign them, and we can get this filed. I'm just ready for this to be over."

"Me too, Carla. I never wanted things to get this far." "Well, you brought it here," she said sharply.

I didn't respond to it. I could tell Carla was still blaming me for everything that happened between us. She bore no responsibility. While I knew I could have done some things differently, I never set out to hurt or do wrong by Carla. I always acted with good intentions, even though it may not have been the best decision at the time. The only decision she regretted was ever marrying me. Although not there yet, I hoped that being able to come to a joint custody agreement again could be the beginning of Carla and I repairing our relationship.

"Alright. See ya." Carla got up and walked away.

"Bye." I watched Carla get in her car before getting up to leave. At that moment, I questioned whether or not I made the right decision for our son, or was I now just thinking about my and Carla's feelings. I hoped I did the right thing. I closed my eyes, put my hands over my face, and said a prayer.

God, I ask that you let this create a new opportunity for Carla and me. Please help us to get back on track and repair our relationship.

Please help us to be great shining examples for Lil Gee and put our own personal emotions aside for his sake. I ask that you help bring both of us awareness so that we may heal from this situation. And so, it is!

20

BREAKING TRADITIONS

L IL GEE FINISHED up his 3rd-grade year at Spark Elementary with all A's and B's. At the beginning of the school year, I had hired a tutor to help him with his reading and math, as these were areas he struggled with the most when he got back to Atlanta. Carla and I decided that he would spend the first half of the summer with her, and the second half with me before moving back to Charleston for 4th, 5th, and 6th grade. For 7th grade, he would move back to Atlanta.

Sending him back was a bittersweet moment for me. On the one hand, I felt good that Carla and I had come to an agreement, but on the other hand, I still worried that things would not change. I also worried that I had made the wrong decision and should have kept full custody of Lil Gee. Would I regret this decision? I was so torn, but I knew I had to just make the decision I had made and move forward. There was no looking back at this point.

Juan and I were well into our first year of marriage, and although our relationship was getting stronger by the day, I still was not completely comfortable being married to a man. It still was not easy to call him my husband. When people found out that we were married, I could see an immediate look of shock on their faces. And most of the responses we got in the community always went something like, "Oh my God! A Black gay married couple? How do you make your relationship work? How did you get to marriage? Who proposed to who?"

The reactions were always shocking to me. While I did know it was rare for two men, especially Black men, to be married to one another, the way that our marriage occurred was not something I was very proud of. We did not get married because one of us decided to get down on one knee and propose. We did not get married because we wanted to take our relationship to that next level. We got married out of necessity. Of course, we loved each other and had committed to being together forever, but marriage was never a goal. Me experiencing romantic relationships with men was against the norm and should've prepared me for feeling abnormal with now being married to a man, but it didn't. Unlike when we first met, I was not proud to post any of the pictures from our beachside wedding. I didn't make a big announcement about it on Facebook or to my family and friends.

When I took the days off from work, I didn't even tell my boss, mostly because he was a straight Black man. Frank didn't even know I was gay; nobody in my department did. Only the people in the call center where Raphael worked knew, but none of them usually spoke with the people in my department. Frank even called me during the weekend to ask me a work question, the night of our wedding, and I answered and dealt with the issue as if I was not celebrating this huge milestone in my life.

The following week, during a one-on-one meeting, he asked, "So, how was your trip? What made you go to New York?"

I froze for what seemed like an eternity. I could feel my cheeks beginning to get rosey, something I always hated because I associated it something that should only happen to White people. What do I say? Do I tell the truth? Do I say, for a wedding? Yes, a wedding!

"I went for a wedding."

"Oh, cool! Whose wedding?"

I blurted out, "Mine." *Mine?* What in the hell? I didn't mean to say that, but it was too late now.

"What?! Congrats, man! What are you doing back already? And why didn't you tell me? I would have never bothered you and your new wife! I am sorry."

Oh, God. I guess I have to come out again as I have had to do many times since I thought I came out years ago. I guess it's a constant thing you have to do when meeting people who assume you are straight.

"Well. 'she' is a 'he.'"

"Oh," Frank replied.

I could see the shock on his face. Frank was about 6'0", 245 pounds, with smooth dark skin and a bald head. He was extremely macho. If the Incredible Hulk was Black, he would look exactly like Frank.

"Surprised?" I didn't know what to say. I just had to break the silence. His face loosened.

"Well, yea. I knew you didn't have such a strong bravado, but I just figured it as just that. But at any rate, congratulations!"

I chuckled. Frank was calling me soft. I wasn't offended, and I didn't take it as an insult. I actually agreed, and I had come to love who I was and how I showed it to the world.

I was also relieved by his reaction. Frank is the type of person I look to the most for validation: masculine, straight Black men. To receive it from him felt good, and it made me more open to expect positive reactions from other masculine straight Black men. At that moment, he made me feel man enough, even though I had just married a man. I still didn't start announcing that I was married, though. It just became something I shared when it came up in conversation. I didn't want anyone to make a big deal about it.

"Do you sometimes feel ashamed to tell people that we are married?" I asked Juan one night in bed while watching The Golden Girls, one of our favorite shows to fall asleep to. I was afraid to ask, but I wanted to know if he felt the same way that I did. I just hoped he didn't think I was ashamed of him. But was I? Just like my mother was with her marriage?

"I wouldn't say ashamed, but I guess it makes me uncomfortable sometimes. Why? Do you?"

"Yes. It's not because I'm ashamed of you, though. I think sometimes I am ashamed of the fact that we didn't decide to get married solely because of our love. We got married because of the custody battle."

"I don't see it that way. Yes, the custody battle prompted us to get married, but it is not the reason. I love you, and you love me. That's why we got married. We wouldn't have done so otherwise."

"You're right. I love you." I immediately felt better.

When Lil Gee's 3rd-grade year ended in spring 2010, we decided to downsize to an apartment so we could save to purchase a house. During this time, Juan had also been laid off from his full-time job a few months prior. We both had aspirations of being entrepreneurs, me running an event production company, and him being a songwriter, so we decided that since I was making enough money to cover expenses, Juan would not go back to work. He would instead focus on starting both of our businesses. Stepping outside of corporate America was a huge deal for me, one that Juan had influenced since the day we met. I always admired his courage to try anything he wanted to.

Juan's focus quickly became G.SPOT Productions, the new event production company, because there was more opportunity to monetize this business quicker than the songwriting business. Juan had also broken up with his songwriting team and wasn't quite sure where he wanted to go musically, so it made even more sense for more of Juan's energy to be placed in the new business. It also helped that he enjoyed the industry. I worked on G.SPOT Productions as much as I could while maintaining my I.T. job.

Our business started off slowly, only getting a couple of clients, so we decided to do weekly club promotions to generate revenue and visibility. We also set out to try and bridge the apparent gaps between the White and Black gay community. After trying to work with several of the White promoters, we quickly realized that there was no interest in bridging gaps. Although they "allowed" us to attend their events, it was apparent there was no desire for us to be there. It felt much like the energy we would often feel at the White-owned gay bars in midtown, where we felt "tolerated" but not appreciated and affirmed as one should when patronizing any business. And you can forget about them attending or supporting our events. Honestly, I'm not sure they were up for the challenge of being the minority in the room. It did not take long for me to discover that the gay community was not inclusive, as it was still filled with racism, just like mainstream society. After a short stint, we quickly discovered that the club promotion industry was not our lane. We knew we wanted G.SPOT Productions to eventually grow into a bar and lounge, but there had to be another path to get there.

Though we still pursued clients to produce their events, I also wanted to create a second chance prom for the Black men that loved men. The White gay community had at least five black-tie galas each year, and I could not figure out why we did not have the same in our community. After being in the closet and hiding who I was for so long, I thought this would be an excellent opportunity to show up arm-in-arm with my new husband, and I knew that many men in our community wanted the same, whether married or not. So, planning "The Gentlemen's Ball" began immediately.

The media perpetuated stereotypes of our community, such as we all dress in makeup and heels, or we were on the down-low or closeted. This was not to put down either my queens or the latter—I was previously on the DL and a closeted man—we wanted to celebrate and fully represent who we were as a community. I also noticed how DL was a term only referred to when it came to Black men when we were not the only men sleeping with men in secret while sleeping with women. White men do it all the time, actually, some very powerful White men, but never are they referred to as DL. This double standard troubled me.

It was Thanksgiving 2010, and Juan and I went to Charleston to spend it at my mom's house, along with my sister, nephew, and Lil Gee. My mom was excited for us to come, which I wouldn't say is rare, but she damn near discouraged us whenever her family would come to town. I knew it was because she still had not told her family that I was gay and married to Juan. She would never admit that this was the reason, but I felt it to be true.

"My family are old-time rednecks, and they would never understand." I never pushed the issue. I knew it was her battle to fight, and her family's opinion never mattered to me. At least that's what I told myself. Whenever I went home, I'd always get Lil Gee, and I'd hate to have to leave him. That Thanksgiving weekend was extra tough because that Wednesday we arrived, he handed me a letter he wrote to me for an assignment in his language arts class. The letter read,

"Dear Dad,

I am writing this letter because I want to tell you what I'm thankful for. I am thankful for a lot of stuff. This is what I'm thankful for: family, my freedom, and my health. I am thankful and grateful for you. My life will be miserable without you. My mom does not give me a hug and a kiss before I go to bed. She goes to Uncle Joe's to play cards. I think if I be down there with you my life would be a breeze. I love my mom, but she don't do that stuff that you do. I told her when I got home off the bus that she should be ready to go over my homework with me. I bet if I ask you that you will do it on the next day I told you. I really love you. Every day I see you, you make me smile. Did you know that?

My freedom is so important I don't want to be in a rage for a long time. I'm glad that I am not a slave because I would have to listen to people.

Health is very good because I don't want to be a sick person every day because a lot of people that are very sick die. That is what I am thankful for. Happy Thanksgiving! I love you!

Greg"

I was crushed. At that moment, I knew I had made the wrong decision by letting him go back to Carla so soon. She must have not been ready because it's so unlike Carla not to have been affectionate towards him. Did Lil Gee still feel this way, or was he just being emotional at the time he wrote it? What do I do? Carla and I were still not speaking. She wouldn't even accept gifts or cards on holidays that Lil Gee would give her that she knew I paid for. "My Mama said not to get her nothing but to make something instead." I knew Carla was trying to tell me to stop buying her stuff, so I did. I even stopped wishing her Happy Mother's Day after never getting a response.

Whenever I would call, she'd just put Lil Gee on the phone, and many times they weren't together, so she'd call her mom's house to have him call me. It had gotten to the point that I just bought my 10-year-old son a cell phone, so I could always reach him.

"Thanks for the letter, Lil Gee. I loved it! Come and give me a hug." I said to him after he ran back into the house from playing.

He hugged me tightly.

"Do you remember what you wrote?" "A lil bit."

"Do you remember the part about your Mom?" "A lil bit."

"Well, you know your mother loves you very much, right?"

"Yes."

"And she may not do some of the things that I do, like kiss you before bed, or go over your homework, but she does a lot of other things to show you she loves you. Parents are different, but we love you the same. Do you understand?"

"Yes," he smiled.

"Well, you know, I bet your mom would love it if you told her you wanted a hug and kiss before bed! You should tell her!"

His eyes lit up like he had heard the best idea in the world.

When it was time for me to leave on that Sunday evening, it took everything in me not to demand Carla let him come back with me. I was so upset with myself that I agreed for him to go back there so soon. I should have waited until she was more stable, but it was too late now. There was no way I was going to go through the fight again, not when we had come this far. As Juan backed out of my mom's driveway, I sat in the passenger seat watching Lil Gee play on the back of my dad's old pickup truck. He was always so good at playing alone. He looked up before Juan placed the car in drive to pull off, and I waved as a tear fell from my eye. I was leaving my baby boy.

On the way home, I decided that I was going to call Carla and read her the letter. I did not want to accuse her of bad parenting or come off as if I was blaming her for anything, so I decided this would be the best approach. It was a shame that I had to walk on eggshells around her when it came to co-parenting Lil Gee.

"Go ahead and call her, Boo. Just try not to be emotional, just tell her what happened. State the facts, not your opinion," Juan said to me.

He was right, so I slowly pulled up "Babymomma" from my contact list, which is how I had her saved in my phone ever since Fantasia sang a song with that title. I even had the ringtone to match.

"Hey, Carla, I don't mean to bother you, but I wanted to read a letter to you that our son wrote to me. Do you mind?" I was always so anxious when having to call Carla.

"No, go ahead," she responded in her usual emotionless voice.

After reading her the letter, I told her about my conversation with Lil Gee afterward, and that I only wanted to share it with her so that she was aware.

"Okay, I appreciate you telling me," she responded. I couldn't tell if she really appreciated it or was annoyed by my call. I immediately felt I should have kept it to myself. I hoped Lil Gee would not get in trouble with her for it.

My coworkers were down at the parking lot enjoying the company's Spring BBQ, while I stayed behind and daydreamed out of my office window. I had come to hate corporate social gatherings and typically stayed out of most of them. While daydreaming, I decided to take the opportunity to log into Juan's Facebook account and check his messages. Juan honestly never gave me any reason to suspect he was hiding anything from me, but it was something I made a habit of doing from time to time. He would even let me do it without a fuss, sometimes in front of him. He actually started the routine by asking for my password once early on in our relationship and went through my phone while I watched. I found it freeing at the time. We've had each other's passwords ever since. I very rarely found anything until that morning in my cubicle. It was a message from Kenneth, Whitney Houston's old assistant, that Juan had met a couple of years back. Kenneth came over to the house a couple of times for parties we had, but other than that, I didn't hear much about him. I did know that he had moved away about three months before.

As I started reading through the messages over the past couple of years, I saw that Juan had been having lunch with him from time to time. Although this was news to me, it didn't bother me much until I read a message he sent about six months ago.

"I am glad I never tried nothing with you. Not saying that you would have accepted any of my advances. Seeing you and Gee give me hope that real relationships can exist, and I am so glad I didn't ruin our friendship based off of a simple attraction. I really respect you guys."

I knew it! I knew there was something between Juan and Kenneth, and this proved it.

Juan responded, "I'd like to think I would have not had given in to your advances either, but that is neither here nor there. I am also glad we've become friends. Thanks for the kind words you said about our relationship. I really am a lucky guy."

While I was happy to read that nothing went on between the two of them, I was still mad when I got home that evening. We shared everything, and this was obviously something Juan did not want me knowing about. When I walked in, I found Juan standing in the kitchen cooking dinner.

"Hey, Boo! How was your day?" Juan smiled and puckered his lip for a kiss. I walked up to him and gave him a quick dry kiss on the cheek. He knew something wasn't right.

"What's wrong? Why the coldness?" He looked rejected.

"I read your Facebook messages today and found your exchange with Kenneth," I said calmly. I waited for Juan's reaction. Nothing.

"Why would he say he's glad he didn't 'try' anything with you? If y'all are just friends, then why would that even been something to talk about?"

Juan still gave nothing. He had a look on his face of a young boy in trouble with his mommy.

"All this time you've been making it seem as if I am just being insecure and crazy when I knew there was an attraction between you and Kenneth?! Why would you try to mislead me and make me feel insecure like that?"

"I just thought he was a really cool guy, someone that I could be friends with! It didn't matter that he liked me. I knew it wasn't going anywhere. I knew you would not want me to be his friend."

I could tell he was being genuine by the way he looked me in the eyes. His eyes looked regretful.

"Why do you have to have a friend that likes you? I don't understand it. And you lying and deceiving me about it does not make it better. I want us to be honest with one another." I softened.

"I'm sorry. I know I should have been honest with you in the beginning. No excuses."

Juan was also starting to remind me of my father a lot. He always seemed quiet and distant. I'd often feel as if I was bothering him when I wanted something, and it felt as if he were holding parts of himself back. It was like he would physically be there, but in another world, even though he'd be sitting right next to me. I'd always feel I wasn't getting enough of him, which came out in ways very similar to my mother, the "Nag." To add fuel to the fire, there was a bit of a control issue going on at home. Juan was not feeling as valuable, not as much of a man, because he was not bringing any money into the home, while I went to work all day and took care of the bills. Meanwhile, I was resenting him for being able to stay at home all day and not having to be a slave to corporate America. I remember calling him from work one day while looking for the number to a mobile car wash company that I used last week. The pollen this spring in Atlanta was ruthless! It was already time for another wash.

"Hey, Boo! Real quick, can you look on the counter and tell me the number that is on the bulletin board next to the fridge?"

"Hey! I can't right now, I'm not at home," Juan responded.

I hated that he had the flexibility to do what he wanted. I knew he didn't have anything to do for the company today, so I wondered what he was doing.

"Oh. Where are you?" I asked, trying my best not to sound annoyed.

"Me and Montell are having lunch at Moe's BBQ." Montell was Juan's friend from L.A. that was staying with us for a while until he found his own place after moving to Atlanta. Although fully self-sufficient, Montell also did not have a job and was pursuing his own business. I was further annoyed and knew I couldn't hold it in any longer. I would already get pissed while thinking about them sitting at home all day having a good ole time while I was trapped in my cubicle, working to bring home the bacon. And now they had the audacity to go out to lunch?

"Must be nice to be able to just up and go have lunch whenever you please. I wish I had the ability," I said with as much sarcasm as I could muster.

"You got something to say, Gee?"

Juan wasn't having my passive-aggressiveness today. I'd been walking around our 1,000 square foot, two-bedroom apartment with an attitude for weeks. I am sure even Montell could feel my resentment. I actually loved Montell, I just couldn't stand his and Juan's daily freedom.

"No. Just call me when you get home. Y'all enjoy lunch. Bye!" Majorly pissed, I hung up the phone. While it was annoying to not have the freedom Juan did, I was mostly pissed that I was having such a hard time with the new transition of him not working. I knew we would have to talk about this when I get home from work.

When I walked into the apartment, I could hear Juan's favorite artist, Brandy, blasting from the speakers in our bedroom as I noticed Lil Gee's bedroom door open, where Montell was staying while Lil Gee was living with Carla. He wasn't in, so I gathered that Montell must have stepped out. I was glad because I knew we were about to have a disagreement, and I wasn't sure which way it would turn. He never did call me to give me the number I asked for, so that was a sure indicator that he was not feeling me. Rightfully so.

I took a deep breath after locking the apartment door before placing my black leather laptop bag and keys on the kitchen counter. As rude as I knew I was earlier that day, my ego wanted to make my actions justifiable. After taking bottled water out of the fridge, I walked five steps to our bedroom door, where I was sure Juan stood, ready to give me the silent treatment and a hard-lipped kiss, something he typically did when he got an attitude with me.

"Hello."

Juan was lying in bed as I leaned over to kiss him between his cheek and the corner of his lips. I wasn't giving him a chance to hard-lip kiss me. Juan didn't respond to my hello. I knew this was his way of making it clear that he was not with my shit.

"We need to talk," I said as I started to take off of my drag attire, which is usually referred to as "business casual" in corporate spaces.

"There is nothing to talk about, Gee. I've decided that this is not working, and I am going back to work. I'm going to find me a job," he said as if it were not up for discussion. He always had a calm way of speaking to me amid conflict. I hated his emotionless responses to me. It reminded me of my father.

"Oh, so just like that! You're ready to quit? Times get a little hard, and of course, you want to abandon me!" I knew the exact buttons to push to make him give me some emotion. I needed him to show he was affected, and that being calm was not the way to express his grievance.

"It's not about quitting! I am tired of you and your attitude, and I know it's because I'm not working!"

My button-pushing worked, and he was partially right. I could care less about him not working, but I wanted to not work too. I was jealous that he got to do it first, and that's why I had an attitude. I felt like it was my company, and I should be the one that got to run it full-time. However, that just was not practical with the timing of Juan's layoff, and I made a substantial amount more than he did. Not to mention, we were trying to get a house, and my credit was the only one that would qualify for a mortgage.

After more petty back and forth banter, we both expressed our fears in the transition that was taking place in our lives. We both were not as comfortable as we thought we were with the new dynamic but still came to the conclusion that Juan would continue to run the business while I stayed at my corporate job until we both could work it full-time.

During this time, we were also looking for a house and were huge fans of the show "House Hunters" on HGTV. We loved it so much that we would watch it all day on Sundays. We loved being able to guess which house the family picked.

"Let's go on the show! I am going to apply! I know they will want us, there never has been a couple like us on the show!" I excitedly told Juan.

"As long as they are paying," Juan responded.

The next day I applied online while at work, and two days later, I got a response asking us to record a video at home, answering ten questions they had for us, showing as much personality as we could. We followed the process, and we soon became the first Black gay couple on HGTV, possibly the first married gay couple. They edited the parts out where we referred to each other as husband or mentioned that we were married. They could have very well done this with other gay couples back then.

Although our marriage was going well, and I was more in love with Juan than I'd ever been, we would often get into arguments about how little we had sex. The opposing views we expressed towards sex when we first met were coming to a head, and I was starting to get sexually frustrated. I had a much higher sex drive than Juan and was often left feeling unsatisfied. One night while watching TV, I had gotten so frustrated that Juan hadn't made any attempts to have sex, that I jumped out of bed, stared at him in the eyes and said, "Why don't you ever want to have sex?"

"We do have sex! And I can't make myself want to have more sex, Gee, and I'm not going to do it if I don't want to!"

"Well, what am I supposed to do? You are selfish! You don't even try!" I yelled. As my husband, I felt like it was his job to make sure I was sexually satisfied. I was frustrated that he did not feel this way.

"I don't know how to make myself, Gee! I am not going to initiate sex if I'm not feeling it. It doesn't even come to my mind! I'm sorry!"

"I am the one that's giving up the ass all the time. I should be the one turning you down!"

In my heteronormative mind, I felt like because he was in the top role the majority of the time when penetration did occur during our sexual encounters, he should be the initiator. Not only was I frustrated at only having sex once, maybe twice a week, I was also growing tired of Juan not allowing me to penetrate him. Over the three years we had been together, I could probably count on one hand how many times I penetrated him, and it rarely went well, except maybe twice. Any other time he would stop me.

"You are too big. It hurts," he would say.

"You have to relax. It's not about my size, you just need to release control. Submit and trust me."

I could always feel Juan's body tense up any time I would attempt to dominate him. It would make me feel rejected, and I would even sometimes experience that same performance anxiety I had experienced many times before.

"No! You are too big, and it hurts!"

Juan was not buying what I was selling, but I still believed. I had experience. Juan was also not buying that, as he would put it, I "suddenly" wanted to top him. He believed it was just a power thing for me, and I was trying to prove something. I could see why it would be hard for him to understand. After all, I had gotten comfortable with being on the bottom for the first two years of our relationship, mainly because I wouldn't have to deal with performance anxiety. Being penetrated was something I had just started to enjoy before meeting him. It was still new to me. That did not mean I didn't want to be on top as well. I was getting to the end of my rope.

"I've had a lot of sex in my life and done a lot of things. A lot more than you, so that's why my sex drive is probably not as high as yours," he said to me as I lay back down in the bed.

I didn't believe that, but I guess it made sense. Before meeting Juan, I was just starting to feel sexually liberated and wanted to express that with him. We had some really exciting sex at first, from doing it in the car at his job, on the front lawn of someone's home who lived around the corner from Blake's, to every corner of our house, and of course, hotel balconies. Juan loved unconventional sex, and so did I.

One night on the way home from Swinging Richard's, a male strip club near our apartment, I blurted out, "Let's not go home. Let's go to Flex." I had never been to a sex club or bathhouse before and was really curious. Juan had been to places like that before and never saw it as a big deal.

"Sure, let's go!" We had talked about how we felt about threesomes and sex clubs before, and I knew he always remained pretty neutral about it. I was the more conservative one when it came to sex, but I was opening my mind up a bit more.

After showing our I.D., signing a release, and paying $25, we were handed a key and two blue towels.

"Room 234. You have 24 hours."

I immediately thought we wouldn't need that long, but I quickly brushed it off. As we headed down the long dark hall to find room 234, there were all types of guys walking up and down the halls, staring us down, trying to catch our attention. Some would grab me as I walked by. The place smelled like a mixture of bleach, sweat, and sex. I tightly held Juan's hand as he led me to our room, which was more like the size of a small walk-in closet with a built-in wooden "bed" topped with a leather mattress. I imagine the leather made it easy for cleanup. A small flat-screen TV played gay porn in the corner. Juan and I took off our clothes and wrapped the blue towels around our waists.

"You want to go walk around?" Juan asked.

"Sure."

As we walked around the bathhouse, there had to be at least fifty rooms spread between four hallways. Some were larger than others, and some had sex swings. Most doors were cracked open where I could see men having sex or masturbating. When we walked into the heated sauna, we decided to chill for a while and watch people have sex and cruise. There was this one guy that caught my eye that sat in the corner masturbating. Juan and I hadn't talked about our intentions for going to Flex, and I wasn't quite sure what I was looking for, but I knew I was interested in him. Apparently, he caught Juan's eye too because I looked over and saw Juan watching him as he watched us.

Juan and I began to kiss and caress each other while the guy continued to watch and masturbate. As things started to heat up between us, I got up, grabbed Juan's hand, and took him back to room 234, giving the nod to the short, chiseled brown boy, hoping he would follow. He anxiously obliged. Juan and I made out for about two minutes before the guy joined in and soon became engulfed in passionate sex. I had always imagined that I would be super jealous of seeing Juan with another man, but it was quite the opposite. I was turned on watching him enjoy our newfound friend, and I could tell Juan was enjoying it as well. Being able to finally be on top was a major relief for me. I needed it more than I thought, and not just physically, but mentally and emotionally as well. I also did not experience any performance anxiety. With Juan being there, I felt less pressure to please or measure up.

Before leaving, the brown boy gave us his number and his name—Horace—and told us to keep in touch. I wasn't quite sure if we would, but he sure gave us a memorable night. Juan and I had to have sex for four days straight following that night at Flex. That experience lit a sexual flame in our three-year relationship.

While I loved the amazing unconventional and recreational sex, I still yearned for deeply connected lovemaking, which Juan and I lacked. He still was unable to fully engulf himself into our sexual experiences without feeling the need to perform, and I still struggled to release my anxiety. I was not able to make him climax, and he rarely orgasmed with me, even through masturbation. This made me very insecure. When I'd start feeling this way, the comments he made at the beginning of our relationship about not being attracted to light skin men, his desire for small penises and men with a belly would come ringing back into my head. I would often ask him if he was sexually attracted to me.

"I am very attracted to you, Boo. I think you are very sexy. Sex is just not a big deal to me, and it's challenging for me to work at it sometimes."

"I think we should go see a therapist. Not only to help us with our sex life, but I think it would be good for us overall just to have a mentor and mediator to help keep our marriage strong. What do you think?" I asked Juan. I had seen a therapist twice in my life—once with Carla and once years after we separated—I really enjoyed it. It helped when I was working through becoming comfortable with my sexuality, and I knew it could help us too.

"Okay. I am cool with that."

"Okay. I will schedule something for when we get back from Charleston after Mother's Day."

The following Tuesday in mid-May, Juan and I went to see Sheila, our Jamaican couples' therapist, for the first time. Sheila was in her late 40s, about 5'7", brown-skinned and top-heavy with an itty-bitty waist and legs. She sported a short Jheri curl with a patch of gray in the front.

"Wah bring ya to me office here tahday, mon?" Sheila asked with a bit of her Jamaican accent coming through. The room was small but cozy and inviting with lots of books and plants. She sat in a brown leather recliner across from us while we sat on a long plaid couch.

"Well, we'd like to just get help and guidance on strengthening our marriage, but we are also having issues getting on the same page sexually. My sex drive is a lot higher than his, and he is not as open sexually as I would like him to be," I answered quickly. I began to give her a history of our relationship while Juan sat beside me nodding his head, agreeing with my sharing.

"Well, first of all, let me say that I very rarely meet a couple that has the same sex drive. Of course, in the beginning, while the endorphins are going, most couples will be in synch sexually. It is not until the second or third year that those endorphins start to wear off, also known as the honeymoon stage being over, that it really becomes a problem because now those warm-fuzzies aren't blocking your view of this real human being standing in front of you. It's quite natural what you guys are going through. In fact, most couples do not make it past this stage because they feel like they are out of love, and the relationship is supposed to be over. Kudos to you two for coming in and working on the problem. I can tell you both love each other very much."

"We do," Juan and I both blurted out at the same time.

"I love him so much, and I want to be able to please him in every way and have more sex, but I can't force myself."

"I want more sex, yes, but it's more than that. I want to penetrate you, believe me I do, but it's more than that. I just feel like you aren't completely open to me. Like I'm giving you all of me, but there's still parts of you that you are holding back."

After hearing us go back and forth for about five minutes, Sheila began to share with us what she felt the deeper issue was. She recognized that it just wasn't about me wanting more sex for physical pleasures. I was yearning for validation and acceptance from Juan, and I was using sex as a way to get it from him. I was not seeing my own self-worth due to my body image issues over the years, as well as the lack of validation I felt from Black boys and men around me growing up, especially my father. My issues had nothing to do with how much sex Juan was giving me, it was only triggering them.

Juan, on the other hand, was dealing with abandonment issues due to his father not being in his life, and his mother's battle with drugs that led them into foster care and being in and out of many different family homes. He was having challenges letting his walls down because he was not use to the security of one person being in his life. He was always waiting for someone to "throw him away." She explained that during a child's formative years, between ages seven to twelve, is when the brain is impacted the most. It is during those years that has the most effect on the issues we will experience in adult relationships. She also gave some suggestions to Juan on how to connect sex with love since it wasn't something he experienced before.

In response to me telling Sheila how I wanted us to connect eye to eye, soul to soul, and heart to heart through our lovemaking experiences, Juan said, "That kind of thing sounds like something out of a romance novel. Not real." Sheila responded,

"It is real, and it is those romance novels that can help you incorporate that into your own life. Start imagining you as those characters in the book. You can have that."

Sheila became one of the best decisions we had ever made in moving our marriage forward. She was able to help us realize our own individual issues that were creating the challenges we were experiencing with each other.

Dorothy also became a strong guide in my life. Dorothy is a clairvoyant that I met through a friend of mine while out at a bar one night. My friend, Dianna, was on the phone with her when suddenly Dorothy asked to speak to me.

"Are you ready for how your life is about to blow up?" she asked me. "Huh?"

"Young man, you have no idea how your life is about to change. You need to get ready for some major changes in your life. I see a lot of big things happening."

Dorothy went on to tell me how Juan and I were going to reach levels in life we had never imagined and that we would majorly impact people's lives. She talked about how we were destined for one another and that our love was meant to last forever. She said a lot on the phone that night that struck me, including how one of us would be questioning our sexuality years into our marriage.

"What?! Well, I know it's not me because I have already been there and done that, and Juan doesn't act like he has any interests in women."

"Well, yea, I'm not really seeing that it's Juan." And then she moved on to the next subject.

I did not give much energy to it while on the phone, but the fear that I once had that maybe Juan would long for that traditional family one day was going to come true. Juan always seemed to be fascinated with pretty women and always seemed to give them a lot of attention when they would come around. I'd find myself getting jealous of how he would always put his hands on them and care for them almost as if they were his lady. It was not uncommon for him to touch their breasts or rub their feet. I noticed this a lot with gay men and women, but it was just something that I could not relate to. I still thought it was disrespectful to touch a woman like that. It was still sexual to me. He stopped doing it once I told him I didn't like it, but it did make me wonder if he wanted to be with women. The fear was fleeting, but it was a fear nonetheless.

Though having HGTV's production crew film us was a bit surreal, shopping for the house was fun. I've always enjoyed shopping for real estate, and this was no different. I really wanted to find a house that needed some rehab work, so we would be able to do some renovations and turn a profit. Juan was not really on board with living in a home that needed a lot of work, so we ended up meeting in the middle and getting a home that just needed slight repairs but would still turn a profit pretty quickly.

Juan and I both have always had aspirations of being on TV and had even tried our hand at a reality show project that never launched, but we never imagined we would be on House Hunters. One thing we quickly learned while doing the show was that reality was not reality at all. There is a lot that goes on behind the scenes that I am not at liberty to divulge due to non-disclosure clauses. However, one thing that surprised me is while every reaction may have been our sincere feelings of the spaces we visited, we had to repeatedly act them out to capture several angles because there was only one camera person. My thoughts of having a huge production crew quickly went out the window. We learned a lot that day about producing reality TV and fell in love with the process.

Through all of this, planning moved ahead toward our big event. With the tag line "Celebrating the TRUE Gentleman," the event evolved beyond a simple second-chance prom, becoming an immediate hit. Everyone loved being able to attend a black-tie event, enjoy live entertainment by S.W.V., and dine on a three course meal in a room full of proud Black same-gender-loving men. Attendees also loved that the Ball raised funds for a local nonprofit.

The event took place on 11.11.11 and was a major success within and outside of the Black Gay Community. While we lost about $40,000 of our own money, local gay and urban press covered the event, giving it a name in its first year.

I felt so nervous the night in February 2012 when our House Hunters episode aired. Juan and I were both so paranoid about how we would look on TV that we only told a couple of people that it was going to air. They tried to encourage us to have a watch party, but we were too nervous. If I said something stupid or God forbid, looked too feminine, I would have not been able to handle it. Feeling this way made me feel like a failure because I still rejected the femininity in me and a hypocrite because of the way I express love for all, both masculine and feminine. Why did I still feel this way?

As soon as I saw our faces pop up on the TV, I was elated. I could not believe how great the both of us looked, and it was even harder to believe that I felt good about what I saw. I expected to be disappointed with how I came across on TV, and it was the exact opposite. It felt so natural for us to be on the screen like we belonged there. It wasn't before long that Juan and I both started getting notifications on our phones from people who were viewing the episode. For months, we were known as "that couple that was on House Hunters."

While that was great for me in Atlanta, I wondered how it would be seen back home in Charleston. I knew it wouldn't be long before word got out, I was sure plenty of people would have a lot to say. I hated that I cared. I especially feared what Carla would say, and it didn't take long for me to find out. One day while we were on our way to a work event, I got a call from Carla.

"Oh, Lord! It's Carla!" I said to Juan while driving down I-20. "Hello?"

"Hey, Greg. I don't mean to call and bother you, but you may want to talk to Gee and your family."

I couldn't tell if she was mad, sad, upset, or angry. I never could.

"Why? What happened?" I asked with fear in my voice.

"Some kids in the neighborhood saw your little House Hunters show and were teasing Gee about you being gay. One of them was your cousin's son, Lil Man. You might want to talk to him about it."

Devastated, my heart sank in my chest. I knew the day would come that he would face kids teasing him about me, but I wasn't sure I was ready for it. Carla didn't say how he handled it, I hoped that he was okay. He never said anything to me, so I knew I had to call him. I was nervous. How would I handle it? How would he?

"Okay, I will talk to him about it. Thanks." I hung up the phone.

"Don't let it upset you, Boo. I am sure Lil Gee is okay, and if not, he will be. Kids will be kids," Juan immediately said. He always knew what to say.

"I know, but I still need to make sure he is okay." I quickly pulled up Lil Gee's number.

"Gee?"

"Hi, Daddy! What you doing?"

"On my way to a work event. What are you doing?"

"Sittin'."

I laughed. No matter how many times he responded with this answer when I would ask him this, it was always funny to me. "Boy, you are a mess! I love when you say that. But I was calling to talk to you about something."

"What?"

"Your mom told me that the kids were teasing you about the House Hunters show on TV. Are you okay?"

"Yes. I was mad at first, but then it didn't bother me. I told them, so what if you are gay? It's their problem."

My face lit up. I was so proud of Lil Gee. "You did? Well, that's a big boy. You know people will always want to tease you about something, right? And that you can't control what people say or do, but you can control how you respond, right? "

"Yes, I remember. That's why I stopped being mad."

"Aww, Daddy loves you. You are so amazing. I'll let you go back to sitting now, and I'll call you tomorrow."

"Okay, bye, Daddy. Love you too."

I felt so relieved. I don't know how I would have been able to handle my son being mad at me for being who I am.

Gee and Lil Gee at Kony's housewarming, Goose Creek, SC, 2010

Juan and Gee entering The First Gentlemen's Ball, Atlanta,
November 11, 2011 (photo: Urban Socialites)

Juan and Gee at a nude photo shoot by renowned photographer Saddi Khali, 2012. Gee was nervous, especially because the photographer was a black heterosexual man.

Juan's surprise 30th birthday party at Steele Restaurant in Midtown Atlanta, 2012

Juan and Gee's mothers happily meeting for the first time at Juan's party, 2012

Kony and Gee, 2012

21

OPEN MINDED

THE SECOND GENTLEMEN'S Ball happened in January 2013, some 14 months after the first Ball. Though well attended, we weren't able to secure many sponsorships, and ticket sales weren't enough; we lost $30,000.

I had been an independent I.T. contractor for the past year and a half before losing the contract, which meant a large portion of our income was going to be reduced. Fortunately, after several more arguments that ended with Juan threatening to go back to work, we finally landed a large six-month event production contract with Audi that required Juan to be on the road for weeks at a time.

We decided that since we had some security for at least the next six months, I would not take another I.T. job and focus on developing more business. While we did get a few contracts, it was not nearly as much money as I was making as an I.T. professional. Not to mention with Lil Gee returning to live with us, we anticipated a move into a better school district. This signaled possible financial strain as the rental property was a lot more than we could afford, and we did not have consistent income to get approved for a mortgage, so we began to explore options.

Still, we happily counted down until Lil Gee would move back with us for his 7th-grade year. He barely passed 5th grade and was now struggling to complete 6th grade. His teachers would complain to me about his homework not being completed, and how poorly he was doing on tests. It was a clear indication of the lack of time he put into his schoolwork at home. Carla's mom's health had taken a turn for the worse, and she was now in an assisted living facility. Carla had also met a man who she and Lil Gee now lived with. She called me one day to inform me about it a month or so before they moved. I hadn't met him, but I heard he was an older gentleman, maybe 15 years our senior, but I was not sure. I did know that he had grandkids, and I liked that he was older. I was also happy that Carla had found someone she loved and hoped that it would help to soften her emotions towards me a bit. I thought, maybe, her still being in love with me was the reason she remained so angry. Like Gracey said, "finding a new love would help her forgive you for all you put her through in your marriage." I must admit, though, I did feel a little threatened by a new man in Lil Gee's life. While I was secure in our bond, I still worried that he may think of his new stepdad as more of a "man" than me.

"Hi, Mr. Smalls. It's Mrs. Young, Gregory Jr.'s guidance counselor," she said with her soft, angelic voice. "I wanted to call you today to voice some concerns I am having about Gregory. I understand you are aware of the issues he is having in class. I do appreciate you keeping in touch with his teachers."

"Absolutely! I thank you for all that you do," I responded, standing in the kitchen while cooking.

"You are more than welcome, Mr. Smalls. He's a fine young man. However, I've been seeing Gregory all year, and he seems to be having a difficult time. I am not sure if he is having issues at home, but he appears to be very sad and low energy. A couple of weeks ago, Mr. Smalls, Gregory told me that he had thoughts of suicide. "

"What?! Are you serious?" I panicked.

"Yes. This obviously made me very concerned, so I reached out to his mom to let her know what was going on with Gregory, and also asked that we schedule a conference. She said that she would get back to me, but I have not heard from her over the last couple of weeks and have followed up. Gregory does not seem to be getting any better, so I thought I'd reach out to you to see if maybe we can get him some additional help."

"Thank you so much for calling me, Mrs. Young! I had no idea that this was going on, and with me being in Atlanta, it's hard to stay in the know. Gregory will be visiting with me for spring break next week, and I will definitely have a talk with him. He will also be coming to live with me for the next school year."

"Oh, I think that would be great. Thanks for listening today, and please let me know how I can help further."

"I will. Again, thank you so much for calling me. Take care, goodbye." I hung up the phone and threw it on the table. I was afraid and sad for my son, and furiously angry with Carla at the same time. *How could she not have told me this? What was she thinking? Why wouldn't she call the teacher back? I feel like she just doesn't care!*

There wasn't even any use in calling her. What would that accomplish besides me blowing up at her and creating an even messier situation? She obviously does not value me as a father to hold something like this back from me. I could not wait until I had my son back in my arms and protection. In a week, I would at least be able to hold him after Juan, and I picked him up in Charleston.

About a month prior, Juan and I had a significant breakthrough in our intimate relationship. One day Juan and I were standing in the walk-in closet of our East Atlanta home, arguing about another failed attempt of me trying to penetrate him when he said, "I feel like you are suffocating me when you get on top of me, and I can't move. When you put your weight on me, I feel like you are just trying to control me by not allowing me to move! It feels just like that time that man tried to rape me!" Tears started streaming down Juan's face.

"What? What man tried to rape you?" I rested my hands on Juan's shoulders as I looked him into his eyes.

"I told you about it. It happened when I was 19 at a friend's party, and this guy I was dating at the time came in the room behind me when

I was putting up my jacket and forced himself on me. He pushed me on the bed on my stomach and got on top of me and started grinding on me. He was over six feet and like 250 pounds."

I remembered him telling me one time this guy trying to have sex with him at a party, but I don't remember it being this extreme.

"When I started yelling for him to get off of me, he kept pushing his weight further and further on to me. I started screaming for help when he finally got off me. I ran from the room and out of the house and never told anyone," Juan sobbed.

I pulled him into me tightly and started caressing his back. He wept in my arms for about two minutes. I pulled back, held Juan's face in my hands, and said, "I'm so sorry. I had no idea this happened to you. I would never want to make you feel that way. I just want to love you and create loving moments between us when we are together. I will do anything to help you heal. You are my everything." A tear fell from my eye, and I pulled Juan back into my embrace. I felt so guilty about the way I was complaining regarding our sex life. I felt horrible that I had caused him to feel like his ex did that day at the party.

Coincidentally that next day, we had an appointment with Sheila. We had still been seeing her bi-weekly, and she was helping us to grow and connect in ways we had never imagined. She helped us realize that we both were brought together to help one another heal old wounds that existed way before we met each other. Our spirits aligned and attracted each other. Not only to love one another but also to help us become more self-aware. She taught us that every situation and conflict that occurred between us were divinely purposed. That meant I was to be a support for Juan to help him grow through each situation. I learned that when we have a conflict, my reactions triggered wounds and insecurities that priorly existed within him. It obviously works the other way around as well. This really helped Juan and me not take things so personally when we had disagreements. Knowing that each conflict was an opportunity for us to learn more about ourselves and our relationship helped me to welcome tough conversations. Self-awareness really started to excite me.

During that session with Sheila, she helped us to realize that we do not own each other. With that being said, he is not here to serve me and to make me happy, and neither am I for him. It is our responsibility to find happiness within each other and ourselves. This allowed Juan to release the guilt he felt about not being able to please me like I wanted, and it also allowed him to take his control back. He was forcing himself to do something out of obligation, which made him resent me and our relationship and blocking the creation of a positive lovemaking experience between us. This new perspective also allowed me to stop holding him hostage to my expectations. Although my sexual desires for our relationship remained the same, it allowed me to release the notion that there was something wrong with our relationship just because we did not connect in the way in which I thought we should. I also now understood that just because he was not able to offer me something I desired for my own selfish reasons, did not mean he was not giving me his all.

Sheila also helped me realize something huge about myself: I was molested by Bernetta. I never considered myself to have experienced molestation because I was a boy, and she was a girl just three years older, but I was traumatized. This played a part in the performance anxiety issues I experienced with both men and women. I always attributed my sexual problems with women to be a result of me being "gay," but that wasn't the case. Actually, my sexual experiences with men helped me realize that falsity as I had similar performance anxiety issues. It also explained how, as I've become more comfortable with myself as a sexual being, my attraction for women started to resurface. I often found myself attracted to trans men and women, and I still have a thing for "tomboys." I experienced arousal when getting close to certain women, waking up in the middle of the night from dreams of fantastical sexual exploits, and once I even dreamt about making love to Carla. As I've been able to free myself from all of the boxes of being gay or straight, or masculine or feminine, I've recognized and come to love my sexual fluidity, even being able to conquer my performance anxiety issues. Dorothy was right all those years ago about me questioning my sexuality again.

After that session, Juan made the decision that he was not going to force himself to be penetrated and would not feel guilty about it. I did not give any pushback and was okay after the new revelation. It actually relieved a lot of tension, which allowed us to have even better sex when we did not fall back into the habit of trying to force things. After five years, we still had great sexual chemistry, and our work with Sheila was helping to keep that alive.

"So how have you been feeling since our last session?" Juan asked.

"I've been feeling good about it, surprisingly. At first, I was like 'How dare he say he is not going to try to please me sexually,' but after I got out of my feelings, I was okay with it. Optimistic, actually. Like I told you, the bright side of not experiencing the full potential of our sexual relationship is having new adventures to look forward to. It keeps it from getting old."

"Well, I'm glad to hear that. Dee also helps keep it fresh, too, huh?" Juan laughed.

Dee was a guy that Juan and I had met at a party that we had threesomes with a couple of times. It was always fun when we got together, and this would keep Juan and me screwing like bunnies the entire week. A departure from only having sex once or twice a week and minimal penetration. It was never something either of us had to do when being intimate.

"Yea, Dee is cool. You know he scratches that itch!"

"And you know I love to watch that scratching," Juan said seductively. He was fascinated by watching me with Dee.

"And I love to be seen," I returned the seductive look.

"That gets me to thinking. How would you feel if me and Dee, or someone else, had sex without you? I mean, since you aren't giving it up, it's only fair, right?" I laughed, but he knew I was serious. We had talked before about open relationships and would even joke sometimes about me having a "boyfriend," so it wasn't a total shock for me to mention it.

Juan chuckled. "Well, while it's not fair for me to have to do things I don't want nor ready to do, and I know it's not fair that you are left unsatisfied. You do have needs, after all."

"Really? Wait, I don't know about that. I think that makes me feel like we have failed or something." Although I wanted to, I was still judging myself.

"Why? It's just sex, Gee. You know how I feel about that. And fail by whose standard? This is our relationship, and as long as we are happy..."

"You are right. But what does that mean for you?" I knew I couldn't handle Juan sleeping around. I felt that if I wanted more sex at home and wasn't getting it, he shouldn't be giving it to anyone else. I also still had a streak of insecurity and would even get an attitude sometimes if I couldn't reach Juan when I wanted. I'd automatically think he was with someone else. I was always so worried about being made a fool.

"Look, how about while I am on the road, you can have sex with other people. But they cannot penetrate you, and I must know when it happens. And it can't be anyone who we know. I don't need to have sex with anyone else. This is for you. You don't have to do it if you don't want but know that the option is open."

Juan made me fall in love with him even more at that moment. It was so refreshing to be able to have these types of conversations with one another and know that it does not affect the love we share. I felt so free with Juan.

22

NOT THE WHITE MOTHER

WE HAD JUST returned from picking up Lil Gee the night before in Charleston, bringing him to Atlanta for his 7th-grade school year at Inman Middle School. A month earlier, we sold the house we bought on House Hunters. With rent high in the new school district, we found a deal that worked for our budget. We had moved into a "show home," which is a house that is for sale, and the homeowner offers it for a fraction of the standard rent to have both the security of a housesitter and the home decorated with our beautiful furniture. Though it was luxurious to live in a very well-appointed house, we often had to leave home for showings, and we never knew when the house would sell. We were in and out of four homes over two years, and most of those times, Juan was on the road, and I had to move by myself.

On that rainy Monday morning in summer 2013, Juan had left for the gym when I heard Lil Gee knocking at the bedroom door. I looked over and saw that it was 9:15 a.m. He never got up this early when he didn't have school.

"Come on in, Bubba. Whatcha doin'?"

"Nothing," he responded.

"You're up early. Come here."

He came to the foot of the bed and stood.

"I've been wanting to talk to you. Mrs. Young called me and told me that you were having some challenges. Is that true?"

"Yes. Kinda."

"She tells me that you have been feeling sad."

Lil Gee began to rub his eyes profusely, something he always did before bursting into tears. My heart began to sink, and I felt sadness take over me. I hated seeing my baby boy, sad.

"Aww, come here, Gee, and lay in the bed with Daddy." I held out my arms, and Gee started crying as came to me. I pulled him in the bed with me and held him tight in my arms as I rocked my 12-year-old son back and forth while wiping his tears. He had gotten so big.

"Daddy loves you, Gee, and hates to see you sad. Let me know how I can help you, son. I will do anything. You don't have to be sad." My heart was breaking, and my eyes welled up.

"I-I-I know Da-Da-Daddy."

"Don't worry, baby; you don't have to talk. Just let it all out and let me hold you."

After about ten minutes of sobbing, he finally let up. "Do you still think about suicide, Gee?"

"A lil bit."

"You know that you can talk to me about anything, right? You never have to kill yourself. Daddy will always help you with whatever you need. Do you know that?"

"Yes, Daddy."

"Did you share with your Mom what you were thinking?" "Well, my teacher called and told her."

"What did she say?"

"She said I shouldn't be telling those White people at school my business. That I shouldn't say things like that to them."

How could she tell him that? I mean, I knew why she would feel this way. After all, it's not uncommon for the Black community to distrust White people in authority. But I was not up for taking the chance, and

I didn't care who he told! It took everything in me to not get angry at Carla and stay in the moment with my son.

"Whenever you feel that way, son, you tell anyone who you feel comfortable telling. I'd love for you to tell me, but if you don't want to, you don't have to. Just tell anyone you want to, even your teachers at school or your mom. We are all here to help you. Okay?"

"Okay, Daddy."

"And don't worry, Daddy will get you more help, okay? I'll find you someone good to talk with. I love you, Baby Boy."

"I love you too, Daddy."

A few days later, I stood in my bathroom, dyeing my beard a light shade of reddish-brown.

"What you doing, Daddy?"

"Dyeing my beard."

"Dyeing your beard? What color?"

"It's going to be a light brown, I guess. We'll see how it turns out."
"Can I dye my hair too? I've always wanted the top part dyed that color."
"Hmm...I don't know if you're old enough."

"How old do I gotta be?"

The truth is I was afraid if I dyed his hair, people, mostly Carla, would think that I was trying to turn him gay. Beyond that, I also was just afraid of the judgment of people thinking that a 12-year-old child shouldn't dye his hair. I knew Carla probably wouldn't approve, but I didn't care much about what she thought because I didn't feel she gave a shit about what I thought the entire time he was with her. After thinking about it after a few minutes, I decided to do it. Why should the only reason I not do it be because of what someone else may think, Carla included?

"We can do it if you are sure you want it. Are you sure? It's permanent, ya know? The only way to get it out is to cut it off."

"I'm very sure!"

I proceeded to dye Lil Gee's hair, and it reminded me of that day, my mom dyed mine and was afraid of what my father was going to say.

Not one hour after dying his hair, I was in the kitchen making a smoothie when my phone started ringing. I knew it was Carla calling about Lil Gee's hair, and it was confirmed when I saw "Babymomma" pop up on my iPhone. I immediately got anxious and started pacing the kitchen.

Should I answer?

What is she going to say?

What am I going to say? Fuck it.

"Hello?"

"Hey, Greg. Gee just called me and said you dyed his hair? You didn't think to call me and see if that was okay with me? I think he is way too young to be getting his hair dyed, and you can't just be doing what you want to do. I have rights too."

"You are right, I probably should have called and talked to you about it first, but I didn't think it was a big deal. Especially not as big a deal as him having thoughts of suicide and you not thinking I should know about it! What kind of shit is that?" I struck back. I knew I wasn't going to be able to hold that in very long. This was the perfect opportunity.

She fell silent for about five seconds before responding. Her voice lowered. "I know I should have told you that, but the truth is I knew Gee was just being emotional, and he was not serious about committing no suicide. He go to school and tell them White folks that mess, and it follows him for the rest of his life! Once they put you in the school system as crazy, they will always think you are crazy! But I do apologize for that."

I could tell she felt bad about it. Or just caught. Either way, she submitted, something she hadn't done in a long time. I didn't give a response to her opinion on what Lil Gee was going through as I knew it didn't matter at that point.

"It's cool, but I do want to find him a therapist that he could talk to about things, so he is not holding things in. I think he does deal with some depression, and he does not always want to talk to us about everything. He is at that age now. I hope that is okay with you."

"Yes, I am cool with that."

Although a bit tense, we were able to at least end the call cordially after a disagreement, which was something we very rarely did.

Carla wasn't the only one concerned about Lil Gee's hair. The other woman in my life also seemed to have a problem but not to my surprise. The next day I posted a picture of Lil Gee and me on Facebook, and one hour later, my mother called. She never really called me just to talk, it was always because she wanted something. She always had the idea that it was our place to call because we were her kids. I never bought into it.

"Hello?"

"Hi, Gregory, whatcha up to?"

I wondered why she was beating around the bush.

"Not much. Just sitting here working at my desk while Lil Gee is outside chasing the squirrels. What's up with you? I know you didn't call to say hey."

"Ha ha ha, very funny. I was just calling because I saw Lil Gee's hair. He wanted that?"

She had her way of trying not to overstep but never did a good job of it.

"Yes, he asked me for it."

"Ohh. What did Carla have to say?" She was always so concerned about what Carla thought.

"She was upset I didn't ask her about it and thought he was too young for it. But she got over it."

"Oh. She didn't think it was gay?"

"Do you think it's gay?"

"I'm just asking! I know how her family thinks over there."

"Or is that how you think?"

"What? I don't think that. Now, I do think he is too young for all of that."

"Oh, okay," I responded dryly.

Our relationship was pretty decent around this time, but there were still underlying issues I had with her that I ignored. Even though I was grateful she finally told her brothers and sisters, one night during a trip to her Mom's house in St. Mary's County, Maryland, that I was gay and married to Juan, it was not enough. Her mother was living out the last couple of weeks of her life while they were sitting around playing cards when her sister asked her how I was doing. I don't know if it was the emotions of her dying mother or the alcohol and drugs that I'm sure they were all partaking in that caused the response.

Out of nowhere, my mom screams, "I don't talk about Greg that much because he is gay and married to a man, and I know y'all don't like that stuff, so I keep it away from y'all!" She burst into tears as she tried to cover her face with her hands.

"Oh, Rita, we don't care about that stuff in this day and age!"

"Well, I always here y'all say faggot this and faggot that, and I know y'all are a bunch of rednecks."

They all busted out in laughter, including my mother. When she told me what had happened, I simply said to her, "I am happy for you. Happy that you finally can release that shame."

"It's not like I was ashamed; I just know how they are."

There was nothing I could tell my mother that would make her understand that, at the end of the day, it was shame. Fear. Just as she used to carry that fear with her to the job for having a Black husband and Black kids, she also carried it with her due to the fact I was married to a man, just like I did when Juan and I first married. Not being able to tell your truth because of fear of someone's reaction is shame and insecurity, plain and simple, but I did not need her to come to this understanding. I was okay with where she was at, and while I was happy she was able to come out, I still held resentment that it took her this long, and she still refused to tell her mother.

"Mama's sick, and she's old. She'd never understand that stuff," she said when I asked if she told her mom too. I knew my mother was afraid to be rejected again after her mother finally accepted her back after all of those years of disowning her. Mom was not willing to take that chance again, and I understood that. That did not mean that I didn't feel she was choosing her over me. It also didn't mean it hurt any less, but I dealt.

Her mom ended up dying on that trip, and neither myself nor my sister made the funeral. My mom didn't even ask us to come.

───────

It was six weeks after Lil Gee started at Inman Middle School, less than a mile from where we lived. One day after school, while he was at the dining table doing his homework, I heard him yell my name while I was in my office about 15 feet away. I knew he must've had a question about one of his assignments, so I stopped what I was doing and walked in to help.

"What's up?"

"I gotta draw a picture and tell a story about the people who live in my house. Can I just say that you and me live here?"

Instantly, my heart broke. My biggest fear had come true: my son was ashamed of his gay dad. I did everything in my power, even moved into this expensive-ass neighborhood that we could not afford, just so he could go to the best, most diverse school, and he was still ashamed of me. I did everything I could, except keep him here three years ago, instead of letting Carla take him back to Charleston. I immediately regretted my decision. I knew they had most likely been brainwashing him into feeling he should be ashamed of me, under the guise of them protecting him. The thought of what they probably told him quickly turned my heartbreak into anger, and I lashed out, but not at the right person. Instead, I lashed out at my baby boy.

"Why? Why do you want to lie and not tell them Juan lives here? Are you ashamed of me? Are you ashamed of your father, Gee?!" I yelled, my eyes beaming with anger and veins popping out of my temples. I reminded myself of my mother.

"I'm not ashamed." Lil Gee could barely get his words out as his eyes welled up with tears.

I immediately felt guilty for taking my anger towards Carla out on him. "You can do what you want to do, Gee. I just encourage you to tell the truth."

I never did look to see what decision he had made; I don't think my heart could take it.

Later that year, in November 2013, Lil Gee was three months into seeing his therapist, Chris. Except for the first therapy session, I sat in my car and read, which is where I was when I received a text from Chris this fall afternoon.

"Can you come inside?"

"Sure," I replied immediately, anxious to find out what was going on.

I entered the small, bright office to see Lil Gee sitting across from Chris on the sofa with his head down. It looked as if he were crying. I sat down next to him and placed my hand on his back.

"What's wrong?" I had no clue what he could have been upset about.

"You want to tell your dad what you shared with me?" Chris asked.

"Sometimes, I don't be wanting to come home from school because I think you're going to yell at me," Lil Gee responded pitifully. His head was still down. What would have made me soften in a heartbeat a few years ago had quickly turned to a feeling of defensiveness, but I knew I could not react hastily. I knew he was right about me yelling at him because I did get on him most times when he got home from school, but I felt it was warranted. I removed my arm from Lil Gee's back, sat back against the sofa, and crossed my arms.

"I understand why you would feel that way, and I apologize for yelling so much. I know that I can be hard on you sometimes, but it's because I want you to do well. You also have a hard time turning in assignments and keeping up with your grades, so I have to check on you."

I was always good at saying the right things, and I meant it, but I was emotionless. It took me back to the days of sitting on the couch with Carla in couple's therapy. Lil Gee reminded me so much of her. I felt like those last three years he lived in Charleston had turned him into his mother.

We were so close to the school that Lil Gee was able to walk home, so every day around 4:15 p.m. before he would arrive, I would check on his school's parent portal to see what grades his teacher's posted for the day and if he was turning in assignments and getting good test scores; most of the time, he was not. He always seemed to maintain a C or a D in one or two classes, with B's and maybe one A in the rest. Any missteps would fire me up so much that I would grill him when he walked through the door.

"Why aren't you turning in assignments, Gee? What is the problem? You sit at the table and do homework every day!"

I was getting so frustrated with myself for not being able to figure it out that I was not seeing how he was being affected.

In the therapist's office, I said, "If you can agree to work harder at school, I can agree to check your grades maybe once a week instead of every day."

"Does that sound like a good plan to you, Lil Gee? What your father suggested? Does that help?"

"Yes."

Lil Gee looked up. I softened and started to feel guilty.

"Can I have a hug?" I opened my arms as he fell into me. "I'm sorry, Baby Boy. I love you."

"I love you too."

That day at Chris's office helped our relationship turn for the better. It relieved a lot of pressure on him and me and opened up our communication.

One Saturday morning, after playing basketball at the park, Lil Gee and I headed to Smoothie King when he told me he had a girlfriend.

"Oh, really! You got a girlfriend, huh?" I laughed. "Yea." He started to blush.

"Well, what's her name?"

"Shenika. She's in my Math class. She's cool." "Well, that's cool. When do I meet her?"

We both laughed. He was 13 and had "girlfriends" before, but there was something different about this time. It just seems a bit more mature. My son was growing up, and I wasn't sure I liked it. Where was my baby boy going?

"What did your mom say about you having a girlfriend?"

"She said as long as it ain't a boy." His eyes got big as if he had made a mistake.

I could tell he didn't want to tell me that and wished he could take it back. I wasn't shocked.

"Oh, she did?" I responded with a slight snicker. Truthfully, I was happy it wasn't a boy too, but I would never say that. Even though I knew better, I still didn't want to take on the challenges that would come along with people, mostly Carla, thinking that I had something to do with Lil Gee turning out to be gay. I was pretty confident that he was not gay, but I still felt the need to say the right thing to him.

"How did that make you feel?"

He shrugged. The look on his face was emotionless. He didn't seem bothered either way.

"Well, you know you can like whoever you want to like, and it is okay, right?"

"Yes, I know that."

"Are you ashamed of me being gay?"

"No, I'm not. My girlfriend knows you're gay. She wants to meet you. Her best friend is gay too. There are a lot of gay people at our school."

I felt proud that he was so open. One of the reasons we moved to the midtown area of Atlanta was so he would be exposed to all types of students and families. It was important to me that he did not feel like an outcast because of me. I wanted him to fit in as much as possible, unlike my experience as a child. I didn't want to be the "White mother" in his life.

Gee and Juan hiding their stress, The 2nd Annual Gentlemen's Ball, 2013

Lil Gee and Gee, winter 2013

Gee, Lil Gee, and Juan volunteering at ChildKind, Christmas 2013

Lil Gee and Gee, Father's Day 2014 (photo: Urban Socialites)

Nephew Jakeem, Kony, Gee, and Lil Gee, spring 2014

Juan, Gee, and Lil Gee in the pool at one of the homes they staged, summer 2014

23

EVERLASTING

THOUGH IT TOOK 23 months to come to fruition, the third Gentlemen's Ball was held in December 2014 and was the most successful yet. The ball featured Nissan and New York Life as sponsors. Thanks to Juan's great idea the year before, we had our second presentation of awards honoring six Black, same-gender-loving men and allies who were committed to creating social change while living their lives authentically. The Gentlemen's Ball had grown into a 501c3 nonprofit foundation called The Gentlemen's Foundation, which not only held the annual fundraiser, but also had a scholarship, mentorship, and mental health program year-round.

When Juan and I first started our company and made a strong effort to bridge the Black and White communities, it was not received. I realized that it triggered the rejection I've carried around with me from my mother's side of the family, specifically from my grandmother Ruby. Reaching out to the White community was my way of asking for acceptance, and I was angry when I did not receive it. However, that rejection and anger were divinely purposeful. I took that energy and used it to build up my community and also myself. Accepting and loving whom I am without needing that acceptance and love from White people was empowering. I was never conscious of the hurt and rejection from not being accepted by my grandmother that I carried around with me. I felt somewhat proud to be able to say that I did not grow up around my White side of the family. It somehow made me feel more Black. But I was hurt and felt rejected—a void. It was when I became aware of this, I started to flourish within my true purpose.

After the foundation was created, G.SPOT Productions morphed into Juan & Gee Enterprises. Juan, who over the years, never got to work on his music, became an equal partner in the business. Because I felt Juan always sat in my shadow within the company, I silently decided to let his name go first on our new brand. He became Chair of the foundation board while I took a back seat as co-chair. We had also started a blog called 'LoveWorks' soon after being asked to publish a monthly relationship advice column in the Urban Socialites magazine. We enjoyed the column so much, and it later grew into an online talk show called 'LoveWorks with Juan & Gee.'

It had been such a great year for us, so we decided to do something a little different for Christmas and took a trip. Lil Gee was with Carla, and it was an excellent opportunity to take our annual trip to New York to celebrate our anniversary. Unfortunately, during this fifth year, we were so tied up with planning The Gentlemen's Ball that we were not able to take it in October as usual.

I've always loved New York City. The architecture, the fast pace, the people, the excitement, and yes, even the smell. Juan, on the other hand, never fancied the city as I did.

"It stinks here. It's old," he'd say.

One thing he loved about the Big Apple, though, was the Broadway shows. We always made sure to attend at least one or two when we visited, and this trip was no different.

"Let's go see NeNe Leakes and KeKe Palmer in Cinderella for Christmas tomorrow!" Juan said to me excitedly as we made our way to The Out Hotel NYC in the yellow cab we caught at the airport.

"Okay! That sounds good to me. I can't wait to see what NeNe does with this character. I am sure she will be good at playing an evil stepmother! And you know we love us some KeKe! We can go to dinner beforehand."

Juan and I arrived at the hotel around 7 p.m. We decided that we would spend Christmas Eve at the hotel and wait until the next day to go out on the town. The hotel had a sauna, steam room, and Jacuzzi, so we had enough to keep us entertained without having to leave the hotel. Not to mention, ordering in and watching movies in bed is something we always enjoyed doing together. I never get bored with Juan, so it never really mattered what we did. Even during the times in our relationships, when things aren't so great romantically between us, I still always wanted to be with him. He is my best friend, and I enjoy spending time with him—the greatest part of our relationship.

"So, how do you think our fourth year of marriage has gone, Mr. Session-Smalls?" Although we had never legally hyphenated our names, we still used it. We had just finished binge-watching the first season of *Weeds*, the same show we watched on his laptop night after night while lying on his apartment floor six years prior.

It was not uncommon for me to ask this type of "relationship" question.

"I can honestly say it's been our best year to date. I feel like we hit some sort of milestone in our relationship. A new level, if that makes sense."

"I feel the same way! Over this past year, I've noticed that I have a new sense of security within our relationship. It's kinda strange, or shall I say surprising? It may sound weird saying this, but I almost feel when we opened our relationship, it started to change drastically. It was like once I stopped holding you responsible for keeping me sexually satisfied, it relieved so much pressure. It allowed me to stop letting sexual frustration block all other aspects of our relationship. It helped me to realize what a small part of our relationship sex really was, and more importantly, I did not own you."

"Ooooh…look who is finally getting it!" Juan laughed. He had always said this about sex, and I was always on the opposite end. Of course he couldn't resist the opportunity to say, "I told you so."

"Oh, shut up! Don't ruin the moment! As I was saying, it really helped me to stop focusing so much on sex between us. It helped me to stop keeping count of how many times we had sex, even though I hardly have sex with anyone! Isn't that crazy?!"

"You don't? I don't either." Juan responded.

I wasn't surprised. Not only because I knew Juan wasn't all that sexual, but also because we spent most of our time together. Juan hadn't traveled most of the year and was working full-time at the foundation and our business. I went back to a corporate job, but with the bonus of working from home. Besides, maybe two more threesomes, neither of us were having much sex outside of the relationship.

Over the years since Juan and I agreed that I had the freedom to satisfy my sexual desires outside of the relationship, the agreements changed from time to time. We initially decided that he shouldn't have sex with other people. However, I could as long as I did not allow anyone to penetrate me, and if I told him right after it happened. Right after the decision, I ran out and had sex with Dee immediately, and then another guy a week later. Both times I felt guilty about it, and it was so hard to tell Juan even though I was not doing anything "wrong." I was still stuck in my traditional way of thinking and judging myself. After I had permission to do it, sex stopped becoming so big of a deal for me. What I noticed most about our agreement was the freedom I felt in knowing that even if I had sex with someone else, I did not have to worry about him leaving me. During the first couple of times, I felt guilty about me having this freedom without Juan having the same. Soon after, I suggested that he also have sex outside of the relationship if he wanted.

"I don't need to, but okay," Juan responded after I told him I wanted to change our agreement.

"It's not about sex, but the release of control and freedom that comes along with that. I want you also to experience that within our relationship."

He did go out and have sex with someone one night while he was on the road in St. Louis. I immediately got jealous and upset when he told me.

"I thought you didn't want to have sex with anyone? How quickly that changed!" I snapped.

It wasn't before long that I realized how ridiculous and controlling I was. I also knew that jealousy would come along with this freedom, but it was a challenge that my ego needed to overcome, not my heart. The jealousy was fleeting, but the release of control and feeling controlled lasted. I perpetually worried about Juan cheating. It had been the deal breaker for me in the past. To remove that barrier opened up so much space for Juan and me to deepen our bond. It was freeing not to worry about what he was doing when we were not together because he could honestly do as he pleased within our guidelines. We experimented with and changed agreements over the years. From having to tell right after, to not having to, and then back again. We went from open to close, to open again, just depending upon how we felt in our relationship. We also allowed each other to change our minds when we wanted.

"Do you think you haven't because of that incident with the boy in St. Louis?" I asked Juan after discovering he hadn't had sex with anyone.

"Kinda, but not really."

Earlier that fall, a blog was posted about Juan and me on RonaldMatters.com, covering The Gentlemen's Foundation and LoveWorks. Under the post was a comment that read, "This is the same guy that I went home with from the club last night! I tell you the gays are a mess! And they call themselves a positive example of love and relationships!"

Juan and I were mortified when I read the comment. Even though he had told me about it, we didn't want our business to get out. Especially not on a blog! Not to mention, the person that left the comment tried to reach out to me on Facebook. I guess to "tell on" Juan. This reminded us not to sleep with anyone outside of our regulars, because of what people might say. We weren't ready for that type of backlash, mainly because we were building a brand. We knew people would think we weren't a "real couple" if our relationship was open. The fact that we still had shame around our agreement did not allow us to be free from opinions.

"Do you want to close it again? I mean, why not? You aren't traveling anymore. To be honest, I do enjoy having sex with other people sometimes, but I enjoy it most when we are doing it together."

"Awww, me too. Let's go back to that then. We'll only entertain others if we are together. I love you, Gee."

"I love you too, Juan. Thank you for being you. You are the best man I have ever known. You truly are."

Juan and I fell into each other's embrace and made love like it was our first time. Not our actual first time, but how our first time was supposed to be.

Christmas 2014 was the most romantic Christmas I had ever had. That entire weekend was magical from that Christmas Eve, to dinner, a stellar NeNe and KeKe performance and skating amidst the snowflakes in Rockefeller Center to Whitney Houston's "I Believe in You and Me." Our relationship over the years continued to prove that Juan was made especially for me.

24

YOU ARE WHITE TOO

THE YEAR 2015 brought more I.T. contracts and my rising frustration with this work. Our contract with Audi was not renewed, so Juan was at home again, putting his energy into growing the business and foundation like he did when we started. We had disagreements on how the business should run. We were also planning the next ball for October, and Juan and I often fought tooth and nail on the details. Even though business was not as bad as it was before, all of this made our home a breeding ground for tension. Soon, Juan returned to the corporate world.

In February, I nervously called Carla, needing to discuss some financial matters. I knew this was not going to be an easy conversation, but I had just a smidgen of hope.

"Hey, Carla. How are you doing?"

When Carla and I first got divorced, a part of our agreement was that we would alternate years when we would claim Lil Gee on our taxes. 2014 was Carla's year, but since I had had Lil Gee the past two years and she was not paying child support, I didn't think it was fair she got to claim him. When we got divorced, we also shared equal physical custody. We weren't anymore but did not update the tax portion of the agreement when going through the custody battle.

"I'm fine. And you?" She was cold and emotionless as usual.

"I was wondering if you planned on claiming Lil Gee on your taxes this year."

"Of course. Why wouldn't I?" she responded in a snarky tone.

"Well, because I have been the one taking care of him all year," I shot back. Carla got under my skin like always.

"How you mean you are the one taking care of him? I buy him clothes, I send him money and get him other things. He is also on my health insurance when that is your job!"

She was right. It was in the agreement that I would take care of his health insurance. However, since I was now doing contract work with no benefits, and she now had a job with benefits, she agreed to cover it. I didn't think that was a big enough deal to claim him. To me, I was the one taking care of him daily, and therefore I should be able to claim him.

"Girl, that ain't shit! I am feeding him and putting a roof over his head every day, but fine! I am not going to fight you on it. Go right ahead!" I was always good at making things a big deal and then acting like it wasn't. I had mastered being passive-aggressive.

"Man, you are something else! You think you so damn perfect, but you ain't shit!" Carla slammed the phone in my ear.

While my relationship with Carla was still on the rocks, life at home with the family was going well. Lil Gee was starting to build solid friend-ships and was liking Atlanta and 8th-grade. We had just moved into a condo on the 40th floor of a high-rise building in Atlantic Station, and he loved being able to walk down to shops and restaurants. It gave him a great sense of independence, one that I knew he enjoyed. The dynamic between him, Juan, and I had also come together. It soon became normal that it was now the three of us going out to dinner all the time and not just me and Lil Gee, or me and Juan. Once I was able to let go of this image in my head of how I felt like they should be in each other's life, things started to fit in perfectly. Sheila helped me to let go and realize that they are going to show up in each other's lives how they are supposed to, and it was up to them to form the relationship that they wanted with each other. I never had expectations of Juan being responsible for Lil Gee, but he was always very supportive of my position as a father. He would often be the one to help Lil Gee with his homework or take him to the barbershop.

In April 2015, Lil Gee was headed to the 8th-grade prom with his girlfriend Kamiyah. He was still able to fit in the tuxedo he wore last year at The Gentlemen's Ball, so he wore that along with his favorite new pair of Air Jordan's, a white shirt, and black bow tie. I remembered Carla calling me after finding out he was going to some "gay event," which is how she referred to The Gentlemen's Ball.

"It's a black-tie fundraiser, not some club event, Carla." Carla was so paranoid that I was teaching Lil Gee to be gay. Something she had said once during her many tongue lashings of me. Something I had been concerned about daily since I came out.

While he was getting dressed for his prom, Lil Gee asked if he could wear some of my favorite cologne, Sauvage, by XL. It always made me feel good when he would ask me that, to wear one of my watches, or help him pick an outfit. It reminded me that he admired things about me, no matter how small they were. While I was coming out of our bedroom with the cologne, I stopped in the hallway as I looked into the kitchen at Juan, helping Lil Gee style his hair.

"See how I'm using the sponge and spinning it in circles all over? That's how you get the spirals in your hair like I have in mine. You have to do this two to three times a day if you want to keep it looking good. Here, you do it." Juan handed Lil Gee the sponge, and he began to swirl it around his head, trying his best to mock Juan.

"Almost, but try to make more circles on your head. Like this." Juan put his hand over Lil Gee's and began to make small circles around his hand, making his hair curl.

"See! You got it!" Juan let go of Lil Gee's hand, and Lil Gee smiled. My heart melted as I sat back and watched the special bond that he and Juan shared, one they created on their own after I was able to let go of my expectations of their relationship. I took a moment and thanked God for allowing me to realize that moment before walking in with the cologne. "Here you go! The one you like the best! You look so handsome, son. You know that, right?"

"Mmhmm." Lil Gee smiled wide.

"Here, let me fix your bowtie." I began to straighten his black and gold bowtie as he looked up at me.

"Man time flies! High school already! Can you believe that?"

"Not really. I am ready, though! I can't wait to get away from these little kids!"

I busted out in laughter! "Lil kids?! Oh, you grown now?! Well, you know that you become the little kid again in freshman year of high school, right? You ready for that?"

"I'm ready! I know I am."

I loved the confidence he had gained over the past couple of years. "Have you given any thought whether or not you will go back to Charleston or go to high school here?" I asked.

The time was approaching, and we needed to prepare. Our lease was up soon, and if he wanted to go back with his Mom, we would probably move out of the school district because of high living expenses. I wanted him to choose us because I feared it would be too easy for him to get caught up in street life if he lived there. I wanted him to be exposed to all of the opportunities that were available to him and did not think that could happen for him in Charleston. I never knew the possibility of who I could be until I had been in Atlanta for over ten years, and I did not want a similar path for him. I wanted him to have an advantage. Although I felt this way, I always did my best to remain neutral when the topic came up. I never wanted to influence his decision one way or the other.

"Yeah, I have. I think I want to stay here," he replied.

I immediately felt a sense of relief but tried not to let it show.

"Oh, really? What do you think will make you sure about your decision?"

"Well, I guess I already know what I want, but I don't want to hurt my mom's feelings."

My heart sank. I knew Carla's feelings would be crushed and did not want her to have to experience any type of rejection from her son. I also ached for my son, who was going to ultimately let her know his decision. I definitely was not going to be the one to tell her. I did not want her to think I had anything to do with his decision, nor did I want to make it seem as if I was gloating that he chose to stay here. It was so bittersweet, just like it was the day I got the call about the custody decision.

"I understand that. You know that you don't have to worry about that, though, right? We are your parents, and we are here to protect you, not the other way around. When making your decision, you should consider only what you feel is best for you, not me, or your mom's feelings. We will be okay with whatever you decide, and that especially includes me. Okay?"

I also worried that he may just be telling me that because he didn't want to hurt my feelings, although he was much more protective of his mom. It was almost as if he felt he had to take care of her. I understood as it was much like the way I felt towards my very own mother. Although we went at it at times, I always had a soft spot for her.

"Okay."

"There you go! Now it's perfect." I finished his bow tie and gave him a hug.

"I love you."

"I love you too."

"Let's go!"

Lil Gee, Juan, and I headed out to drop him off at the prom.

That next month the three of us went to Charleston to see my mom for her 60th birthday. We all had planned to cook dinner for her and her friends while she sat back and enjoyed herself. We made strawberry martinis, grilled filet mignon, lobster tails, and shrimp along with mom's favorite, a buttery baked potato, and broccoli. They were in heaven all evening and couldn't get enough of the strawberry martinis. My mother always loved a good drink, and so did her friends!

Around 8 p.m., after all her friends had left, my nephew Jakeem and Lil Gee were sitting at the computer desk in the den, while my mom, sister, Juan, and I talked and laughed about random things as usual when the topic of using the N-word came up. It was something we never discussed in our house, nor did I ever hear it.

"Nowadays, these kids don't even know the meaning of the N-word, and anyone uses it," Juan said.

"I know!" I said. "That's why you have to teach them the history of it, so they don't continue to let anyone call them that. Jakeem, Gee! Do y'all White friends say the N-word?"

"Yeah. It ain't nothing, Uncle. It's just a word. Nobody cares about that stuff anymore," Jakeem replied.

"What?! Boy, don't you let no White boy call you that word! You shouldn't be using that word yourself. It was created to humiliate and demean us!"

"I think if you continue teaching the hate over and over, then racism will never die," my mother quickly said, putting in her two cents. She seemed to be passionate about her statement.

"That is not how you get rid of racism! You cannot forget your history. That is what America wants us to do now! Like nothing ever happened!" I screamed. I was upset that my mother did not feel the way I did and could not understand. It reminded me of our difference.

"Dang, I didn't know you felt so strongly about the N-word," Kony said.

"How you mean? I didn't know that you didn't!" I replied.

"I guess it just doesn't bother me like that." "Well, it bothers me!"

"You better not forget you're half White too, ya know!" my mom yelled. She was getting angry at my defensiveness.

My mom still did not see me as a Black man, somehow thinking her White contribution to my racial makeup diluted the fact that I was still a Black man. She proved this more than once by making comments like, "Lil Gee looks just like a black version of Greg" and posting on Facebook that she feared for her Black grandsons during these times of police brutality, never making mention of me. It was further confirmation that she would never be able to understand or relate to my experience as a Black man.

"Show me where being half White means anything! I am Black. You are White. There ain't no such thing as half White in America! I am a Black man with a White mother!" I was furious and screaming at my mother.

She was stunned at my reaction and didn't know what to say.

"You know what? You know what? Oh, nothing, Greg! Just nothing!" she yelled back.

"What? Say it if you want to!"

"You act like you are so perfect while you sit here and scream and disrespect me in front of my grandchildren on my birthday! Thanks a lot for ruining my day!" My mother threw down her glass and grabbed a paper towel as tears rolled down her face.

I immediately weakened. I felt so conflicted because, while I hated to see my mother sad and crying with me being the root cause of it, I was also furious that she could not get me. No matter what, she would never be able to relate to me in that way. She was a White woman. I was a Black man. I wondered how my father dealt with this difference in connecting with my mother. When they first got together, he had to have had many experiences as a Black man that he needed the woman he loved to console him on. How did she console him? How did this affect their relationship? Did he see me as a Black man?

The thought quickly passed, and I took a deep breath. "You are right, I should not be yelling and screaming at you like this, but I am upset. I apologize to you for that, and I also apologize to you, Lil Gee and Jakeem, for disrespecting your grandmother. I should not be speaking to her like this, and don't you guys use this as an excuse to do the same thing. Y'all know better, and so do I. I am sorry again, Momma. I will leave it alone. I did not mean to ruin your day." I meant what I said, but the feelings were unattached.

The next morning we were finishing up breakfast at a local restaurant before heading back on the road to Atlanta. As usual, we acted as if nothing happened the night before and had the typical surface-level conversation. It was definitely in true Smalls fashion.

"Love you, Gregory."

"Love you too."

We hugged, and the three of us were back on the road. I left feeling quite different on this trip. The situation with my mother the night before would not settle within me. I realized that the fact that neither of my parents treated me like a Black boy growing up explained a lot about the way I felt about fitting in and being accepted as a Black man. How could I fully embrace myself and even feel accepted as a Black man by others if the very two people that made me did not see me that way? How did this influence the way they raised me, especially my father? It was his job to ensure my mother knew that although I was mixed, at the end of the day, I was still Black. But maybe he didn't know or didn't feel that way. I would never find out. While the discovery was painful, it also brought me some clarity. It made sense why he may have never talked to me about race.

Something else interesting happened not long after at my Momma's house. About a year later, when visiting for Thanksgiving, it would be my Aunt Pam who'd say the word so frivolously one night after a few drinks. It was just before commenting on how she had been to the same liquor store all week without a bother but noticed the change in White employees' behavior after walking in with Juan and me.

"Wow! They couldn't stop following and asking us questions! They didn't do that when I was in here before."

Juan and I didn't even notice. It was normal to us but quite noticeable to Aunt Pam, who never walked around with Black men.

Later on, in conversation, she went on to talk about her grandson and my cousin, Jude.

"Jude loves him some Black people. All of his friends are Black. I sometimes wonder if he wants to be Black!" The more she talked, the more she came off with an offensive tone—as if to be Black was a bad thing. It started to make me uncomfortable. I wondered if my sister and Juan, who were also in the room, were feeling the same way. My mom was at work.

Aunt Pam was about five margaritas in by now as she carried on. "Oh, and he gets so mad when I say that word talking about the students!"

That word? Is she referring to the N-word in regards to the student who rides the bus that she drives for D.C.'s inner-city public school system?

"He'd say, 'Grandma, you can't use that word! Stop saying that!' And I'd be like, 'This Ni Ni Ni always acting a fool on my bus!'" Aunt Pam mumbled it under her breath.

Did she really just say that? Did Juan and Kony hear it? Why am I surprised? I knew she was still a Trump-supporting redneck from the trailer parks of St. Mary's County, Maryland. But why was she so comfortable saying it in front of me? Did she not consider me a nigger? What about Juan? I was caught off guard and did not know how to respond, but I had to say something. Juan and Kony didn't seem to be reacting to her.

"Jude is right. You should not be using that word. It's extremely offensive."

Aunt Pam just kinda laughed and went on to the next drunken story. I decided not to share with Momma what happened that night. I'm not sure if it was because I did not want to start a fight between sisters, which was quite common, or if it was because I was afraid of what her response would be. I do not think I was prepared not to have her come to my defense.

25

NO RULES

IT WAS A week before heading to Miami with my mom, sister, nephew Jakeem, and Lil Gee for summer vacation. Juan and I were hanging out at the pool at our condo with some neighbors and friends. Juan was moving back and forth from the grill while I was in and out of the pool. Our neighbor Reggie, who lived a few floors up, was also hanging out and being extra flirtatious with me. Juan and I met him the week before at the pool when I mentioned that I thought Reggie was hot. We never did have an issue with this type of exchange. Reggie was in his upper 20s, caramel brown skin with a chiseled chest and six-pack. He had beautiful pearly white teeth and confidence that everyone fell in love with. Reggie was also in a wheelchair, which for some reason, intrigued me. The week prior, he shared with us that he was in a skateboard accident that left him paralyzed from the waist down, but he was in physical therapy and expected to walk one day again.

"Yes, it still works," Reggie laughed.

"Hey, I wasn't going to ask but good to know!" I replied and laughed. Juan did not seem amused.

Something about Reggie in that wheelchair turned me on. I wanted to have sex with him and knew that he would be down for it by the way he flirted that day.

"You want to see if Reggie wants to go out with us tonight?" I asked Juan while he flipped burgers. I knew he understood what I meant: I wanted to have sex with Reggie.

"Sure," Juan replied. Juan typically went with the flow and did whatever I wanted. That included any man I wanted us to have a threesome with. I was always the initiator. It never really seemed to matter to him, although he would enjoy it. It had been since New York during our Christmas trip that we indulged, and I felt it was overdue. Juan and I had been monogamous for six months, having sex maybe once or twice a week if I was lucky. That was not nearly enough for me, so I was horny and sexually unsatisfied. Juan still could care less about sex, no matter how hard he tried or how many times we went to see Sheila.

We had a great day at the pool, and Reggie was on board to hang with us that night. However, by 10 p.m., Juan was passed out from all the sun and drinking. I was still pumped and ready to go, as were our friends.

"Juan! Wake up! Let's go!" I nudged him on his shoulder.

"I don't want to go. You go ahead and go. I'm staying home."

"Come on! Are you sure?" I wanted him to go. We had a threesome to do.

"Yes, I am sure. You go."

I was disappointed, but I knew how Juan got after a day of drinking, so I did not fuss about it. Not long after putting on my shoes, I get a text from Reggie.

"Hey man, I am going to stay home. Y'all have fun."

I laughed to myself and thought it wasn't meant to be.

"That's cool. Goodnight!" I texted back, and off I went to Swinging Richards with our two friends.

About four drinks later, at the end of the night, I called an Uber to head home. While I waited, I could not stop thinking about how bad I wanted to have sex with Reggie, so I sent him a text even though I knew I shouldn't have.

"You up?" I asked.

Reggie replied right away. "Yes."

"Want some company?"

"Sure."

My excitement grew in my head and my pants. He was going to be mine tonight, and I deserved it. I justified my actions by thinking of how Juan and I weren't having sex as much as I wanted to, and he knew I was not sexually satisfied because of my complaining. Not to mention, my itch for being on top was not being scratched. I thought he wouldn't care. Earlier, I told him what I wanted it so many ways.

Reggie had told me that the door would be unlocked and that I could come straight back to his room. As I entered the dark, empty apartment, I could hear and see the shadows of the TV playing in his bedroom to the left of me. Straight back were the floor-to-ceiling windows that were identical to ours.

In the bedroom. Reggie laid with one arm behind his head against the headboard and the other between his open legs. I could tell he was naked because of how low the comforter rested around his small waist.

"Come join me," Reggie demanded, and I stripped naked and laid next to him. I thought about that moment all day...only Juan was not there. For a quick second, I thought I should go home, but it wasn't long before Reggie had his head between my legs. I had gotten what I came for then went back home to bed. Even through the sexual satisfaction and drunkenness, I felt guilty about what I had done. I knew I had to tell Juan.

"Good morning," I said as I came back with coffee for the both of us as Juan stood up and stretched. I often brought him coffee on Sunday mornings.

"Hey, good morning. Thanks for the coffee. How was your night?" Juan asked. I immediately grew nervous but not as nervous as I thought I would be.

"Well, it was fun. I had a good time. I do have to tell you something. I broke one of our agreements." I thought this was the best way to say it since we always said if we broke an agreement, we would need to tell one another.

"What did you do?"

"I had sex with Reggie last night."

Juan's eyes grew big, and he pressed his lips against each other, something he did when he was trying not to show emotion.

"You did what? How did that happen?"

"Well, I texted him on the way back and asked if I could come over."
"So you cheated?" he asked firmly.

"I guess I did." I had never thought of it as cheating. I held my head down and immediately felt even more disappointed in myself. I was becoming my parents. I didn't expect him to react like this. I didn't even think it would bother him.

"That's very disrespectful. We were hanging out with him all day, and now you go and have sex with him?"

I didn't know what to say. I felt like I made it clear that was the intention all day, although it was for the three of us. Juan was acting as if this came out of the blue like he did not know I wanted to have sex with Reggie. Or maybe I made it up, assuming he knew.

"You are right. I apologize for disrespecting you and for sleeping with him. I know I had no business doing it."

Juan fell silent for a few minutes before he got up and went into the shower. He didn't seem as bothered anymore. After a few minutes, I got up and joined him.

"Hey," I said to him with a slight smile.

"Hi," he replied. I couldn't read him.

I pulled him into me and kissed him on the lips. He pulled back. I got the hint, released him from my embrace, and sat on the granite shower seat while I watched him bathe. I felt a bit confused by the energy because he was clearly aroused, so I felt like he wanted to be near me, but his actions were saying something different. I knew that he needed to hold his ground to let me know that it was not okay for me to break our agreement, even if he was not bothered by the sex. I understood and gave him space.

Although I had felt a bit anxious about our beach trip with the full family, things turned out great. Typically, Juan and I just took Lil Gee and Jakeem on vacation, but this time my mom and sister joined us. We had a great time together, and it reminded me of that first time we all went to Disney World when Juan first met them. I love my family, no matter how dysfunctional we are.

On the way back from dropping them off at the airport, Juan turned down the music and said to me, "So, I've really been thinking we should go back to opening our relationship. I don't see the need in putting those boundaries on us. I wasn't really bothered by you having sex with Reggie. Hell, it even turned me on a little bit, but I did not like that you broke our agreement. Then I thought, why do we have that agreement? What is the real point of it?"

"For me, I know it's just about feeling like it's the 'right thing,' even though it doesn't naturally feel like the right thing. It's like even though I know there is nothing wrong with an open relationship, it still conflicts with traditions and rules of how I was brought up. It's about breaking those old thought patterns. That's the challenge."

"Yea, you are right. I say we need to work on being free from that, and not conform because that does not work. We know what we have and share. Sex does not define or break that. It never has for us."

"Ha, you are right about that! We would be over a long time ago if that were the case!" I laughed.

"Sure would have! So we good? No more of those rules?"

"Yes, we are good. Let's just focus on growing together and being free from norms. Let's continue to create our way. We are so much more than husbands. We are partners in life. I love you for allowing me to be so open with you. I love you for loving me and all of my fuck ups and mistakes. Thanks for being the most security I have ever experienced in my life, Juan." If it were not for Juan, I would not have been able to reach my present level of self-awareness. It is because of the space in which we allow each other to grow that I am who I am today. We understood that we weren't here to control or change but to acknowledge and accept one another in the ways we show up in the world. He cannot make me happy, nor could I make him happy. We got the point. This was a pure unconditional love that I have never shared with any other human being. We knew that it was love with no conditions and love with no limitations. That's the kind of love every soul desires, ours included. We allowed each other that kind of love, and it is because of this love that Juan and I have been able to continue to evolve and journey together in life.

"Aw, baby, there are no fuck ups. We are just growing. I will always be here, and I know you will always be here for me. You are right; we are partners in life, which is so much bigger than marriage. Let's go through this life together forever. I love you too, Gee."

"Speaking of being open, I have one more thing to bring up. I know you've heard of PrEP, the pill that prevents HIV? If we are going to have sex with others, what do you think if we got on it? As an extra precaution?"

I had learned about PrEP through the work we were doing at The Gentlemen's Foundation. PrEP is a daily medication that reduces the risk of HIV by 99%. I thought it would be a great idea if we both got on it, just in case we had any "slip-ups," and we have definitely had our drunken night slip-ups before. After all of the times we dodged the virus before meeting one another, I thought it would be irresponsible for us not to take advantage of all that's out there to protect ourselves. I can only imagine how much farther along we would be if this were available to use twenty years ago. How many lives would be saved? Besides, I also know that many men contract the virus from a partner they trust and thought they knew everything about. We had to do it, I just hoped Juan would be on board.

"You know, I've been thinking about that too. Why not? Better safe than sorry, right?"

"Exactly, I am glad you are down. I will schedule an appointment with the doctor next week."

It was the end of summer, and we were leaving dinner at Tenth and Piedmont after closing a deal with the CDC to do some HIV awareness marketing campaigns using LoveWorks and events. We were pretty excited about it and decided to walk across the street to Blake's to celebrate with some cocktails.

Upon walking up the ramp, we were greeted by a young, blonde White guy who asked for our I.D.'s. As I was fumbling through my cardholder to find my driver's license, I couldn't help but notice the new dress code that was posted on the door. It read:

No hoodies
No oversized tank tops or tee shirts
No sagging pants or excessively baggy clothes No sweatpants
No bandanas/do-rags No sunglasses after dark No oversized purses
No athletic wear
No oversized chains or medallions No headphones
No weapons
No bad attitudes
WE RESERVE THE RIGHT TO REFUSE SERVICE TO ANYONE

I was immediately confused. Blake's was an old dive bar with sticky floors and a smell that always reeked of a dirty mop. All the tables and chairs wobbled, and the bar was barely standing. This was no place for a dress code. Most people came directly from Piedmont Park across the street after playing sports or some other park activity. Who were they kidding? Who made up these new rules? This dress code was a not-so-subtle message to let Black people know they were not wanted or welcomed. All of the items on this dress code were stereotypically clothes, and fashion Black men would wear. I was never a big fan of Blake's because of the racist undertones, but it had never shown up like this before. Now it was clear. Again, the non-inclusiveness of the gay community was showing up.

"Umm, excuse me, sir. How long has this dress code been in place?" I asked the guy at the door.

"As of about ten minutes ago," he responded.

"Wow. Okay, thanks." I responded and quickly snapped a pic of it with my phone.

We made our way to the bar and ran into some friends of ours. "Hey, did y'all see the dress code they posted?" I asked.

"Yeah, I saw that. Crazy, huh?!" one of my friends answered. "Yeah, it is. It seems blatantly racist," I responded.

No one in the group seemed to be bothered much about the new dress code, but I couldn't stop thinking about it. By the time I was done with my Tito's and soda, I was ready to go.

"Want another drink?" Juan asked.

"No. I am ready to go. I don't feel good being in here anymore." "Okay." Juan looked a little disappointed. I could tell he did not want the night to end since he was enjoying himself.

On the way home, I posted the picture on my Facebook page, asking what everyone thought of Blake's new dress code. I wanted to know if I was the only one who felt it was a huge slap in the face to the Black men in the community, many of whom patronized the place religiously. It wasn't before long that a flood of comments, likes, and shares started coming in, with most everyone being just as upset by the new dress code as I was. I felt validated in knowing that I was not the only one. I wasn't just being sensitive.

By 9 a.m. the next morning, I got a call from the Georgia Voice, a local LGBTQ newspaper, asking me about the posted picture. They wanted to know if they could quote me on my thoughts about the new dress code and how I felt about racism in the community.

I immediately felt fearful. Was I Black enough to speak on behalf of the Black community on the racial climate, not only at Blake's but here in Atlanta? Am I a proper representation? Would people question me and my experience? I knew I could not be silent on it, despite my insecurities surrounding my racial identity and acceptance.

"Sure, that would be fine. I believe the dress code was clearly stating that Black folks are not welcomed, without coming out and directly saying it. There are many bars in the midtown area where we feel we are not welcomed, and Blake's is just one of them. Unfortunately, there aren't many places for us to go, so we go anyway. It's time to put a stop to it. I am calling for all of my brothers and sisters, and those who are our allies, to boycott Blake's. Stop spending your money where people do not want you."

This was also around the time Marriage Equality was occurring. I never really felt connected to the movement, which surprised many seeing as though I was married, but with so many other issues plaguing our community, it just didn't seem like a Black person's fight. I was proud that the first Black President of the United States, Barack Obama, was the one to validate that love is love, and he was even more proud of how the Black community rallied behind him as a Black man, despite his racial makeup. It made me feel affirmed as a biracial Black man, though there were still comments made that he wouldn't have gotten into the oval office if he had been dark-skinned. It didn't bother me to hear that anymore because, as an adult, I know many reasons why this statement holds true. It's no secret that America tends to be more inviting to us "light skins," and it would be irresponsible of me not to recognize that privilege. It doesn't take more than looking at the skin tone of the men who are most vulnerable to police brutality to prove that fact.

The dress code and bar boycott started a big uproar in the community. While many of the Black men stopped going for a while, it wasn't long before everyone forgot about it, and things were back to business as usual. In a way, I felt I had failed in my attempts to bring awareness to what had occurred and the issues that permeated our community. Below the surface, I knew that I was not strong enough to lead such a movement. I was still trying to reassure myself that I was Black enough and worthy enough to be the voice the community lacked.

The 3rd Annual Gentlemen's Ball with Gee, Juan, and Lil Gee, his first time attending and the first event with corporate sponsorships, 2014

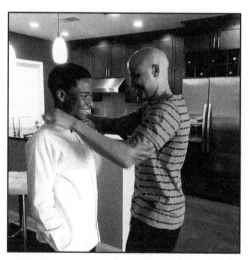

Gee readying Lil Gee for 8th Grade dance, 2015

Gee and Mom, Charleston Crab House, Mother's Day 2015

Juan and Gee at first live show for their web series, Center for
Civil and Human Rights, 2015 (photo: Urban Socialites)

Family trip, Miami, 2015

Juan and Gee being interviewed for a documentary
on masculinity in black men, 2015

26

A NEW MR. SMALLS

IL GEE HAD been at Grady High School for three months now, and I could not tell if he was adjusting well or not. He started to stick to himself more and not opening up as much to me or hanging out with us anymore. Very seldom would we go out to eat or to the movies like we used to do. We still ate together every night because that was mandatory, but he didn't say much and wouldn't even watch movies or TV with us afterward as usual. Instead, he went to his room and closed the door.

Earlier that spring, Carla's mom had passed away as well. I wasn't sure if that could have been bothering him, but they never appeared to be too close, and he said he was not very affected by her passing. When Carla called to discuss picking up Lil Gee for the funeral, I didn't know what to say. Carla and I were not on speaking terms by any means, but I wanted to be there for her just as she had been for me when my Dad, who shared much of the same struggles as Carla's mom, passed away. I was sure Carla would never accept me being there for her in that way, and I was too much of a coward to offer or even show up to the funeral. I was too afraid of how being in a church full of "Team Carla" would make me feel.

Lil Gee was growing up and becoming his own man. I tried to get him interested in extracurricular activities at school, but he didn't even play basketball anymore. After trying out for a few days, he quit. He used to draw all the time, and I also got him more art supplies. I told him to "have at it" on the walls in his bedroom, but he never wanted to paint. He got interested in modeling once, but shortly after Carla discovered pics from his first photo shoot on my Facebook page, he quickly lost interest.

"She gonna think that modeling is just for girls," Lil Gee said to me after I asked why he hadn't shared with his mom that he wanted to be a model. I am not sure if Carla was still worried about him turning out to be gay or if it was just Lil Gee still protecting her, but he gave it up nonetheless.

He was also not doing very well at school. His grades were always up and down, and I put major restrictions on him. One day while I was in my home office working, I got a call from his teacher.

"Hi, Mr. Smalls. My name is Ms. Lawton, and I am your son's home-room teacher. I wanted to bring an incident I had with your son today to your attention."

"Okay, you have my attention." I immediately grew concerned.

"Today, in class, I had to ask Gregory several times to turn around and stop talking to his classmate, India. It seems that he was upset with her and wouldn't leave her alone. After growing frustrated, he stormed out of class even after I asked him to stop. I had never seen his temper like that before. It is very unlike Gregory, and he hasn't been himself for a while now. I had to write him up, Mr. Smalls. He is suspended for three days, and you will need to pick him up now."

"Thank you for telling me, Ms. Lawton. I will be sure to have a talk with Gregory and get to the bottom of this. I am on my way."

I was furious with Lil Gee. Why was he acting out like this? What am I going to do? I had already done all the punishing I could do, and it didn't seem to matter. I couldn't get him to talk to me about anything. Was he even talking to his therapist?

On my way to pick him up, my anger grew to worry and sadness. What was my son going through? When I entered the disciplinary office,

Lil Gee sat in the chair with an angry face and his head down. I signed him out and waved for him to follow me. When he jumped in the car, I was confused by his demeanor. Instead of looking sorry and regretful, he looked pissed and mad as hell as if somebody had done something wrong to him versus him being in trouble for acting out.

"What's wrong, Gee? This is unlike you. What made you want to storm out of class?"

He could tell that I was more concerned than angry. He relaxed a bit. "Nothing. I just was outraged and felt out of control. I had to leave."

"Well, I applaud you for doing something to take care of yourself.

You are not wrong for doing that."

I knew he meant that he was going to cry and did not want anyone to see him. I knew how he cried when he got really upset.

"But you have to figure out what is making you lose control. What happened?"

"Nothing." Lil Gee shook his head.

I knew it was something, obviously, but he wasn't going to share it with me. I also knew it was probably India.

"I want to help you, son. I can't help if you won't share with me what's wrong. I am on your side."

Lil Gee shook his head again. I knew I would not be able to get it out of him. We stayed silent for the rest of the ride home.

Lil Gee was walking in front of me as we entered the condo when I stopped him by pulling his shoulder, and he turned around to face me. I pulled him forcefully into me and wrapped my two arms around his 16-year-old body and held him tightly. He returned my embrace, and I could feel his body collapse into mine as he started to weep. My son was hurting, and I had no idea what was making him hurt. I began to weep with him as tears streamed down both of our faces. It was the first time in a long time that I had held my son like this. Affection no longer came naturally between us. The more he grew into a man, the more uncomfortable it became for me to show affection. Every hug, every gesture, became intentional. I had to remind myself to do it. Much like with his mother. Much like with Juan. Much like with my family.

"I love you, son, and I want to help you. I want you to be happy and feel peace. If you don't share it with me, I can't help. You can trust me with whatever it is. If it's me, you can tell me. I promise I won't be mad. I just want you to feel better."

"It...it...it's nah-nah-not you." He was crying so hard that he could barely get his words out.

I hadn't seen him cry like this since he was a kid. While I hurt for him, it also made me feel good that he trusted me with his tears. It reminded me of the day he lay in bed with me after we talked about his thoughts on suicide.

"Well, whatever it is, Gee, you can tell me whenever you are ready. Take your time. And if you're not ready to share with me, share it with somebody else. It will be okay, Gee. I love you."

I knew my son was heartbroken over his girlfriend. I knew she had done something that got to him. He reminded me a lot of myself when it came to relationships. He loved to love and commit himself to someone. He loved relationships, but he would often find himself with girls he never trusted. I sometimes wondered if his being away from his mother affected him and his choice of girlfriends.

I held him tightly, and we stood in the doorway for about five minutes until we got all of our tears out. While our voices were silent, our hearts and souls said a lot.

<hr/>

A few months later, I had made it down to Miami for a getaway just weeks before my 39th birthday. By this point, I was feeling pretty good about whom I had become as a man emotionally, spiritually, mentally, and finally physically after years of hating the body that carried me around. Ever since the first day, I experienced my old college roommate Aiden walking around naked around our apartment, I've longed to become as comfortable with my body as he was. Over the years, I realized how that experience was more about my admiration for his freedom than being sexually aroused. I, too, wanted to feel that freedom, and it was this year that I would experience that at Haulover Beach. I hadn't been to this nude beach since my weekend at Sizzle nine years before when I had a drunken quickie under the DJ booth at Club Space. Miami had become a breeding place for my sense of freedom since that day, and for the past couple of years, I had made it a point to take a solo trip every year during my birthday month. This year, I was going to release all inhibitions, which included removing my clothing at Haulover Beach. I wasn't as nervous as I thought I would be amidst the sea of strangers on that mildly sunny day. After paying the sexy Cuban "Chair and Umbrella Guy," I quickly removed all of my clothing. Feeling the ocean breeze in every crevice of my body, I inhaled the smell of the ocean mixed with sand and tanning oil while closing my eyes to face the springtime sky. And for the first time, I knew exactly how Aiden felt walking around our apartment in all his naked glory. I felt a sense of gratitude and peace for how far I had come to love all of who I was, including this body that went through so much trauma. I felt liberated.

Since that day, going to beaches that aren't nudist-friendly became quite mediocre despite my lifelong love for beaches. There is just something deeply spiritual about feeling all of nature on your skin without the shield of clothing. There is nothing like it.

Things were also going well with LoveWorks and The Gentlemen's Foundation. The audience for our web talk show was growing, and the foundation was finally getting the attention of corporate sponsors and other funding sources for both our programs and The Gentlemen's Ball. Generally, most funding funneled to the LGBTQ community always went to the White organizations, leaving the Black organizations only with funding for HIV. So the support from corporations like UPS, Nissan, New York Life, AARP, and others, allowed us to have the ball annually in October. We even grew to include honoring the women in our community as well, something we were excited to do. And two consecutive years of being out of the red with the event signaled success for us.

Juan had started to grow a friendship with James, the guy who did the production on our show. I knew that James and Juan dated about six months before Juan and I met. Juan told me that after nearly two or three months of dating James, he stopped talking to him abruptly when he found out that he had contracted HIV. I had also come to get acquainted with James over the years socially and from doing some of the same community work. He was a cool guy, but he always seemed a bit uncomfortable around me.

"You should ask him why," Juan would say any time I would mention it after having contact with him.

James and Juan both experienced the same type of depression, something that I could not relate to, so I liked that Juan had someone he could talk with who understood. They became accountability partners.

One night Juan and I were at a party when we ran into James. While Juan was at the bar getting us drinks, I went over to James and said, "Hey, I wanted to ask you a question."

"Sure, man! Shoot!" James said with a smile.

"Why does it seem you always are uncomfortable around me?"

"Well, I wanted to tell you, but Juan told me I shouldn't."

As soon as James said that, Juan walked up with our drinks.

"Huh? What?" I was confused. What would Juan tell him not to tell me, and why? "James just said that he's been wanting to tell me something, but you told him not to."

Juan's face looked like a deer in headlights. James' face was soon identical to Juan's.

"I'm sorry. I didn't mean it," James said.

"Don't be sorry. Sorry for what? What do you want to tell me? What does he want to tell me, Juan?" I was furious and embarrassed. I could not believe I sat between my husband and another man who shared something that I did not know. I felt foolish.

"Let's go," Juan said.

"No, we don't have to go. Let's stay. I'm good!" I said as I downed the drink.

I was not good. I was getting increasingly upset but still trying not to look like a fool in front of James and whoever else might be watching. I was starting to feel out of control like Lil Gee. I needed to leave, so I walked out. Juan followed.

As we jumped in the car, I immediately started yelling at him. The fact that I was slightly drunk did not help my temper.

"What the fuck does James want to tell me, and why did you tell him not to? You know how stupid I looked in there?! That is the one thing that I always told you not to do! Never have someone have something over me like that! Nobody should know nothing about you that I do not!"

"I am sorry, but it really is nothing! I did not want to make it a big deal. James told me that he still had feelings for me and loved me, but he respected our relationship. He wanted to tell you for whatever reason, but I told him not to because I did not want to lose his friendship. I knew I did not feel that way about him, and it would go nowhere, but I also knew you wouldn't want me to be his friend if I told you. I know I was wrong."

"Why do you always need friends that want you? Why do we always have to go through this?" It was happening again, just like with Kenneth.

There was also another guy after Kenneth. And now he had gained another friend that liked him. Why did he need this?

"I promise nothing ever happened or ever will happen! I don't like him." "I'm not worried about that. I don't like that you hide things from me or always need friends that like you."

It was the truth. I had no doubt in my mind that James and Juan had nothing going on. It was not about that at all for me. I hated Juan sharing secrets with someone else. Why did he feel the need to hide it from me?

"I am sorry," Juan said.

I did not speak to him the whole ride home. I was angry that he allowed James into our home, our work life, and our personal life with this secret being held from me.

I woke up still angry the next day and went into a shell. I had no words for Juan, and he didn't seem to have any words either. He stuck to himself and did not speak. It made me even angrier that he was not reaching out to me, trying to make things better. He was the one that fucked up, but he's giving me the silent treatment? Who did he think he was?

By the third day of not speaking, I had had enough of him not saying anything to me. So as he was in the kitchen making dinner, I walked in and started yelling at him.

"How can you walk around here like I am the one who fucked up and did something to you? How can you be giving me the silent treatment? I can't believe you! You know what? FUCK YOU!"

I knew this would pierce his soul and make him see that I was serious. Juan and I never cussed at each other, and he knew how I felt about speaking to each other like this, but I was angry. He was stunned; I had gotten his attention. Just as my mom and Carla did when they said it to me.

"I am not giving you the silent treatment. I just don't know what to say to you. It seems like we have grown apart this year like we don't really connect anymore."

I couldn't understand where he was coming from. I know that over the past couple of months, we weren't as in sync, and we had even had a horrible vacation a month ago, where we argued the whole time during Memorial Day weekend in Puerto Rico. I didn't think things were that bad. He would always complain about me not hearing him or understanding him. I could never figure out what he was searching for in me.

"You are always saying that, but you are never specific. It's like you don't even care," I responded.

"Sometimes I wonder if we have reached the end of our time together. Like maybe we have helped each other grow as much as we can," Juan said.

"Oh, so you think we should get a divorce?" I asked with a shocked look on my face.

"Sometimes," Juan responded.

I could not believe my ears. Was he serious? His words were not resonating with me at all. It was strange; it seemed I should have been devastated hearing those words—and part of me was—but overall, I did not feel threatened. I knew Juan was just going through the motions. I also knew that it was a part of his character to retreat when things got bad. He had abandonment issues. I knew he wasn't going anywhere, and I wasn't going to let him, even though things were rocky. He would soon realize again that our relationship is great. My anger quickly went away. He was hurting too.

"Wow. I didn't expect that. I'm not sure what to say."

"Can we go and talk to Sheila about it?"

Juan had never suggested going to see Sheila. This made me feel good.

"Sure, schedule the appointment. I am always down to see her."

As always, Sheila helped us achieve another breakthrough. It seemed that every time we go through one of these major challenges, she shows us how it is always about what each of us is experiencing individually and our need to release control, to allow each other to simply be.

I learned that I needed to stop trying to control Juan's relationship and self-discovery. I learned that I needed to allow him to figure out why he needed friends around that liked him. It kept happening over and over again no matter what I did, and why was I trying to stop it? What was I afraid of?

Sheila also helped us discover and own the energy each of us brought to the relationship. It seemed as though since Juan and I got together, we would always have this power struggle between us that I could never figure out. Sheila explained masculine and feminine energy and how both are needed to make a relationship work. Opposites are always drawn to one another, and it has nothing to do with being a male or a female. The masculine energy is the "doer" in the relationship or the person who moves with actions and solutions. It is typically the person who drives the relationship forward while maintaining a functioning life. That was definitely me. The feminine energy we learned is the "feeler" or the person who brings the emotions to the relationship. That was definitely Juan.

Throughout our entire relationship, I was trying to make Juan into a doer. I subconsciously always felt that all men should be doers, just as my father taught me, and I expected Juan to be one too. I didn't see the value of the emotions he brought to the relationship and would resent him for not being more of a "man." I was doing to him, what was done to me. I often referred to him as irresponsible or accused him of not taking the initiative in our relationship and life. I always had to be the one to make sure responsibilities were taken care of. Learning this helped me release and accept not only Juan for who he was, but also accept more of who I am. I embraced my role as the doer and Juan as the feeler. This revelation made a significant impact on our marriage. It took us to another stage in our life partnership.

Like in our relationship, we were finally able to settle into our roles and release control, also allowing a positive environment within our business. We decided that I would be the CEO of our company, and Juan would be COO. I let go of my I.T. contracts once and for all so that I could pour all attention into our business and passions. With a new contract with Lexus, Juan got back on the road, which put me back at the forefront of our business and the foundation. Having to do press and meetings on my own helped me rekindle the flame that I dulled because I felt it would make Juan feel more secure when we started the business together. I now realized that a large part of that was me not being ready to let my light shine. The time apart also forced both of us to rediscover ourselves and who we are as individuals, and not just "Juan & Gee," which is something we struggled with most of our marriage. Now in the right positions, we began to thrive individually and together.

"I think I want to drop Session and just become a Smalls," Juan said to me while on the way home from voting in the controversial 2016 Trump/Clinton presidential election.

"Really? Where did that come from?"

"Well, I was thinking as I saw my name on my voter's card that I never related to it, so why am I keeping it? That's just the name of my mother's boyfriend of a few months that she had at the time I was born. It's not even my dad's name. And then my cousin, Peaches, kinda put the thought in my head last week when she asked why I kept that name. You and Lil Gee are my family, so I am a Smalls. That's what resonates with me," Juan replied.

My heart got full, and my eyes welled up. I may not have been a feeler, but he sure knew how to bring a tear to my eye.

"That makes me so happy. I would love for you to carry my last name."

By the end of 2016 and after eight years of relationship and seven years of marriage, we were officially the Smalls family. I almost felt like we are extra-married after he changed his name. Somehow it made us more official.

27

IF IT WASN'T FOR THE KIDS

MY FATHER NEVER let us forget that if it wasn't for my sister and me, he would have been gone a long time ago. From where I stood growing up, my parents didn't have an excellent relationship. They argued often, and we rarely spent time together as a family except for the holidays. My mother had her friends, and my father had his. My father seemed to do his best to stay out of my mom's way, but he never could escape all of her "nagging."

"Quit naggin' Rita," often spewed from my father's mouth to my mother.

I remember their arguments would get so heated sometimes, I would lie in my bed at night and cry until they stopped. My mom would often jump in my father's face and even push him sometimes. She was the ultimate agitator. I never saw my father hit my mother, but once I walked in from junior high school and found my mother crying over the sink in the kitchen, holding a bloody paper towel to her head. My eyes widened in shock.

"Yo...Yo...your father hi-hit, me," she said to me as she was trying to catch her breath. I immediately knew she had finally pushed him too far, and he struck back. And although I knew my mom probably hit him first, my anger quickly grew for my father. I would later find out from my sister that it was my father's watch that caused the bleeding. It cut her forehead after he snatched his arm away from her as she tried to grab ahold of him. I walked to the back of the house and opened the door to the patio to find him there sitting in a chair, smoking a cigarette. His forearms rested on his thighs as they swayed back and forth. I could tell he felt anxious, shameful, angry, and regretful. He could not even look up at me.

"Your mother keeps pushing me, Greg. She keeps pushing me. If it wasn't for you kids, I wouldn't be here."

That was always his thing to say when he got mad with her. He made it clear to me that he wasn't here because he loved my mother. Hell, that wasn't surprising. I never even heard either of them say it to one another. And while I genuinely believe that he expressed this with good intention, for him to say, "Look at what I'm sacrificing for my kids," never made me feel good. It made me feel like my mother was a bad person or unlovable, which in turn built resentment for my dad for feeling this way about her. It also made me feel as if I were the reason for his unhappiness. I was a burden, something he wished away.

"If it wasn't for the kids...," rings so loudly in my head.

"If it wasn't for the kids..." "If it wasn't for the kids..."

I knew that hurt my mother to the core. And it wasn't until 2017 while talking to Mom on Mother's Day that I was made aware of just how deep that statement hurt.

A couple of months earlier, while planning my fortieth birthday, I decided I wanted to start off by celebrating with family and friends I grew up with. I wanted to host the celebration under my mother's roof, the only home I lived in for 18 years before moving to Atlanta. I wanted to reconnect with everyone who'd helped make me into the forty-year-old man I'd become. However, when I presented the idea to my mother, she immediately shut it down with all types of negative rhetoric on why it was not a good idea and how she didn't want people in her house. But that was my mother. In hindsight, her reaction had nothing to do with me and everything to do with her. It's just how she is. However, at the moment, I was extremely hurt and offended.

This incident brought many issues I was holding on to, regarding my mother, to surface. It reminded me of the time she forgot that it was my 11th birthday and started asking me to do all types of chores around the house. I was visibly upset that she was not only asking me to do chores on my birthday, but she also was not acknowledging it. Her brother, my drunken Uncle Tommy, who was sharing a bed with me at the time, reminded her that it was my birthday. Instead of being apologetic or showing sympathy, she brushed it off with jokes about me being a little boy and wanting a toy for my birthday. That crushed me. It made me feel insignificant like I didn't matter. My birthday or any other time I am celebrated has been an awkward time for me ever since. I never really forgave my mother for that, or for making me share a room and bed with her unfamiliar brother who often came home late at night drunk. I can still smell the liquor coming out of his pores. I literally would have to run to the bathroom to throw up by the time I woke in the morning because the smell in my 150 square foot room was so strong.

She not wanting to host my fortieth birthday party made me feel humiliated. Stupid. Unloved. Silly for wanting to be celebrated. Foolish for wanting to spend it with her. I was that eleven-year-old little boy all over again. I got so upset with my mother, but I showed the nonchalant, "ain't-shit-wrong-wit-me" type of anger. I wouldn't call. Conversations were dry. On the rare occasion we did talk, everything was always "fine." The connection was undeniably broken, and she knew it. In classic Momma fashion, she complained to my sister about how I was acting. My sister told me, and I, in turn, talked about my mother. Typical circle of family drama.

Well, it all came to a head two months later on Mother's Day. For the past ten or so years, I made it home for every Mother's Day. This year, I decided I was not going to go.

"She never comes to see me, not even when invited for The Gentlemen's Ball, so why should I continue to make an effort to see her?" I was fed up. I was tired of feeling unsupported by the one person I wanted the most support and approval from. I was being petty because I was hurt.

Although I decided not to visit, I knew I had to at least call. I wasn't so upset that I would not recognize the woman who gave me life. It was around 11 a.m., and I was still lying in our king-size bed while gazing out of the window of our hi-rise condo.

"Happy Mother's Day." It took everything in me to make the call.

"Thank you, Gregory. What are you up to? About to head to your event?"

This was the excuse I gave her for not going to see her. I didn't have the balls to just tell her why at the time. And I wasn't in the business of deliberately hurting my mom's feelings. I do and always will have a soft spot for her, but I did want to make the point. She got it. It was now time to confess.

"I didn't have to work. I lied because I did not want to come to see you. I lied because you really hurt my feelings on my birthday, and that really brought up a lot of stuff for me, a lot of deep-rooted issues that I've been holding on to."

I started to feel vulnerable. My wall of protection started to come down as I poured my heart out to her.

"Sometimes, I just want my mommy, and you never could give me that. Sometimes I just want you to reach out and be held in your arms and hear you tell me you love me. Cradle me. Coddle me. Tell me it's going to be okay. Tell me how proud you are of all the work that I do. Tell me how you see greatness in me. Tell me that anything is possible, and I can do anything I put my mind to. Show sympathy and concern for things that I go through. I've always felt like I was a crybaby."

I could hear my mom sniffling on the other end of the phone. It hurt me to listen to her cry, but I knew I needed to get it all out for us to get past it. I'd been holding on to it for years.

"You always made me feel like my feelings didn't matter. That I was making a big deal about whatever I wanted to express to you. You made me feel like I shouldn't feel. Boys aren't supposed to cry. Tough it out. I remember as a child, I would always long for you to tell me you loved me. You only did if I were away for the summer, and we were about to get off the phone. And I remember each time you told me, I would cry as I said it back. That's just how much it meant to me to hear that from you. I think it was because I wasn't sure that you did. Just like Daddy, I always felt like a burden around you. I could never do anything right. I didn't know why you always yelled at me."

"When you immediately shut down my hopes of celebrating my fortieth birthday party at your house, I felt like a burden all over again. I couldn't understand why you never wanted to celebrate me, and it hurt me."

All of this came out within a matter of a minute. I never planned to express myself in this way, although I knew I would tell the truth about why I did not come down for Mother's Day. What I did not expect is for all the old wounds I thought were healed to resurface. I don't think she expected it either, but I could tell she needed the release too.

"I am sorry, Greg. I knew you were upset with me. I could tell something was wrong. I kept telling Tawny that, but she wouldn't believe me. I never meant to hurt you, and that's not what it was about when I acted that way about your birthday."

"I know I can be hard sometimes," she continued, "and I can't help it. It's just the way I grew up. I always said when I had kids, I would not treat my kids the way my mother treated me. She treated me like shit!"

My mother began to sob while telling me the story of how she grew up and the way her mother treated her and how her grandmother treated her mom. And while what my mother was telling me was not new, as a forty-year-old, I heard them differently this time. I wonder if my mother ever heard the words, "I love you," from her mother as a child. I doubt it.

She continued. "When Mom died, it was important for me to be there and make peace with her. We were able to rebuild our relationship over the years, and it helped me to understand her better and forgive her. I know we have to do the same thing."

Not only was my mother forgiving of how her mother Ruby treated her as a child, but she also forgave Ruby for disowning her after giving birth to my sister. My mother also shared some back story on her and my father's relationship.

"When I met your father, he was in love with another woman. We were sneaking around to see each other. He would only come over to my house, and he could never bring me around his friends."

This was news to me. I knew they didn't get married until years after I was born, but I had no idea their relationship started out that way. After about a year of being the side chick, my mom got pregnant.

She was terrified and wanted to get an abortion. She said she was afraid to raise a Black child by herself, but my father pleaded for her to keep it, promising to never leave her alone. Although a scared 22-year-old, my mom put her faith in my father.

She was in love with my father, crazy over him, really. I sometimes wonder if she got pregnant on purpose to have him as her own. I wouldn't put it past her or fault her for her decisions. I see her as not just as my mother but as a woman with a story of struggle, hustle, and triumph. She was a survivor and a fighter. Her life choices were all based on the decisions others made that impacted her life. She is not unlike many other women.

With the promise of my father, she decided to keep the baby, and nine months later, Kony was born. My father couldn't have been happier. She said she had never seen him so proud. They even had to make him leave the nursery because he was so loud with excitement. My mother felt my father so strongly wanted her to keep my sister partly because he wanted light-skinned children.

She believed my father carried depression with him all his life due to the way he was treated as a child. Their stories were similar, except in his case, it was his father and paternal-side of the family who treated him like shit, partly because of the rich, dark skin he had that mirrored his mom's side of the family. My father's side of the family's skin was lighter. I never knew this was a part of the reason he was rejected by them. I wondered if my father hated his black skin, too, and if he ever came to love the skin, he was in. I wondered if he deliberately picked my mother because, consciously or unconsciously, of feeling White was better. I wondered if he admired my light skin as I admired his dark skin.

When my mom reminded me of how my father was rejected and treated by his own dad, it made me realize that my dad, in a way, repeated the same pattern as his father. Maybe not to the extent of creating another family, but he did repeat the pattern of creating a family while in a committed relationship with another woman. But he chose differently. He married his mistress years after having two kids with her and moving them down to the Deep South. He was determined not to be like his father, and he held true to his word. He never did leave my mother, although they had their breaks. It makes so much sense finding out the full story and gives the statement, "if it wasn't for these kids," such a deeper meaning. The entire marriage started out as a duty to fulfill an obligation, and so he did.

What is so interesting is that I always told myself I would never stay in a marriage and be unhappy for the sake of the kids, and I didn't. I learned from my father what not to do, as he did from his.

That day, my mother and I really bonded on the phone. We had a mature conversation, one that allowed us the opportunity to see each other for who we were and the story that shaped us, separate from being mother and son. I also learned much more about her and my father's relationship than I had ever known. She told me stories of how bad they were abusing cocaine in the '80s and early '90s, which led to a lot of parental neglect. They even used and sold angel dust. I knew they partied a lot but never knew to what extent. I had also known my mother used a bit because I would often search her coat pockets and find cocaine straws and wads of cash. My dad? I was totally shocked. I knew he was an alcoholic, but I had no idea that he also used drugs so much, even up until his last few years of life.

I could not only forgive her, but I also understood her on a new level. I know my mother loves me and shows me the best way she knows how. This gives me peace. It also helps that she always refers to me as her "favorite" son. It is her way of showing affection and telling me she loves me. I love her for that.

Mom and I have had a couple of conversations like this in the past, at different stages in my life. But, just like any relationship, it takes constant communication and forgiveness to keep the bond. The thing about the parent-child relationship, though, is that as children, we are not able to express our hurt feelings or concerns we have with our parents. We are just supposed to listen and obey their every command. We aren't to let them know that we are displeased with their behavior towards us, or when they have hurt our feelings, so we bottle them up. The thing about bottling up emotions is they never go away until they are expressed. Just because I am an adult does not mean that one time when Daddy allowed his friends to poke fun at me is forgotten. I never forgot that time when I asked him to stop smoking cigarettes, and he told me I needed to stop eating so much because I was fat. I still get to have these conversations with Mom because she is still here. My dad isn't.

Although my dad never had a problem telling me he was proud of me, I rarely heard, "I love you," again after that one time he said it to me over the phone, after my mom had told us about her beating his girlfriend's ass. He did always share his wisdom with me any chance he could get. I appreciated that about him. I remember him giving me some advice once while fishing. The sun was blaring down on our backs as we sat in the small motorboat in the middle of the Wappoo River, with our lines cast out in the water.

"Bub, let me tell you something about relationships," he said. "When arguing, it's not about winning or determining who is right or wrong, but it's about finding a solution. Always focus on the solution."

I had to be in my early teens at this time. I believe the night before, he was arguing with my mom and venting in a roundabout way to me. I never did forget that nugget of wisdom and have carried it with me ever since. I always wonder what advice he would give me about Juan, or if he would have accepted Juan. Even accepted us. I always wondered if "as long as you're happy" would still have been his response to my life's big decisions. That was, until the night I ran into Lakara, the lady I'd met while on a group vacation in Puerto Rico during Memorial Day weekend of 2017 when Juan and I argued the entire time. I didn't get to have much personal time with her while on the trip, but I could tell she was a nice lady. A month later, as I was smoking a blunt on the patio with some friends at a bar on Auburn Avenue, Lakara approached me.

"Hey, Gee, is your son named after your dad?" she asked.

"Hmm, well, he is named after me, and my middle name is my father's first name, so in a way, he is," I replied curiously.

"Humph. Is his name Fred? Is that your son's name?"

"Umm, no, but that is my dad's middle name!" I astonishingly replied.

"Your dad is here, and he won't let me leave here without saying something to you. I hate doing things like this, but he is really adamant about it."

At this point, my mouth dropped open, and I was having these rushes of emotions. *What is this lady saying? How did she know my dad's name or that my son was named after him?* I believe we are all spirits, and some of us are just temporarily in a human form, so I didn't deny that my father could very well be present. However, it still took me by surprise.

"What's this island he keeps talking about? Did you grow up on an island?"

"Yes! I grew up on James Island. It's off the coast of Charleston." "Well, he is definitely making it clear to you that he is here." "Wow! Well, what he want?" I joked.

Lakara spent the next two hours in the corner of the patio, sharing these things with me that my father wanted me to know. She started off by telling me that he is always around me, protecting Lil Gee and me. Not only is he protecting me, but he is also guiding me in all the work that I do. He brought up my mother. He said their purpose of being together was to raise my sister and me, and they were soul mates. They loved each other. They were friends. They may not have been soul mates in the romantic sense, but they were meant to be together to raise the both of us. We were his purpose. And he knew love. He didn't want me to think he never experienced love, because he did…and there was plenty of it, including love shared with my mother. She said that my father wanted me to know that neither he nor my mom ever saw color in a way that everyone else did. They could not even understand on a human level why they were drawn to each other, but they were because of who you are becoming. You needed them as your parents. They both came from very strict and troubled childhoods and battled with anxiety and depression most of their lives. They found love and acceptance within each other, unlike anything they had ever experienced and were meant to be together.

He just didn't know how to express himself very well because he had never seen a healthy relationship. He had never seen men express emotions. He said he knows he made a lot of bad decisions when my sister and I were younger, but he never did quite figure out how to navigate an interracial marriage and raising biracial children. But he did know he did not want you to experience what he did as a Black man. He got mistreated as a Black man back then, especially in the military. It is why he always told you that he never wanted you to enlist and why he did not instill in you his plight. He wanted better for you. All of his life's struggles took a toll on him, and he never recovered, not to mention he never got over the death of his mom. This led to his alcohol and drug abuse.

He wanted me to know that he always knew about my sexuality but also knew I had to come to terms with it on my own. Besides, he really wanted a grandson who could continue the family name, so he wasn't about to stop that from happening.

This is so my dad! I thought back on Calvin, my old "hairstylist" who my Dad used to take me to so often. He and Calvin seemed to have a friendship. I wondered if my dad took me there because he knew Calvin and I were the same in many ways. I wondered if it was less about the fact that the regular barbers would not know how to cut my hair because they surely didn't seem to have an issue once I started to go to them in middle school.

"Your dad wants you to know that in this life that he was your father, it was complete. There was nothing more that he could have offered you, nothing more that he could have taught or shown you. He couldn't have taken you farther in life than he had already taken you. That is why shortly after his passing, he sent you Juan. He knew Juan was going to challenge you to make you into the man you are today and will continue to become. He said the night you all met, you both were headed in separate directions, but he redirected both of you so you could meet."

I started to cry.

"He knew that Juan would be the only one who could help make you the man you needed to be. No one else could do it. And he wants you to know that your journey together is just beginning. You all may think you have been together for a long time, but it's just beginning. If you ever wonder if your father would have accepted you, you do not have to wonder anymore. Not only does he accept you, but he also did this. He is making this happen for you, so you never have to question it. He is very proud of you."

By now, tears were cascading down my face as I realized that Daddy not only knew about me, but it was okay. He loved me for who I am, as I am.

Lakara interrupted the flow of my tears by ending with, "Oh, baby, your dad is taking all the credit for your life! He is saying, '*The Gentlemen's Ball? I did that! LoveWorks? I did that!*' Your upcoming TV shows—yes, shows!—he's doing that too! He's doing it all! He wants you to know that he knows you want to be a millionaire, and you will! He is saying you must finish the book. Are you writing a book?"

I stopped laughing and said, "Yes! I am, but I have not written in a while."

"Well, he says you have to finish the book. This book is not about you. It is not personal. This book is about freeing other people so that they don't have to go through the same struggles you went through. It is going to open the hearts and minds of so many people. And don't worry about what you are writing about yourself or your experience with others. Not even me. You will help other fathers with sons just like you. Your life will not change due to anything you write in this book. Of course, you will make lots of money, sell many products, go on Oprah, and all those things, but the truths of your experiences will never hinder you. They will only free you and others."

It was just five days before Father's Day, and through Lakara, he had given me the healing I didn't even know I needed.

Lil Gee, Gee, and Juan, The 5th Annual Gentlemen's Ball, 2016
(photo: Just4lovephotos)

Juan, Jakeem, Lil Gee, and Gee at Jakeem's High
School Graduation, Charleston, SC, 2016

Juan, Gee, and Lil Gee, family photo, January 2017 (photo: Ty Xavier Turner)

Gee on 40th birthday, first time going nude, feeling
completely liberated, Haulover Beach, FL, 2017

28

RELEASE, RENEW

"HEY, GEE! I'VE got the perfect role for you!" I read the text in the back of an Uber on the way to a friend's party. It was a week after I had spoken with Lakara, and Juan was back on the road. The text was from Henderson Maddox, CEO of Signal23TV, a network geared towards same-gender-loving Black men. Henderson lives in my building, and I'd always joked with him about casting me when I would bump into him in the lobby or elevator. We both knew I was only half-joking. My childhood passion for acting never went away.

Oh, gosh, I hope it's not a role where I have to show my body.

Signal23TV is known for its very sexy scenes, and I was not ready for all of that. He had offered me one or two roles before, but I was always too fearful of seeing it through.

I felt ready this time, so I texted, "Tell me more!"

"The character is the father of a 17-year-old son who is discovering his sexuality, and he is uncomfortable with his son being gay. Your role is a cop named Darnell. It's a comedy!"

I almost dropped my phone. Darnell? Seriously? The name of the very first character I auditioned for at seven-years-old and didn't get cast because I wasn't black enough? And now here I am being offered the role as a grown-up Darnell who has a son exactly the same age as mine? I knew this had to be the role for me. Although I was coming up with all types of fearful reasons I could not do it, I decided to suck it up and take the role. I knew God had sent this to me, and after reading the script and seeing that Darnell and his son were going through some of the same father-son challenges that Lil Gee and I had just gone through, affirmed my decision. And not only was I playing a Black father with one of the Blackest male names ever, I was also playing a cop, one of the most hyper-masculine professions out there. God sure did have one hell of a sense of humor.

As we approached the end of his sophomore year of high school, Lil Gee decided he did not want to spend it in Charleston like he normally would.

"Why not?" I asked him.

"It doesn't seem like there is anything down there for me. It seems like everybody down there is always so negative and so far behind. They don't do nothing with their lives. All of my friends from 'down the island' are either selling drugs or dropping out of school. I want to stay here and work."

Without me even saying it to him, Lil Gee had observed it on his own. I was glad that he was able to experience both worlds and see the difference.

"Well, you are going to have to tell your mom that."

"I already told her. She don't really want me down there either. She says there is nothing for me there, but she just wants to make sure I don't sit around doing nothing."

I was surprised to hear him say that and replied, "That's one of the reasons I wanted you to grow up here. I wanted you to see more possibilities in life that I knew you wouldn't be exposed to in Charleston."

"Then why didn't you fight for me to stay here?" Lil Gee looked up at me with the biggest look of confusion on his face.

"I did!" He was 16 now, and I guess it was by far time I told him. "You don't remember that day we all went to court? You were about eight years old."

"Yea, I do remember something like that, but I never knew why I was there."

"Well, it was because me and your mom did not agree on what should happen with you, so we had to go to court. Me and your mom have not really gotten along since then. I made a lot of people mad by taking her to court to fight for custody of you."

"I knew she didn't really mess with you like that. I never knew why, though."

"Well, that is why. She got really upset at me for taking her to court. Let me tell you a little history about the both of us." I began to tell him the story of his mom and me, from the time we met up until the present day. He learned about how I hid my sexuality, married her, divorced her, and then ended up taking her to family court. He sat with an amused look on his face like he was excited that all of that was going on over him. I could tell it made him feel loved. I always wondered if the fact that his mom and I did not get along affected him, but it seemed as though he was unbothered. He never remembered us having a different relationship than what it was, so I guess it was normal to him. It seems we both did an excellent job of keeping him from getting in-between our mess. I was at least proud of us for that, even though we could barely be in the same room with one another.

I felt good about being able to tell Lil Gee that I did fight for him. That very moment made all of those years of struggle worth it. I could not imagine what my response would have been had I never fought for him.

During the summer of 2017, I got Lil Gee a job as a prep cook at a restaurant where one of my friends worked as a chef. He caught the Marta train there five days a week and then hung out with his friends and new girlfriend during his free time. Besides eating dinner together when he was home and playing basketball every so often, my relationship with Lil Gee began to waver. By the time school had started back, Lil Gee was becoming more and more distant. We would go through spurts where we would have real deep, life-changing conversations and bond, but then his grades would start slipping in school, and I'd have to be strict and punish him again. This always caused a strain on our relationship. I had gotten to the point where I did not know what to do with him anymore. No matter what restriction I put on him, from making him sit at the table for hours to do homework, removing his room door, and even taking away his social media didn't make him care about school. He didn't seem to care about anything.

The week before Christmas break was approaching when I was doing one of my routine checks through Lil Gee's room while he was at school. I did this periodically just to see what he may have been up to that I did not know about. While searching through his desk drawer, I found his old iPhone 3.0 that he had a couple of years prior. I didn't even know he still had it and was curious to know what he was doing with it. I powered it on, only to be blocked by a passcode request that I did not know.

At about 7 p.m., he walked through the door after staying after school to get extra help from one of his teachers, something he did at least two or three times a week.

"Hey," Lil Gee said.

"Hey, Gee. How was your day?"

"It was good. How was yours?"

"It was good, nothing special. I did find this phone while going through your room. Here, unlock it." I removed the phone from my back pocket and handed it to him. His eyes grew big, and I could tell he was nervous.

Lil Gee took the phone out of my hand and quickly put in a four-digit passcode.

"What was that you put in?" I asked. "You did it so fast."

"3287," he said with his head down.

"Thanks. I'll take a look at it later."

By the look on his face, I could tell the phone was going to reveal things he did not want me to know. I was not looking forward to going through the phone. I really feared what I would find. However, I knew it was necessary. Although I talked openly with him about sex, drugs, alcohol, relationships, and general life challenges, he didn't always speak openly with me. Over the years, I learned to stop taking it personally, realizing that I was still "Dad" at the end of the day. No matter what, my son was not going to tell me everything. He was a teenager, after all.

When I have searched his phone in the past, I have found things like pics of him smoking weed, and who he had sex with, but the most disturbing was the personality he put on when he's around his friends. It's almost as if he turns into 21 Savage, one of his favorite rappers. I've always felt all of these were things he could come and talk to me about, but he never did unless he got caught. I remember when I saw this personality he was putting on, it really made me question how he saw me as a man. Why was he acting like some thug off of the street? Why did he feel the need to mimic this personality? I did not act like this and have always tried to teach him how to be a respectful gentleman. I started to question myself and my impact on his life. Was I Black enough and man enough for him as a father? After having a discussion with him and asking him to name three Black men who he thought were positive role models, he mentioned me. I then relaxed, realizing this was normal teenager stuff.

I had already figured that he was using the secret phone for social media, something I restricted him from until he brought his grades up. That had me pissed already because I put a lot of trust in Lil Gee to follow the rules. For the most part, he obeyed, but again, he is a teenager.

It was around 11:00 p.m., and Juan had already fallen into a deep slumber next to me as my eyes started to get heavy while watching "The Golden Girls." Deciding that it was time to call it a night, I grabbed the remote and turned the TV off. As I turned over to turn off my lamp, I saw the old iPhone sitting on my nightstand. I had forgotten about it, and as tired as I was, curiosity still got the best of me, so I put 3287 in and unlocked the phone. Of course, the first thing I notice was Snapchat and Instagram, his two favorite social media apps. His Snapchat was pretty clean due to the 24-hour expiration time of all of its posts, but I was not ready for what I found while scrolling through his text messages, Instagram, and DMs. My son had been posting videos of him cutting class while smoking weed, riding down the highway in the backseat of his best friend's car. There were his alleged sexcapades, and I also found private messages where he was meeting up with students to sell weed edibles at school!

My son was selling drugs?

The very thing I fought so hard for him not to get into, the biggest fear I had of him growing up in Charleston, yet here he was right under my roof, and I had no idea what he was doing.

What kind of father was I?

How could I not know what was going on?

Did I influence him to be so fascinated with weed?

Not only did I find out all of the mess he had been getting into, but I also found several disturbing posts he had made about me. The worst was a screen-recording he posted, of videos I posted on Instagram, saying things like "Look at this ugly ass nigga!" or "This nigga ugly as fuck!" and "Man, he lame as fuck!"

I could not believe what I was hearing and seeing. My heart instantly broke at the sounds and visuals of my son, demeaning me on social media to his friends. Did he really feel that way about me? Was he really that upset with me that it would cause him to make such a video? Lil Gee had never shown this type of anger or disrespect towards me before.

As I scrolled through a year of posts and messages, there were times where he would cuss me out for putting such strict rules on him. He also posted about how I didn't care about him anymore and how I've given up on him after being more lenient. I had even seen where he posted about committing suicide after he and his girlfriend broke up. She commented, "You ain't gonna do shit, nigga! You always talking that shit!" Was he using suicide to be manipulative? Is this what he did before as well? Was his mom right when she said he was just emotional back then? With every word, my heart broke more and more.

Four hours had passed, and I still could not fall asleep or stop thinking about all of the things I had found on the phone. Tears ran down my face from feeling the heartbreak when I was not feeling anger and fury from all the lies and deception Lil Gee had kept up. I could not stop thinking about where I went wrong and how I could have prevented him from taking this path. I just did not know what to do. I had tried everything that I knew to do to help him get on track, but he still was not responding. I felt like such a bad parent.

Is this my fault?

Was I not talking to him enough?
Was I not spending enough time with him?
Should I have made him hang out with me all of those times he said no?
Should I have made him do more in school? Was I too lenient?
Did my smoking weed influence him?
Should I have always been so open with him?

The slam of the door and turn of the key woke me up out of my light sleep. It was 7:20 a.m., and Lil Gee had just walked out the door to head out for school. I had drifted off to sleep around 4:30 a.m. after my emotions had finally settled a bit. Juan was in a deep slumber, still at least two hours before he would be getting up. I felt like I was wide awake, so I decided to head to the gym to get in some early morning cardio. I could use the stress relief. I just did not know what to do, and I was so angry at Lil Gee. I knew I had to call Carla to let her know what was going on, which was something that I dreaded doing. Carla and I still did not speak very often; in fact, we could go months without as much a text to one another. I knew Carla would blame me for what was going on, and she probably had every right to. What kind of parent was I to have raised a son that felt he needed to turn to the things he did to validate him? I was so afraid for my son. Raising a young Black man in America was a terrifying thing for me, especially during these times of prevalent shootings, the corrupt prison system, and modern-day lynching of Black men by police officers with no protection from the leader of the "Free" World, President Trump, aka "#45." I felt like I was failing miserably at protecting him.

Maybe it was time for him to go live with Carla. How else can I save him from continuing forward? It was clear to me that I did not have the power to influence his decisions, and there were people and things around him that outweighed me. Maybe stripping away his comfort zone and giving him a new environment is what he needed to make a change in his life. Here he was living on the 40th floor of a high-rise condo in Midtown Atlanta with two dads, but he was acting like he was from the streets, even calling his old iPhone his "trap phone." He was taking his life for granted, and maybe some time down there in the country where his mom lived would do him some good. Leaving a high school of over 3,000 students and switching to one with less than 200 would really shake things up for him. I am sure Carla would love the opportunity to have him back with her. She had even bought a brand new house in a great neighborhood and had a room set up for him. It would also be nice for him and his mom to spend some quality time together before he graduated high school. I know they both needed it, especially her.

But is that really the right thing? How can I live without him?

Will he get into even more trouble if he moves? Will he resent me?

After taking the last sip of my protein shake, I rinsed out the reusable bottle and placed it in the sink. I could start to feel myself get incredibly anxious as I prepared to call Carla. I knew she was going to let me have it.

"Hello," Carla answered, her voice as dry as usual.

"Hey, Carla. How are you?" I wondered if she could hear the nervousness in my voice. I hated that she still had this power over me.

"Fine, and you?"

"I'm okay. Well, actually, I'm not so okay. I had to call you to let you know what your son's been getting into. I was going through Gee's room and found an old phone he's been using for social media, and he's been really doing some fucked up shit." Conveniently, she's her son now.

"What has he been doing? What happened"? Her dryness quickly turned into motherly concern.

"Well first off, he's been cutting class to hang out and smoke weed. And then there's what he's posting. His social media profile is pretty much full of posts acting as if he's a porn star and drug dealer. Which he has been doing too."

"What? He's been dealing drugs? What kind of drugs?"

"Well, he's been selling weed edibles. This was about two months ago. It doesn't look like he still is, but I have yet to ask him about it because I just found this out last night. And he's been selling them at school! I just don't know what else to do with him, Carla. Gee knows better. We have these talks all the time. He knows he can go to jail and get expelled from school. He knows better than to post all that dumb shit on social media!"

I knew Carla couldn't wait to go in on me, but she was pretty calm.

"You know, I have these talks with him too, Greg. It's like you can only talk to him so much. He's gonna do what he wants to do. You can't control them, teenagers, these days."

I was shocked to hear Carla respond so calmly. She wasn't blaming me?

"I think it might be a good idea if he comes down there to live with you. He needs to get away from his friends, who are all doing the same things. He is really taking his life for granted here, acting like he is some big dope boy from the streets. Let him go down there in that country and be a big bad boy! I am so mad at him, I can't even talk to him right now!"

"Yeah, I think that might be a good idea too. I'll get his room and everything set up. I am also quitting my daytime job next week, so I will have a lot of time. He might need that change." I could hear Carla's voice get excited at the thought of it. "When you thinking he should come?"

"Winter break. It's perfect timing for it. "

"Oh, okay. I'm definitely going to have a talk with him when he gets out of school."

Carla and I talked about thirty more minutes about Lil Gee and our parenting over the years. It was really good to have this type of conversation with Carla. It was something that I always missed. Maybe this could be the start of something new for us.

"Well, let me know how your conversation goes with him," Carla said.

"Okay. I don't even know what to say to him right now, to be honest with you. I am just so hurt and angry."

"I understand. Try not to stress yourself. I'll let you know how our conversation goes too. I appreciate you telling me."

"No problem. I'll talk to you later. Bye."

"Bye."

The call went a lot better than I expected. I took a long, deep breath. I just knew that Carla was going to blame it on me. Hell, I blamed me. Here I am thinking I am this amazing father, and all along, my son is right under my nose has an entire life that I had no clue about. I felt like a complete failure at the biggest job I had in the world, one that I took very seriously, one that I took pride in. When Carla and I first divorced, I made a point not to abandon my son. I wanted to do everything in my power to not be one of those deadbeat dads or even a part-time dad that only saw his kid every other weekend and on holidays. I refused to have people say that I left my wife and son to be gay.

When Carla took Lil Gee to Charleston back in 2008, I started to feel I was becoming one of my biggest fears: a part-time dad. And when Carla did not hold up her end of the bargain and treated me as if I had no rights, I felt even more threatened. My son was slipping through my fingers, and I refused to let it happen. All I ever wanted was equal say, and I was going to do all I needed to do to have it, and I won. Not only did I win, but I gained more than I asked for. The court took all of Carla's rights away and saw fit that Lil Gee would be best if he were raised with me. But was he? Was Carla right back then? Was Lil Gee better off with her? Would things have turned out this way had I never taken Carla to court?

Now I see how my emotions took over my heart and mind back in 2009 when I took Carla to court. I was so upset at her for denying my rights and so fearful of losing my place as a father in Lil Gee's life after "turning gay" that I used all I could to win custody in court. I still believed that the best place for Lil Gee to be at the time was with me, but I can also say that the picture that was painted of her in court was not who she was. Although it was the environment in which she lived, Carla never drank, smoked, or used any drugs. She actually hated it.

And was Carla's then-boyfriend Tank a real threat to my son sitting behind bars for ten years? Sure, Carla may have been a little naive for being in a relationship with him, but I know that Carla would never put our son in the danger of drugs. She's always been firmly against any drugs, and I know she would do all she could to keep Lil Gee away from them, even if I didn't think she was making the best decisions. She had hoped that Tank would do the right thing after being released. At that time, I also really felt she was using the relationship, throwing it in my face. After becoming conscious of how the criminal justice system is set up to keep our Black men in prison, it makes me feel like a complete sellout for bringing Tank, my childhood friend, into the court case. I did not see how this could have been damaging to him, and I still don't know if it was or not; however, it makes me feel bad knowing that my bringing his name into our custody case, could have caused him harm as he navigated our oppressive judicial system.

That day in court was the last day Carla allowed me any room to hurt her again. She never gave me the opportunity, no matter how many times I tried to reconcile with her. Offering her apology after apology, she never opened that door again. Gracey would always say she thought Carla was still in love with me, and that's why she hated me so much, but I now understand the real reason. She refused to open herself back up to me after hurting her over and over again for 18 years. She would never allow herself to trust me again, or better yet, trust herself around me. I was her kryptonite. I finally get it, and I cannot blame her, no matter how tough it's been to co-parent through it all.

I sat at my desk, anxious for Lil Gee to walk through the door from school. I was fuming and had no idea what words would come out of my mouth. At 4 p.m., his key turned the lock, and I immediately sat up. As I heard his footsteps walk towards my office, my heart started to race.

"Hey," Lil Gee said. He was either trying to act as if nothing happened, or he was hopeful that I hadn't checked the phone yet.

I swiveled around my white leather chair to face him as he stood in the door.

"Hey, Gee. Come in here and let me talk to you. I have several questions, and I don't want you to lie, or I am going to be even more pissed than I already am."

"Okay." I could see the fear in his eyes.

"Were you selling drugs?"

"I was like two months ago. Not anymore." He said without emotion, acting as if it was not a big deal.

"What the fuck? You mean you been selling drugs? How many times have we had this conversation, Gee? What the fuck is wrong with you? Who do you think you are? Some trap boy? You live in a high-rise with two dads. You are no trap boy! You are just a wannabe! I trusted you, and all you want to do is cut class to smoke weed? You don't give a shit about nobody or no one! Not even yourself!"

"Yesss, I doooo."

"Shut up! No, you don't! And you want to get online to make fun of me calling me some ugly ass nigga? I'm no fucking nigga, and don't you ever disrespect me like that! You might want to disrespect yourself, but you not going to be disrespecting me! And I've already told your mother what's going on, and you are going to live with her! Get the fuck out of my face!"

Fuming, I could not believe how I lost control like that. Lil Gee's face was stunned, but he would not crack. He just left as if I had just yelled at him for getting detention. He really did not care, and I couldn't understand it. I was so angry and hurt, I could not see clearly. Did my son even respect me?

Later on that night, I laid in bed and told Juan what was going on with Lil Gee and how it made me feel. I hadn't remembered feeling such pain since the death of my father. After all the hearts I've broken, especially his mother's, I just knew that one day I was going to have my heart broken too. I just never thought it would be my son who did it.

"I just can't believe this is happening. I feel like such a failure, Juan. Here I am supposed to be some Life Coach and running a foundation that's all about being an influencing respectful gentleman, and I can't even influence my own son. What kind of father am I?"

Tears were falling from my eyes as Juan wrapped his arms around me tightly from behind, spooning me as I laid in the fetal position.

"Don't say that, Gee. You are a great father! An amazing father! I can't even think of a better father than you, and don't you worry, Lil Gee is going to see that one day. He is just being a teenager right now."

"You should have seen how he looked at me! Like he didn't even care. He was unbothered. No remorse at all! Even if I was to consider him staying here, I couldn't even let myself do it! He needs to learn a lesson! If I don't do something drastic, he will not learn."

"Are you sure you're ready for that?"

"No!" I busted out in tears and sobbed as Juan held me tighter until I drifted off to sleep. I was losing my son.

The next day Lil Gee posted a long message on his Instagram page about what he was going through. I have no idea how he was posting it, and I didn't even have the strength to try and find out. The message read, "Well, it's over for me. I am busted. My dad found my trap phone and found out about all the things I've been doing. Selling drugs, cutting class, the weed, the sex, everything! I have never seen him so mad at me in my life. I really fucked up this time. I know my mom won't even be able to look at me. My dad is giving up on me. He is kicking me out and making me move back to Charleston. After the court case and how hard he fought for me to grow up here, now he don't give a fuck. I can't believe this. I am going to miss all of y'all!"

Kicking him out of the house? Giving up on him? Is that how he really felt?! Was he playing a victim? I did not even have time to think about it, although it tugged at my heart.

It was the last day of school before winter break, and I hadn't spoken to Lil Gee for four days since he stood in my office when all I could get out were cuss words. Christmas was that following Sunday, and I had decided to let Lil Gee go over his Aunt Nikki's house even though it was my year to have him. His mom was going to be there, and I thought it would be best if he spent it with her seeing that I still was not able to talk to him. The day before, he had come into my office after school, trying to apologize.

"Can I talk to you, Daddy?"

I turned around in my chair and faced Lil Gee at the door.

"Sure, what is it?"

"I just wanted to apologize for lying to you and posting those videos of you on Instagram. It was just a joke. I did not mean it." Lil Gee's eyes looked intently to see what my response was going to be.

"Okay. Thanks." I turned back around, and Lil Gee exited. I was still angry.

I was also still checking his text messages and saw one that he sent to his best friend that pissed me off. It read, "This nigga still walking around here mad and shit. He still ain't even talking to me. He all in his feelings. He really is doing too damn much."

I had no words for my son. I decided that I would need to wait to speak to Lil Gee until we were able to book a session with Chris. I had also never felt so lost as a parent in my life, and I was desperate for his help. He was the only one I could trust that could help us through this, and Lil Gee trusted him too. After all, he had seen him ever since he moved back five years before in 2013.

After picking Lil Gee up the day after Christmas at his Aunt Nikki's house, we said hi and then headed straight to Chris's office without saying another word.

"So, guys, what's going on?" Chris asked. "It's not too often that I get to see both of you."

Lil Gee stayed close to the corner of the couch with his head down. I sat on the other end of the couch with my arms folded.

"Well, Chris, a lot is going on. Last week I found a backup phone that Lil Gee's been using, and I found out a whole lot about him." I went on to fill Chris in on my findings and about the solution of sending him back to Charleston.

"Oh, wow! That's a lot."

"Yes, it is." Tears started to roll down my face. "No one has ever made me cry like this before. I am just so afraid for him. I just don't know who he is. He thinks he is some trap boy on the streets while cops are just dying to kill boys that look like him! I don't want to have to bury my son! Black men in America cannot afford to act like this! We don't get second chances!"

I wept, and Lil Gee turned at me and started aggressively wiping his eyes. He always did that to try and hold back his tears, but it wasn't working.

Chris asked, "Do you have anything to say Lil Gee, about how your father feels?"

"I am sorry, Daddy. I am sorry, I just get so caught up in this other person I've created, and I don't know how to stop sometimes. I am sorry." I moved over and held Lil Gee.

"Son, you only have to be yourself. You are perfect just the way you are, and I just wish you could see that and love that about you. You are such an amazing young man that I am proud of. You do not have to impress anyone. You have people that love you so much. I love you so much, and this is not me giving up on you. This is me trying to save your life. I would never give up on you. I love you more than you will ever know, and I will always fight for you. "

"I love you too, Daddy, and I understand having to move to Charleston. I think it is best, too, even though it will be hard."

Lil Gee and I hugged and cried for a few more minutes until we heard the alarm go off, notifying us that our time was up. It was the best session we had ever had together, and even though we had to go through some mess to get there, Lil Gee and I felt closer than ever. It was what we needed.

Carla and I decided to meet in Augusta, so neither of us had to drive the entire way. The last time I had seen Carla was at one of Lil Gee's basketball games in the 7th grade. She sat on one side of the gym, and I sat on the other, but we did say hey to each other in passing. I was somewhat looking forward to seeing Carla. I was hopeful that our interaction would be a lot more pleasant or at least less awkward than it did in the past.

I cried all week as Lil Gee packed his things, keeping a few items he wanted to leave here in Atlanta and throwing away the rest. Watching him pack was very hard for me. I felt like I was losing my baby boy. But I wasn't looking at a little boy anymore; I was watching a young man. As he was putting the last few items in his suitcase that gloomy Saturday morning, I watched him and questioned myself on where the time went. It seemed it was just yesterday that he sat across from me at the booth of The Cheesecake Factory, asking me for a turtle cheesecake. Now it feels like I am sending him off to college a year and a half early, never to return again. He had turned into a man before my very eyes.

Juan was driving, and Lil Gee sat in the back seat. Over the past week, Lil Gee and I really got to spend a lot of time together talking and mending our relationship. I was proud of him for how he took responsibility for the mistakes he had made and for his attitude towards starting a new life in Charleston. He was looking forward to how the change would impact his life for the better. His self-awareness astounded me, and although I was hard on myself through this whole ordeal, I knew the impact I have had on him as his father contributes to that. Keeping self-awareness is one thing that I am most proud of impressing upon him. I know that this lesson will take him very far in life.

We pulled up to the Dunkin' Donuts, where we had agreed to meet, and Carla was running about thirty minutes late. It was not unlike her to be late, and it was not unlike me to be early, so neither surprised me. When they did finally pull up in their big gray SUV, I could see Carla in the passenger seat talking on the phone. Juan and I got out of the truck and headed towards the back so we could unload Lil Gee's belongings while Lil Gee went up to the passenger side to say hi to his mom. Carla put the window down and said hey to Lil Gee, while her husband Leroy got out to help us load up their SUV.

Leroy extended his hand to me. "Hey, man. How are you?"

"I am well, and you?" I responded, putting my other arm around him for a half hug.

"I can't complain. I'm enjoying the mild weather." Leroy was always pleasant when I saw him, although it had only been a few times.

"So am I, especially for December!" Leroy and Carla got married shortly after they moved in together years ago. One day Lil Gee came home from a week's vacation with her and told me his mom had gotten married the weekend before. I was happy that Carla had gotten married again.

The three of us loaded up the SUV while Lil Gee watched, and Carla sat in the truck on the phone. I couldn't believe that she wasn't coming out to speak. I was hoping that this would be an opportunity for us to start working together, but Carla still refused to let me in.

"Hey, Carla!" I yelled through the back of the SUV.

"Oh, hey, Greg. My bad. I'm coming out there. Let me get off this phone," Carla responded but continued to chat on the phone.

I knew she had no intention of getting off, and it was okay.

We put the last of the bags in the truck, and Lil Gee went over to give Juan a hug.

"I love you. Be good!" Juan said to Lil Gee. "I love you too," Lil Gee responded.

I always appreciated that they told each other they loved one another.

Lil Gee walked over to me with that bashful smile on his face while looking down, something he's done since he was a baby when he was embarrassed about his vulnerability towards me.

"I love you, Gee, and I am going to miss you. And just in case I didn't make it clear to you, I forgive you for everything. I am always here for you. I'm proud of how you are handling this. Be good, and love on ya Momma."

"Thank you, Daddy. I love you too."

Lil Gee and I hugged for several seconds before he gave me one last squeeze and jumped in his mom and stepdad's SUV.

As I watched them drive away, I realized for the very first time that I was able to let Lil Gee go without any guilt or need to control what was going to happen to him. I knew that he was his own person, and just like I had to experience my own journey and relationships to help me be the person I am today—he does too. This move, with all of its heartaches, was a part of that. As kids, we see our parents as the be-all, end-all. We always look for their love and approval, never realizing that they are just humans trying to figure out life just like us. Unfortunately—or fortunately, depending on how we look at it—our parents' decisions, challenges, and bad days can have lasting impressions on us well into adulthood. Just as I've had to heal wounds and mend fences with my parents as an adult, I know Lil Gee will one day recognize the wounds I have layered upon him. Although I've done my best like my parents, I know my best was not always enough for Lil Gee. I only hope to make it as comfortable as possible for him to confront me with those things when he does his own soul searching.

I also thought of how Carla finally got what she wanted. She had her son back with her new husband in their beautiful home. And she had also become a very successful caterer in Charleston, even featured in local magazines and on news stations. And although it did not look like how I imagined it would, we still co-parented Lil Gee through his entire upbringing. I know each twist and turn of our story was on purpose, and Lil Gee is the amazing person he is today because of it.

But I can't help but wonder what life would have been like had Carla and I never divorced. I do often wish that she could get to know the man that I've become today. Would she love me? When I first started to recognize my attraction toward boys, I didn't understand it. Despite my attraction towards girls and my relationships with them, I was still called "gay" or "faggot." This confused me. I never understood why people would think I was gay. They could not fathom that a less than masculine boy really liked girls; to them, I had to like boys. As it turned out for me, we both were right. The problem is once I started to open myself up, or should I say, once my attraction toward men increased and my discipline for keeping that contained decreased, I thought that meant they all were right. How could I like females when males made me feel this way? It had to all be a lie. I had to always have been gay, but I kept it bottled up for so long and never really liked females, right?

Well, as I got more acquainted and comfortable with my same-sex attraction and the curiosity of it all wore off, I found this "either/or" societal norm to be untrue for me. Out of all the labels, I finally felt most comfortable with "fluid" or "same-gender-loving," which is a term coined by my friend and mentor, Dr. Cleo Manago. Gay, queer, straight, and all the others never seemed to suit me, although it doesn't bother me to be called any of them...well, you can keep straight.

I can't stop what people call me, much less what they think of me, but it only matters that I stand confident in knowing who I am so I can share with others. I know that now.

The truth is, I've never stopped loving Carla. When we were together, I just didn't understand, much less know, how to show up and love in a relationship. Aside from my fluid attractions, I was only 22 when we married. Since then, I have learned that to truly show up and love someone, I must first show up and love my self fully. I neither gave Carla nor myself the chance to grow within our relationship. Carla bared all while I bared nothing. I projected all my insecurities onto her. I did not know how to express or manage my emotions. I thought that my struggles with my sexuality meant that what I had with her could not be authentic. I felt that my inability to show affection toward her meant that I was not attracted to her. I thought that those failed sexual experiences with females meant that I was not attracted to women anymore. But after experiencing all of those things with men too, it caused me to dig deeper and know better.

It would take years for me to learn these things. Unfortunately for the fate of Carla and me, I didn't know who I fully was, back then. But fortunately, that is not how life works, and I got to take the journey that was meant for me. I would do it all over again if I had to.

"Are you okay?" Juan looked over and asked as we were about thirty minutes into our hour and a half drive back to Atlanta. It had been quiet since we pulled out of the Dunkin' Donuts parking lot, and I knew he had to be worried about how I was handling all of this, especially after seeing the highly emotional month I had.

I sat back, relaxing comfortably in the passenger seat of Juan's 2008 Jeep Commander. His hand rested on my thigh since leaving Augusta, and I placed my hand on top of his. Juan always had a way of making me feel secure with the slightest touch. I loved this about him.

"Yea," I replied, while nodding my head and smiling. "I'm ok."

Juan and Gee on red carpet at the Cassius Launch,
The Gathering Spot, Atlanta, summer 2017

Gee and Lil Gee leaving The Cheesecake Factory, summer 2017

Gee and Juan riding bikes, Miami, 2017

Gee, Lil Gee, and Juan, The 6th Annual Gentlemen's Ball, October 2017

Juan with Gee as he addresses The 6th Annual Gentlemen's Ball, 2017

Lil Gee and Gee, the last pic in their condo before Lil Gee
moved to Charleston to live with Carla, January 2018

ACKNOWLEDGEMENTS

Hands down, writing this book has been the longest and most dramatic emotional rollercoaster I have been on in my life! But over the past three years, I've learned so much about myself. I would do it all over again. Putting my intimate struggles and truths into words is the most vulnerable thing I have ever done. People often ask me why I share so much about myself, and my response is, "Well, why not?" The truth cannot hold you hostage when set free, and if I've learned one thing along this journey, it's that nothing bad can ever come out of speaking truth. These truths have shaped me into the man that I am today, and I can finally confidently say that I am in love with me—all of me and all of my journey. People tend to only keep things to themselves that they are ashamed of, fear judgment about, or think they could lose. I don't feel any of those things about what I have written. In fact, it makes me feel powerful to share my story.

I had to write this book. It has not been easy for some people to accept this as my calling. I am truly grateful to those people for allowing space for my writing to breathe freely and go deeply, despite the contrast it may have brought to their lives.

One of those people is my mother, Rita F. Smalls. I could not have chosen to be born into this world to a more perfect mother for me. All of your journey and all of who you are helps define the man I am today. Your strength inspires me, although I will never be as strong as you. You have fight inside of you, and it is something I admire so much. I still want to make you proud and hope you can even feel every ounce of the love I have for you, Momma. Thank you for loving me with all that you have and for always reminding me that I'm your favorite son.

My father, Virgil F. Smalls, although no longer here in human form, continues to guide me. Ever since Lakara Foster, a medium, approached me that night at the bar with an urgent message from my father—thank you so much!—I have felt his presence and been talking to him ever since. Thank you, Daddy, for giving me the very best parts of you and leading me along this journey of life, especially when the road tends to swerve. Thank you for sending me my husband soon after you left; you knew exactly what I needed. What a gift you have been and continue to be to me. Please continue to help guide my steps and show me the way. I know that as long as you are watching over me, things will be okay.

My sister, Tawnya Smalls, my "Kony." You have been the most consistent person in my life, ever since I was a little boy climbing into your bed after having a nightmare. Still, to this day, you make me feel safe after having one of life's nightmares. I never have to question whether or not you will have my back, and for that and more, I thank you, Sis! I love you.

There are so many reasons to be grateful for my ex-wife and son's mom. You were my first true love and the first person after my sister to ever make me feel protected. Thank you for how you helped shape me and for co-creating Lil Gee, the person that means the most to us both.

Gregory V. Smalls, Jr., Lil Gee, my son, my forever babyboy. I have never been more proud of wearing a title than I am proud of wearing the title of "Father." Thank you for making me into a man, showing me who I am every day, and loving me even when I don't make the highest choices. Know that there has never been anything I have done in my life with more passion, intent, caution, thought, and love than I have put into being your father. Since the day you were born, I have lived to make you proud of me, both as your father and as a man. You inspire me to be better, and your opinion means the most to me. It is something I will always cherish and hold dear to my heart. I know you will succeed at whatever you want in life as long as you continue to use your gift of intuition. It is strong; use it. Continue to grab each of your experiences boldly while never playing the victim, but by always walking away with ownership and wisdom. As you continue on your own life's journey, know that your "Pa" will always be here to support you. I love you more than you will ever, ever know.

To my homeboys who I've known since I was damn near in Pampers: J.T. Brown, Jerome Gilliard, Twan Campbell, and Nicky Kornicky. Thank you for always embracing me through each of my differences and never making me feel less than. Some of my best childhood memories are with you. Thomas Brewer and Nard Goodwine, y'all fit right in after J.T. and I came to Atlanta for college. I will never forget the good times in English Oaks! N3, baby!

Taka Wiley, I still think you're beautiful. You showed me I was worthy of love from a Black woman despite what society said, and I am forever grateful for that. Years later, I can honestly see that I still had a lot more growing up to do and was not ready for the kind of love you had to give. Thank you for being you!

Lyndsay Kim, dude! Although our lives have taken us in separate directions—how classic—I still feel like we are the best of friends. The years we shared together will forever be ingrained on my soul, and I know you feel that! Let's indulge one day again!

Brandon Freeman, my GBF, my birthday twin, the first true friend I met when discovering what it meant to live life as a same-gender-loving man. I remember both of us being fresh out of the closet and so naïve when it came to "tha life." It sure didn't take us long to catch on! LOL! I love you, man!

Jennaaay, you my mufukin bitch, and I'm proud of you! #thasall

QBEEEEEEE, I'm not sure if you know how much you inspired my journey. You were my first life coach before that was even a thing. You helped me to believe in myself because of how much you believed in me. You always saw me. Thank you for sharing your energy with me, Deanna Scott. Much love wherever you are. (smile)

I cannot forget to thank those brothers who have had my back throughout the process of writing this book. First, thank you to Byron Jamal for practically making me sit down to start this book. You are so good at what you do! Darnell L. Moore, you inspire the fuck out of me!

Thank you for allowing me to blow you up and never making me feel like a bother during this writing process! I love you to the moon and back! J.L. King, thank you for always telling me to stay on it! You've done that since I first met you years ago, and I will never forget it. Dr. Cleo Manago, you helped to get me woke, and I thank you! I promise not to go back to sleep.

To my book coach, Wayne South Smith, thank you for pushing me beyond the limits I put on myself. You were very instrumental in my writing process, and I am forever grateful.

To Rebecca Bennett, Dr. Yvonne "Momma" Freeman, Dr. David Malebranche, Dr. Daniel Black, and Al Washington, thank you for reviewing my book and offering your detailed feedback! And my gratitude to Merri Sheffield for her keen proofreading.

And to my therapist of over nine years, Cheryll Thompson, I am grateful for the tools you have taught me to become more aware of myself. Teaching me that self-awareness is the purpose of relationships has helped me tremendously with the people in my life, especially my partnership with the love of my life, Juan Smalls.

Juan, words will never be able to express the gratitude I have for being able to have you as my partner as we both walk through this journey we call life. We have learned so much together, and I'm not sure where I would be without you. You pushed me to tap into my creativity, take risks, stop letting life control me, and walk into my greatness! I've told you since the day we met that you are my dream come true, and you continue to be that dream for me. You have allowed me to grow every day, never holding me hostage to the man I was yesterday, and have even managed to stay interested in the person I continue to evolve into. How could I ever ask for a better friend, lover, husband, or partner in life? You complete me, and I don't care who thinks that's an unhealthy statement. We are still here working out this thing we call life together, and I look forward to holding your hand for the rest of our life's journey. I love me some you.

A special shout out to my fellow James Island natives for helping to raise me, and to my Atlanta community, both in and outside of the Black LGBT community, for helping to make me into a man. I will forever call these two places home. #proudgeecheeboi #fila

There are so many others who have supported me along my way that I could write another book just full of thank you's! To anyone who has ever shared space with me from near or afar, you have helped to make me. Thank you!

ABOUT THE AUTHOR

Gregory "Gee" Smalls is a father, husband, entrepreneur, life and relationship coach, and restaurateur, owner of Virgil's Gullah Kitchen & Bar in historic College Park. Born into the Gullah Geechee culture of Charleston, South Carolina, Gee is the only son of a White mother and Black father who raised him during a time when mixed-race marriage was unaccepted in the south.

Gee knew since childhood that his mixed-race was not the only thing that made him different from most of his peers, but like many in the LGBTQ community, he suppressed his same-sex attraction for most of his pubescent years. His young journey led him to fall in love with and later marry his high school sweetheart. No longer able to stow away his truth, at 26, he was a divorced father with shared custody of a young son while simultaneously trying to navigate his life as a biracial, sexually fluid man. At 31, he met Juan Smalls and was smitten by the handsome man who he eventually dated, fell in love with, and married in 2009.

With a Bachelor of Science from DeVry University and a Master's degree in Project Management from Keller Graduate School, Gee worked for twenty years in the Information Technology industry in roles that transitioned from corporate representative to IT consultant.

In 2010, Gee co-founded Juan & Gee Enterprises, which included the web-based talk show series LoveWorks with Juan & Gee, relationship and life coaching services, as well as custom event design services. He has been featured on HGTV, PeachtreeTV, V103 Atlanta, WAOK, as well as in publications such as *Ebony, Swerve, Kontrol Magazine, RollingOut, The Huffington Post*, and more.

In 2011, Gee and Juan created *The Gentlemen's Ball*, an annual black-tie fundraiser that has grown from 75 attendees to over 600 who come from across the nation and abroad. The event has honored and attracted allies and members of the Black LGBTQ community and has raised thousands of dollars in scholarships.

In 2014, the annual fundraiser expanded with "The Gentlemen's Foundation" whose mission is to promote the holistic development of Black men in the Same Gender Loving (SGL) and LGBTQ community. The foundation has awarded scholarships, established mentorships, and advocated health and wellness through media outreach and support groups. The nonprofit foundation attracts corporate sponsors and partnerships from organizations such as UPS, Mercedes Benz, Nissan, AARP, New York Life Insurance, Home Depot, and Gilead.

In 2019, Gee became a restaurateur and opened Virgil's Gullah Kitchen & Bar, alongside his husband, Juan. Named after Gee's father, the restaurant is located in Historic College Park, a suburb of Atlanta.

Gee has been awarded several community service awards, along with being included amongst *Business Equality Magazine's* "40 LGBTQ Leaders Under 40."

Black Enough, Man Enough is Gee's first book. Gee lives with his husband Juan in Atlanta, Georgia.

For more information, please visit www.geesmalls.com or email connect@geesmalls.com. Follow him on Instagram and Twitter @geesmalls or on Facebook at MrGeeSmalls.

CPSIA information can be obtained
at www.ICGtesting.com
Printed in the USA
LVHW091037210720
661192LV00004B/24/J

9 781733 082808